THE AMERICAN CRIMINAL JUSTICE SYSTEM

THE AMERICAN CRIMINAL JUSTICE SYSTEM

How It Works,
How It Doesn't, and
How to Fix It

Gerhard Falk

 PRAEGER

AN IMPRINT OF ABC-CLIO, LLC
Santa Barbara, California • Denver, Colorado • Oxford, England

Library of Congress Cataloging-in-Publication Data
Falk, Gerhard, 1924–
   The American criminal justice system : how it works, how it doesn't, and
how to fix it / Gerhard Falk.
      p. cm.
   Includes bibliographical references and index.
   ISBM 978-0-313-38347-2 (hard copy : alk. paper) — ISBN 978-0-313-
38348-9 (ebook) 1. Criminal justice, Administration of—United States. I. Title.
   HV9950.F35   2010
   364.973—dc22   2009048614

ISBN: 978-0-313-38347-2
EISBN: 978-0-313-38348-9

14   13   12   11   10   1   2   3   4   5

This book is also available on the World Wide Web as an eBook.
Visit www.abc-clio.com for details.

Praeger
An Imprint of ABC-CLIO, LLC

ABC-CLIO, LLC
130 Cremona Drive, P.O. Box 1911
Santa Barbara, California 93116-1911

This book is printed on acid-free paper ∞

Manufactured in the United States of America

CONTENTS

INTRODUCTION

The Constitution of the United States is the basis of the American criminal justice system. Because that document is over 200 years old, it has been interpreted and amended numerous times, so that the criminal justice system has changed over the years to reflect the beliefs and needs of each succeeding generation.

At the beginning of the twenty-first century, in the light of such scientific advances as DNA testing, the need to improve the criminal justice system is evident. It is thus the purpose of this book to exhibit the current shortcomings of the system with a view of providing suggestions for reasonable alterations in the system.

During a parliamentary debate in 1947, Winston Churchill, former prime minister of England, said, "Democracy is the worst form of government, except for all the others." Those words may also be said of the American criminal justice system. It is not the intent of this book to denounce the entire criminal justice system, however, or to seek to invent a different system. Instead, it is hoped that the discussion presented here will serve to improve what we have, making our approach to criminal justice more equitable and more attuned to the needs of the United States of America's twenty-first-century citizens.

Police, in particular, should be more aware of our current needs in criminal justice because the police are the one branch of the criminal justice system with which the vast majority of Americans come in contact. Neither the courts nor the prisons are known firsthand by more than a fraction of Americans, despite the fact that we have a greater incarceration rate than any democracy on earth.

This book also explains some of the history of our criminal justice system. For example, it is generally unknown that criminal prosecution was at one time a private matter and that citizens had to calculate the cost of prosecuting an offender before doing so. Even the police began as a private force, remaining so until the beginning of the twentieth century.

Some of the most important changes in the administration of criminal justice in the United States revolve around the effort to abolish the death penalty and to ensure that the innocent are no longer penalized, as has been the case for so many years. Both of these goals seem within reach as the century progresses because methods of detection and the unreliability of such evidence as eyewitness testimony have become suspect. In fact, so-called lie detectors have proved to be a lie themselves, so that polygraph results are no longer accepted by American courts.

Even as efforts to protect the innocent are improving, the criminal justice system is being burdened more and more by a flood of white-collar crimes. Such crimes are on the increase, even as crimes of violence have decreased during the two decades preceding 2009.

This book concludes with an epilogue suggesting those changes in the criminal justice system that will ensure the system's continued usefulness to the American people.

Chapter 1

THE AMERICAN POLICE

The police are the only branch of the American criminal justice system well known and visible to most Americans. The other branches of the system, that is, the courts and the prisons, are encountered by only a few citizens despite the immense number of Americans, over 2 million, imprisoned in the United States in the first part of the twenty-first century.

THE SHERIFF

The earliest police force to exist in English-speaking jurisdictions was the office of the sheriff. That word "sheriff" is derived from *gerefa*, which became *reeve*, and referred to a local administrator representing an Anglo-Saxon king in medieval England. Such officials were already appointed in the tenth century. However, no certain date for such appointments is available. Therefore, the sheriffs of England declared 1992 to be the 1,000th anniversary of the creation of the sheriff's office because it is certain that sheriffs existed in all of England in 992.[1]

In English folklore the Sheriff of Nottingham is a vile figure whose deeds are told in the legend of Robin Hood. This legend is the product of the invasion of England by the Normans under William the Conqueror, who defeated the Anglo-Saxons at the Battle of Hastings in 1066. The Norman French were able to win that battle and rule England thereafter because England at that time was only a geographic expression but not a unified country. The English lived in separate villages and small communities without a centralized government. Therefore, the protection of life and property was private and uncertain. After 1066 the sheriff became the king's representative in each shire or county. He was the direct agent of the Crown who served a writ to anyone charged with a crime and thereby created security and permanence in the new English nation. The office of sheriff later became part of the American colonial government and functioned in the new world as it had functioned in Europe.[2]

The office of sheriff was continued in the American colonies when the settlements in Virginia adopted the office of sheriff to replace the military regime with a civilian government. In 1635, the Crown officially appointed a sheriff to represent the king at the earliest English settlement in America at Jamestown, Virginia, founded in 1607. The function of the sheriff was to keep the peace.[3]

After the American Revolution (1775–1783), sheriffs in the United States and in the western states were elected locally and thus served local interests. The Puritan community of Massachusetts was exempt from this practice, however. Because of frontier conditions, American sheriffs based their powers on the concept of posse comitatus, or "power of the county," which refers to the local sheriff's power to enlist citizens in law enforcement by deputizing them to help deal with one or another problem at the time. Such deputized citizens were not part of the sheriff's permanent force but only helped out on some occasions.

Because sheriffs were elected democratically on a county basis, they were active in protecting the community. They enforced the law, administered the prisons, provided security within courts, enforced court orders, served subpoenas (under penalty), and provided police protection in mostly rural America. These functions are still the duty of present-day sheriffs, who are the only police to patrol rural areas in the United States today (2009).[4] Sheriffs are responsible for maintaining county jails even in urban areas. This responsibility is possibly the most difficult and unproductive task a sheriff has to fulfill because no expenditure is less popular among taxpayers than the cost of maintaining jails.

The cost of maintaining county jails is approximately $129 per person a day. The number of Americans in local jails at the end of 2007 topped 780,000, which meant that 259 of every 100,000 U.S. residents were then in jail. Of these, blacks were five times as likely to go to jail as whites.[5]

The cost to the taxpayers of incarcerating so many citizens in local jails exceeded $19 million in 2008 and has become a major source of dispute concerning the feasibility of releasing nonviolent offenders earlier than expected. Consideration should be given to the fact that between 1982 and 2006, the cost of jailing in this country increased by 600 percent.[6]

The crowded conditions in American jails place great stress not only on the prisoners but also on the staff. In many American jails, there are four men where one ought to be; hammocks are strung between beds and bunks. Gymnasiums have been converted to huge dormitories, and so inmates cannot exercise or engage in other stress-relieving activities. Such conditions lead to a good deal of staff absenteeism. One additional consequence of jail overcrowding is that a number of American jails are under court order to reduce crowding.[7] This problem would be soluble if the sheriff had authority to admit new prisoners. These additional inmates, however, are sent by judges without consent of the sheriff and those who run the jails for him, or by the police who arrest possible offenders in the first place.

Such overcrowding can, of course, be eliminated by allowing suspects to go home "on their own recognizance" or sending arrested drunks to a detoxification center.

One principal reason for overcrowded jails is the attitude of prosecutors. They are viewed as protectors of the public from marauding criminals who need to be locked up. Prosecutors who do not run as many offenders as possible into jail are seen in the media as "soft on crime" and are unlikely to be reelected. Unthinking "lock 'em up" policies have great benefits for prosecutors and judges; however, the sheriff who runs the jail is left with the consequences of these policies. Prosecutors are also responsible for the length of time a defendant spends in jail, since the severity of the charges affects the amount of bail imposed. Moreover, pretrial diversion is also in the hands of prosecutors. "Diversion" refers to the discretion a prosecutor has in allowing a defendant to visit a psychiatrist or social worker or alcohol clinic instead of going to jail.

In addition, jail overcrowding could be alleviated by pretrial release. Because so many of the persons charged with petty crimes are assigned a public defender, the public defenders are also responsible for a good deal of jail overcrowding. Many defense attorneys delay the trials of defendants again and again because they know that witnesses forget what they saw or are no longer in the community when a delayed trial is held. Meanwhile, the defendant, unable to make bail, stays in jail.[8] Sheriffs not only are responsible for administering the local jails but also are expected to enforce laws pertaining to "public order crimes," which some observers have called crimes without victims. Such crimes are usually related to sex offenses, including child pornography; substance abuse, including drunken driving; and illegal gambling.

American sheriffs are usually responsible not only for patrolling the rural areas of any county, investigating possible crimes, maintaining communications, and operating the local jail, but also for servicing the courts. That responsibility consists of screening all persons entering a courthouse to prevent the introduction of weapons and other contraband, providing security for judges and jurors, and dealing with prisoners in court. An example of the kind of security needed but that failed in court was the conduct of a defendant in Fulton County Court in Atlanta, Georgia: the accused overpowered a sheriff's deputy in court and then fatally shot the judge, his assistant, and a federal customs agent.[9]

Sheriff's deputies also serve warrants, summonses, orders of protection, and eviction notices.

In counties that contain large cities, the urban police are much more involved in the patrolling function, although the sheriff is regarded as the highest-ranking police officer in any American jurisdiction.

A BRIEF HISTORY OF THE URBAN POLICE

The first police officers, other than a sheriff, in an English-speaking jurisdiction were established by the novelist Henry Fielding (1707–1754). Fielding was not only a writer; he was also a lawyer. Fielding lived on Bow Street in London. There, he persuaded six former "constables" to join him in apprehending thieves and other known criminals. These men came to be known as the Bow Street Runners. They worked for the reward money but were later paid a weekly sum and a bonus for each successful prosecution.

It was not until 1829 that the London police force was organized by Sir Robert Peel, then prime minister. The members of that force were called "Bobbies" because of Peel's first name.[10] New York City was the first American community to establish a police department, in 1845. Prior to that, New York had a "night watch," as did other American towns and cities. The night watch was responsible for defending citizens against criminals and for sounding an alarm in case of fire.[11] The members of the night watch were viewed by citizens as wholly ineffective, and the *New York Gazette* wrote that they were "idle, drunken, vigilant snoopers, who never quelled any nocturnal tumult in their lives; but would be as ready to join in a burglary as any thief in Christendom."[12]

As the nineteenth century progressed, a number of improvements were achieved among the American police. The first of these improvements was the hierarchical (holy rule) organization, which imposed on the police a command and communications structure resembling the military. This structuring became possible after the police department was located under the executive, rather than the judicial, branch of government. Beginning with the reforms of the nineteenth century, police began to wear uniforms. This second improvement was at first ridiculed by citizens. Nevertheless, the wearing of a uniform had several salutary effects: the uniform increased citizens' access to police officers, since their visibility became apparent; the increased visibility also helped the officers' supervisors to locate them at once. Finally, the police received regular salaries after the start of the twentieth century, which made them more responsible than was true when fee collection was their main source of income.

An unexpected consequence of the change—from giving reward money and making payments only for successful prosecutions to providing police officers with regular pay—was free prosecution of offenders. Prior to the payments of salaries to the police, the victim had to calculate the value of stolen items before calling a constable, who collected a fee. Another unanticipated consequence of paying salaries to police officers was the corruption of the police into political hacks who prevented some people from voting while promoting the interests of whatever political "machine" employed them at the taxpayers' expense.[13]

Between 1850 and 1880, uniformed police spread across the entire United States, leading to more and more riot control. Riots had been part of the American scene for years and were common in New York City and elsewhere. In fact, New York City endured eleven riots between 1806 and 1900.[14]

Because welfare in the nineteenth-century United States was entirely a local affair, police were used to dispensing welfare in various forms. City government was responsible for the homeless and orphans, for delinquent children, and for mentally ill citizens. Therefore, station houses had rooms in the back where temporary shelter was given to persons found on the streets. No one was allowed to stay more than a few nights, and so these accommodations did little to alleviate the misery of the poor.[15]

The welfare assignment did not last long. As the police became more professionalized and as social work became a profession, police officers relinquished such housing duties; consequently, by the beginning of the twentieth century, the police were no longer in the welfare business. Instead, police officers focused on crime control and on being the keepers of public order. They began to dispense "justice" at once on the street. The belief in a "dangerous class" was common in the nineteenth century, so the police were free to deal as they pleased with immigrants, racial minorities, and deviants of every kind.

In any case, crime control became the principal focus of police work beginning with the 1890s, and so the welfare activities of the police were gradually discontinued until they disappeared entirely by the 1940s.[16]

As crime control became the sole occupation of the police, policing evolved from just another job to a career and later to a profession. This transition also led to a decline in the age of new recruits to police departments. At the beginning of the twentieth century, that age was around 30. Thereafter, it dropped to the age of high school graduation, which usually occurs at age 18. In the nineteenth century and in the early twentieth century, labor disputes were common in many

American industries and led to strikes, which were resisted with force. Often employers retaliated against union organizers and strikers by using the lockout, which became an effective tool when union members no longer had money to buy food or pay their rent. Employers also used "goons," or strikebreakers, to physically attack strikers and lock out workers.

In 1892, the Homestead plant of the Carnegie Corporation hired 400 Pinkerton agents to attack striking workers. In the ensuing melee, 10 men were killed and 60 wounded. The fight was provoked by the shared belief of management and government that workers had no right to strike.[17] An excellent example of the attitude of the American upper class concerning laboring men and their rights is an article published in 1894 by a lawyer concerning the right to strike. According to the author, Artemus Stewart, laboring men had no such right. He argued that the workers in the Homestead Steel mill could not voluntarily leave their jobs. He drew an analogy with surgeons, who, according to Stewart, could not suddenly leave in the middle of an operation just to demand more money. His commonly used arguments often led to the employment of police as strikebreakers, a role also played by Pinkerton detectives and other private enforcers.[18]

Police were used not only as strikebreakers. After Congress passed the National Labor Relations Act in 1935, labor unions became entitled to bargain collectively and to strike. The legislation put an end to much labor unrest in the country and curtailed the strikebreaking role of the police. However, racial unrest was in its infancy; as fighting escalated, the police became more and more involved in race riots at the end of the nineteenth century and thereafter. These riots were aggravated by the housing shortage during World War II.

RACE RIOTS AND THE POLICE

On August 7, 1898, the *New York Times* printed a story entitled "The 'Hell's Kitchen' Riots." Referring to an area in New York City in the vicinity of Tenth Avenue and Twenty-ninth Street, Hell's Kitchen was so named because those who lived there were poor immigrants. Evidently, the rioting started when a number of men living in the area fought in the street, so that two men were killed and a number of others wounded. A large contingent of police officers were employed until the rioting subsided.[19]

Such riots were subsequently recorded regularly in the *New York Times* and other American newspapers throughout the twentieth century and into the twenty-first century. So many such riots occurred in those years that they cannot all be mentioned here. However, a sample of stories will suffice to show that the principal reason for street riots involving the police were, and continue to be, racial and religious tension.

While the predominant majority of such riots involved so-called white and black disagreements and hostilities, Afro-American assaults on the New York Jewish population are responsible for religion-based rioting. On August 16, 1900, the last year of the nineteenth century, a large contingent of white men assaulted numerous Negroes, as the *Times* then called blacks, to avenge the death of patrolman Albert J. Thorpe, who had been killed the day before by "a drunken Negro." Police were called, and the *Times* reported that the rioting ceased within 20 minutes.[20]

Five days later, the *New York Times* reported that a delegation representing "The United Colored Democracy" had visited the mayor of New York City and complained that the police had taken part in the assault on "Negroes" conducted by "whites" on August 16.[21]

On July 20, 1905, another delegation from the black community visited Police Chief McAdoo of New York City and the district attorney and once more complained that during a recent race riot, the police had sided with the "whites" and shot an unarmed "Negro," who was dying at Bellevue Hospital.[22]

"Race Riot Laid to Lax Police Rule" proclaimed the July 8, 1917, *New York Times* headline concerning a race riot in East St. Louis, Missouri. The *Times* reported that in a population of 83,000 inhabitants, the police force consisted of only 63 men. It was later claimed that the riot began when white joy riders shot into a church during a Saturday evening service and that the police did nothing to prevent this incident or apprehend the offender.[23]

In Tulsa, Oklahoma, the police chief was indicted on June 26, 1921, because the grand jury found that he had failed to enforce the prohibition law, failed to enforce firearms laws, conspired to dispose of stolen automobiles, and had done nothing to prevent "armed Negroes" from marching into a white neighborhood, leading to a race riot.[24]

Chicago fared no better than Tulsa. There, too, race riots plagued the city in the '20s, leading to a commission report by six white and six black citizens as to how such riots might be avoided in the future. It was reported by the commission that the chief cause of the riots in Chicago was the habit of "white hoodlums" bombing the homes of "Negroes." Additional recommendations included the restriction on the sale of firearms, the closing of so-called athletic clubs as havens for the aforementioned "hoodlums," and the development of a police action plan and increased awareness to defend blacks against aggression.[25]

On July 1, 1937, the *New York Times* reported on a congressional inquiry conducted by Senator La Follette concerning the deaths of seven men shot in the back by the Chicago police in order to force the end to a strike at a Republic Steel Corporation plant. La Follette confronted police officials with photographs showing police captains standing idly by while several police officers beat a man on the ground with clubs and fists. The police excused these killings and beatings by claiming that their victims were "reds" or "Russian spies."[26] By 1943, during World War II, rioting in American cities became particularly intense. On June 21, 1943, federal troops in full battle gear moved into Detroit, Michigan, to end a race riot in which "twenty Negroes and three white persons" had been killed and over 600 citizens had been injured. The Associated Press, which reported these riots, did not give any reason for the fighting in Detroit. The anonymous reporter commented only that "Negroes" were seen shooting from windows in a tenement house. A two-hour gun battle developed that led to the killing of two tenants by the police and the wounding of a police lieutenant.[27]

Likewise, St. Louis endured a race riot in July 1943 not only because of a housing shortage but also because of the propinquity of Jefferson Barracks, an army base including many "Negroes." The black soldiers stationed there sought to drive through nine miles of a white neighborhood to get to the black neighborhood. This act, together with the competition for housing among defense workers, led to "an explosive situation." Here, too, the police force was blamed by both sides for providing insufficient protection.[28]

Detroit once more made the headlines when race riots broke out in that city on June 21, 1943. This time, the National Association for the Advancement of Colored People (NAACP) accused the local prosecutor and the police commissioner of dereliction of duty for failure to enforce the laws against whites. The prosecutor and the commissioner argued that twice as many whites as "Negroes" were injured in these riots and that 56 percent of violent crimes in Detroit were committed by just 10 percent of citizens, who were black.[29]

Also in 1943, in the midst of World War II, rioting occurred in Harlem, a section of Manhattan in New York City. These riots led to the killing of 5 and wounding of 400 persons as hundreds of stores were looted and property wrecked in the estimated amount of $5 million. All the injured and wounded except two police were "Negroes," so that racial conflict was not a factor in these outbursts. The *New York Times* attributed the riot to "hoodlums."[30]

Between 1947 and 1951, the Chicago area became the scene of a number of race riots, culminating in a severe altercation in Cicero, a suburb of Chicago. These riots were principally provoked by efforts of black citizens to move into areas previously all-white. A grand jury, assembled in 1951, indicted the Cicero chief of police for failure to enforce the law when a black bus driver moved his family into an apartment house in Cicero, leading to rioting on the part of the white population.[31] Rochester, New York, was the scene of a race riot in 1964, when the police arrested a black man for disorderly conduct, only to be confronted by a large number of his supporters, who assaulted police officers and threw rocks and bottles. A number of white citizens rushed into the fight to help the police, leading to numerous injuries, the burning and looting of stores, and the deployment of 500 police in an effort to restore calm to the city.[32]

Racial tensions continued throughout the 1960s, 1970s, and 1980s and led to severe disturbances (too many to list here). In the 1990s, race riots continued. The police beating of Rodney King, a black motorist in 1991, led to the trial of two police officers, Stacey Koon and Lawrence Powell, for beating King after his arrest for a traffic violation. Koon and Powell were found not guilty when tried for assault in a state court in April 1991. That verdict led to the worst urban riots ever recorded in the United States. The riot lasted three days, led to the deaths of 55 people and the wounding of 2,300, and resulted in the destruction of 1,100 buildings. Subsequently, both Koon and Powell were tried once more and convicted on federal charges of violating King's civil rights.[33]

Rioting has never been absent from American life. At the turn of the twenty-first century, Philadelphia, Seattle, and Cincinnati became locales for rioting, which invariably involved the police. In April 2001, Cincinnati, Ohio, experienced a race riot after an African American was gunned down by the police. A 19-year-old man, unarmed, was shot to death by a white police officer. Reacting with rage, the black community smashed store windows, set fires, and vowed revenge. Cincinnati is 43 percent black and racially divided both geographically and socially. Blacks claim that constant police brutality endangers their lives each day. The police claim that they are facing hostility and lack of cooperation from citizens but are nevertheless expected to enforce the laws and protect those who do not respect them.[34]

THE FEDERAL POLICE AND THE "REDS" SCARE

Although Americans have traditionally sought local control of government and particularly the police, the effort at retaining power in the hands of the citizens came to an end when, in 1908, the attorney general of the United States, Charles Bonaparte, organized a federal investigation service that was then, and is now, highly controversial.

That controversy is based on the belief by many Americans that local government is a far better guarantor of American liberties than is the remote bureaucracy in Washington, D.C. Nevertheless, when Theodore Roosevelt became president in 1901, following the assassination of President William McKinley, the so-called progressives in American politics were successful in imposing the federal government on American citizens in far greater fashion than had been known before. Theodore Roosevelt believed that the federal government could do things better than any local government and that the country needed a federal investigative service. As time went by, this idea was gradually taken for granted, so that the corps of special agents of the Justice Department, first organized in 1908, has grown into the vast bureaucracy of spies and informers now called the Federal Bureau of Investigation (FBI), with over 30,000 employees and a budget of $6.04 billion.[35]

By the time the FBI was a decade old, the bureau had begun to abuse its power by seeking to suppress political dissent. This abuse became evident when the Bureau of Investigation, as it was then known, conducted so-called Red Raids, leading to the imprisonment of American citizens whose sole crime was participation in organizations believed to have "revolutionary goals." In January 1920, 10,000 women and men throughout the country were arrested by the Bureau of Investigation on the grounds of being communists or communist sympathizers. It was the intent of these raids, organized by the General Intelligence Division of the Bureau of Investigation, to deport as many aliens as possible among those arrested. Among those seized were numerous people who had nothing to do with any communist party. They were detained solely because they may have attended one or more lawful meetings or social functions of any group then deemed subversive by the director of the General Intelligence Division, J. Edgar Hoover.[36]

Nearly 3,000 people were jailed and held for deportation as a result of these raids. The targets of these raids were allowed no lawyer, nor were they given any protection as required by the U.S. Constitution. Even the dean of the Northwestern University Law School argued that the Constitution could be suspended in face of the "threat" that the alleged communists posed to the United States.[37]

Despite the hysteria surrounding such activities, and despite public approval of the government's illegal activities, numerous lawyers and others came to the defense of the victims of these raids. Using the habeas corpus provision of the U.S. Constitution, these lawyers challenged the government in court and won in some instances.

Nevertheless, the Bureau of Investigation, headed by Hoover, used innumerable legal and illegal tactics to harass critics. Even someone who allowed a possible suspect to stay at his home one night was placed under surveillance and investigation. Authors of journal articles, financial backers, and defense lawyers of people accused of "socialist leanings" were among those harassed by the Bureau of Investigation. This harassment also extended to members of labor unions, all of whom were viewed as communists.

The activities that characterized Hoover's tenure as head of the bureau were criticized widely by those still anxious to uphold civil liberties in the United States, particularly after a labor lawyer, Felix Frankfurter, defended a number of falsely accused and falsely convicted union organizers. Frankfurter later became a Justice of the Supreme Court.[38]

Hoover then directed his staff to investigate Frankfurter, making special reference to Frankfurter's Jewish religion. Hoover also demanded that Zechariah Chafee, a professor of law at Harvard University, be dismissed on the grounds that he had publicly criticized the Justice Department. No such action was taken, of course; but Hoover's stance displayed his contempt for the constitutional rights enjoyed by all Americans.[39] Hoover remained director of the FBI until he died in May 1972. He did nothing to oppose organized crime and even claimed that the Mafia did not exist. However, he was obsessed with those who disagreed with him in any manner and used his powers to harass anyone with opinions not to his liking. Hoover also displayed hostility toward ethnic minorities and was particularly interested in labeling Jews as "un-American." Neither the presidents in office during Hoover's long tenure nor Congress ever questioned Hoover's tactics.[40]

The conspiracy theories of the 1920s concerning "reds" receded as many of the accusations by the Justice Department proved to be unfounded. In addition, the public turned against these raids when many of the accused were denied the right to counsel after they were arrested without the authority of a warrant and jailed in abominable facilities although innocent. Furthermore, prominent members of the legal profession defended the acting labor secretary, Louis F. Post, after the Justice Department attempted to have him impeached for defending the Constitution.[41]

One of the outcomes of the "red"-baiting era was the achievement of power by a number of government agencies that claimed to participate in fighting the danger of the communist conspiracy. These included the Central Intelligence Agency (CIA), the Secret Service, the Immigration and Naturalization Service (INS), and most important, the FBI.

THE FEDERAL POLICE AND THE MAFIA

"Mafia" is a Sicilian word related to the Arabic and meaning "defenders." This word became a part of another conspiracy theory in American history after a number of Italians had come to the United States under our unrestricted immigration policies prior to 1923. In that year, Congress adopted a quota system, so that entrance to the United States was limited to the proportion of any nationality already in the country as of 1890.

It was in that year that the Mafia first came to the attention of the media and the American public when the New Orleans superintendent of police, David Hennessey, was found murdered on the street. This killing was attributed to the Sicilian community in the city, although there was no evidence that Sicilians had murdered Hennessey. Nevertheless, a number of Sicilians were put on trial for the murder and acquitted. Before the accused could be released, a mob attacked the prison in which they were held and shot or lynched 11 Sicilians, of whom 5 had not been on trial. The news of the alleged involvement of the Mafia in the Hennessy murder spread all over the United States and led to suspicion that all Italian immigrants were somehow "Mafiosi."[42]

This first Mafia scare did not involve the federal police. However, the second Mafia scare was fostered by the federal government and involved not only the FBI but also the Federal Bureau of Narcotics. When the U.S. Senate investigated the so-called Mafia threat in 1951, that investigation was conducted by a committee chaired by Senator Estes Kefauver of Tennessee. These hearings were televised, and thus that new invention brought the "threat" of the Mafia into American living rooms. In 1957, the Mafia was again a topic of wide interest as a group of top organized-crime leaders were arrested when they fled the home of a major "Mafioso" in Appalachian, New York, where they had been meeting to discuss business. The local sheriff raided the meeting and thereby achieved nationwide publicity for himself and those "conspiring" to commit crimes.[43]

In 1963, a minor "soldier" in organized crime, Joseph Valachi, testified before the McClellan Committee of the U.S. Senate. That testimony led to widespread interest in organized crime and facilitated the entrance of federal law enforcement in seeking to suppress this "Italian conspiracy." In 1967, the President's Crime Commission reported that "today the core of organized crime in the United States consists of 24 groups operating criminal cartels in large cities across the nation."[44] This report led the Federal Narcotics Bureau to ask Congress for a large budget with which to fight the importation of drugs into the United States, a business attributed to the Sicilian Mafia. In fact, the Mafia, or its American version, La Cosa Nostra, did not engage in the drug business but concentrated much more on labor racketeering and on prostitution, liquor violations, gambling, loan sharking, and other offenses. During the lifetime of J. Edgar Hoover, organized crime was hardly prosecuted because Hoover denied the existence of the Mafia. Some researchers have claimed that Hoover would not investigate organized crime lest the Mafia expose his homosexuality.[45]

Hoover's power came mostly from his having investigated the private lives and family members of everyone in Congress and other elected officials. He remained chief of the FBI until his death because all politicians from the president on were afraid of what he might reveal if anyone sought to remove him.[46] Nevertheless, Congress passed the 1968 Omnibus Crime Control and Safe Streets Act and, in 1970, the Organized Crime Control Act. These laws were mainly the product of efforts by Harry Anslinger, who had been appointed federal narcotics commissioner and who needed to expand his agency's budget and his power. To do so, he linked the widespread use of narcotics to foreign sources and claimed that the Chinese communists and other foreigners were responsible for introducing drugs into the United States. Anslinger's tactics worked so well that he boasted of having sent more criminals to jail per agent than had any other federal enforcement agency.

Supported by journalists, the Mafia concept became popular and was merged with communism as the source of the United States' drug problems. Now Italian Americans became the targets of law enforcement throughout the 1950s and beyond as the FBI and the Bureau of Narcotics benefited from ever-larger budgets to deal with these "threats."[47]

After Hoover died in 1972, President Richard Nixon appointed L. Patrick Gray as director of the FBI. Gray appointed the first women as special agents. It was during the administration of Patrick Gray that the Watergate scandal led to the resignation of Richard Nixon from the presidency of the United States. Gray's involvement in the events that led to the Watergate break-in forced his resignation on April 27, 1973, and led to the appointment of William Ruckelshaus. Ruckelshaus likewise served only a short time as FBI director, as he was replaced by Clarence Kelley, who remained in that position until 1978. During Kelley's tenure, the resignation of Vice President Spiro Agnew was followed by the resignation of President Nixon.

Kelley was succeeded by William H. Webster, who had been a federal judge. At the time of his appointment in 1978, terrorism had become widespread around the world and therefore became the fourth priority for the FBI. The three other priorities in Webster's FBI were foreign intelligence, organized crime, and white-collar crime. Webster also organized the National Center for the Analysis of Violent Crime.

It was during Webster's administration that the FBI uncovered the spying operations of John Walker, a naval officer assigned to the National Security Agency. Walker had sold numerous military secrets to the Russians for large amounts of money. He also used his son, a U.S. Navy officer assigned to an aircraft carrier, to give him salable information. Both father and son were convicted and imprisoned for life.[48]

It was also during Webster's term of office that the FBI discovered the so-called Pizza Connection involving the heroin trade in the United States and Italy. Webster remained FBI director until 1987 and was succeeded by William S. Sessions after the brief interim appointment of John Otto. The "war on drugs" occupied most of the FBI's time, and government agents actually visited schools and warned children of the dangers of drugs. This new focus led to the FBI's expansion to include over 23,000 employees. It was during the tenure of William Sessions that the FBI organized a national DNA index.

On July 10, 1993, President Bill Clinton removed Sessions from his position of director of the FBI on the grounds of ethics violations. Clinton then appointed Louis J. Freeh director. During Freeh's term in office, the FBI was involved in the investigation of the Murrah Federal Building in Oklahoma City, the Unabomber investigation of Theodore Kaczynski, and the Ruby Ridge, Idaho, and Waco, Texas, FBI aggressions against American citizens. In 2001, Louis Freeh resigned and was succeeded by Robert S. Mueller. Only one week later, on September 11, 2001, the United States was attacked by Arab terrorists, leading to the passage of the U.S.A. Patriot Act. This law allows the FBI to accept the responsibility of protecting the country from future terrorist attacks. As of August 2008, this legislation had succeeded.[49]

THE FEDERAL NARCOTICS POLICE

As fear of the People's Republic of China became a major political issue in the 1950s, Anslinger now claimed that Communist China was surreptitiously sending vast amounts of illicit drugs into the United States in order to weaken the country. This story became particularly effective when the United States fought North Korea, which was supported by China in its effort to invade South Korea.[50]

All this suspicion led to the passage of the Narcotics Control Act of 1956, which increased penalties for the importation of narcotics and in some cases included the death penalty. It also allowed the Federal Bureau of Narcotics agents to carry firearms, serve warrants and subpoenas (under penalty), use wiretaps, and make arrests without warrants.

In the 1960s, when hostility to Cuba under the dictatorship of Fidel Castro became widespread in the United States, Anslinger linked drug trafficking to Cuba and claimed that Communist China and Communist Cuba conspired to send heroin into the United States and that "the United States had been free of cocaine addicts for twenty years until the Cuban traffic began."[51]

After Anslinger retired in 1962, the punitive approach to drug use was temporarily converted to a treatment-oriented approach during the Kennedy-Johnson administration. This approach was followed by the war on drugs initiated by President Richard Nixon and continued after Jimmy Carter by the Reagan-Bush and Clinton-Bush years.

Now the Justice Department persuaded Congress to allow the department to seize property of possible drug dealers by demonstrating "probable cause" before a federal judge. This meant that citizens only suspected of drug offenses could forfeit their houses, cars, money, or other property. As a result, the U.S. Department of Justice seized $2.5 billion in assets between 1982 and 1992. Eighty percent of this money came from people never charged with any crime.[52] In 1986, the Anti-Drug Abuse Act was passed by Congress and the Bureau of Narcotics and Dangerous Drugs was formed under the Drug Enforcement Administration (DEA). These developments led to a considerable increase in the prison population in the United States, so that in 2008 more than 2 million Americans were incarcerated. The DEA investigates violators of controlled substances at the interstate and international level. To that end, an intelligence network has been assembled that operates in the United States and in foreign countries. The DEA also seizes assets from those who have used the assets for drug-trafficking purposes as well as those suspected of intent to do so. In addition, the DEA enforces the Controlled Substances Act, dealing with the manufacture, distribution, and dispensing of legally produced controlled substances, and also deals with foreign countries in an attempt to limit or eliminate the drugs sent to the United States from abroad.[53] As of 2009, the war on drugs has not succeeded. The use of illicit drugs continues in the same fashion as alcohol was used during the years of Prohibition.

OTHER GOVERNMENT POLICE

There are at least 26 federal police units operating in various branches of the U.S. government. Bloated beyond recognition by those who founded the American Republic, the federal government has become a vast bureaucracy devoted to perpetuating itself. To that end, a large police force is employed whose purpose is to guard the beneficiaries of the federal bureaucracy, that is, the bureaucrats.

Thus, the U.S. Postal Service, the Internal Revenue Service tax collectors, the U.S. Government Printing Office, the parks police, the Occupational Safety and Health Administration, and an endless array of other government agencies all employ police departments. Among these many federal government police units is the Military Police. In addition, each state employs state troopers, who usually work the highways of each state and have responsibilities toward such elected officials as the governor.

PRIVATE POLICE

Private policing in the United States is as old as the Pinkerton National Detective Agency, an organization that served the interests of large corporations during the nineteenth and early twentieth centuries. Private police usurp a government function and therefore escape scrutiny by legislative oversight committees. Yet, the state is always implicated in private policing because the state allows private police to exist.[54]

Private police were not only used by business interests to crush labor union efforts. In the nineteenth century, many citizens relied on private watchmen and police to protect them because the urban public police force either did not exist or was inefficient and corrupt. Furthermore, the average public police officer was poorly trained and lacked the communications equipment now common and reliable.

In 1905, the *New York Times* reported that "more than 4,000 special policemen are employed from dusk to daylight."[55]

Private police were rewarded financially by citizens whose stolen properties they recovered. This practice continued even after public policing became more prominent, so that formerly private police now serving in a public police unit took money for recovering stolen goods. Many of these private-turned-public officers had connections to underworld informers.

When it became prohibited for a member of the city police department to take money for apprehending a suspect, the New York City police joined an organization called "Independent Policemen."

Business owners and banks engaged the services of private police to test the honesty of their employees. In rural areas where there were few if any public police, the private police organization was frequently the only force protecting the citizens.[56]

Railroad companies whose trains traveled through multiple jurisdictions, some of which had no police force of any kind, turned to private police firms. Of these, the best known was the organization founded by Alan Pinkerton, who was repeatedly charged with using such questionable methods as threatening people who sought to talk to the public police force. Private detectives were also employed in divorce actions. These detectives were hardly to be trusted, so their testimony was given little weight in court. These detectives were also accused of using excessive force and entering private property without permission.[57]

Most notorious were the private police officers used to fight the demands of workers seeking to organize into unions during the nineteenth century. The Homestead strike in 1892 became the symbol of the manner in which wealthy business owners sought to prevent unions from gaining living wages for their members.

In June 1892, a three-year contract between Carnegie Steel and the Amalgamated Association of Iron and Steel Workers came to an end. The contract was to be renegotiated at a time when Andrew Carnegie had returned to Scotland. Carnegie appointed Henry Clay Frick as manager of the steel company. Frick hated unions and therefore ordered the construction of a solid steel fence around the factory. The company then shut out the workers so that the entire workforce was locked out when the contract expired.

The union then surrounded the plant to prevent "scabs" from working there. Thereupon, Frick hired 300 Pinkertons, who came on barges down the Monongahela River with a view of entering the steel mill. Workers therefore met these barges as they docked, whereupon the Pinkertons fired into the crowd and wounded several workers. These workers, in turn, fired on the detectives from ramparts of steel, iron, and scrap. In the end, the 36-hour fight led to the surrender of the Pinkertons. Seven workers and three detectives were killed, and many were wounded. Consequently, the governor of Pennsylvania sent in the National Guard. This reinforcement led to the end of the strike, the discharge of union workers, the blacklisting of many others, and the defeat of the union. For 40 years thereafter, until the Franklin Roosevelt administration, unions had difficulty organizing because the law and some public opinion were usually opposed to strikes. Nevertheless, the Homestead strike and other such confrontations led many Americans to view the private police with disdain and as unreliable as witnesses in the courts. Yet, as labor unrest became less frequent and as it became evident that the public police did not have the human resources to guard everything at all times, private police gradually gained more acceptance.

During the years since the 1930s, private police gradually began to cooperate with public police. Such cooperation became important during World War II, when private police in defense industries were seen as guarding against sabotage and other acts that could have damaged the war effort.[58]

During the 70 years ending in 2008, information sharing between private and public police has become common. This kind of cooperation is no longer surreptitious. Instead, it is open and accepted. For example, the Business/Law Enforcement Alliance of California deals with such offenses as check fraud, which concern the private members. This alliance also includes contacts with executives of the private police organizations and public police representatives for mutual benefit.[59]

In view of the attacks on the World Trade Center on September 11, 2001, such privately owned utilities as gas and electric companies and telephone companies have become members of the InfraGard network. This network consists of the private police forces of these utilities as well as public police. Networking permits private corporations to receive information concerning threats affecting telephone or gas lines, electric networks, or other vulnerable segments of the American infrastructure that could be subject to a terrorist disaster.

The American police have many more functions than have been related here. Furthermore, there are a good number of police organizations in the United States in addition to the sheriff, the urban police, the federal police, and private police. Each state operates a police force, as does the military.

All share the ideal "to serve and protect." Yet, all are also a threat to American civil liberties as guaranteed in the U.S. Constitution. This dilemma is particularly evident in our judiciary system and is most pronounced in the offices of American prosecutors.

SUMMARY

The police, whether federal, state, or local, constitute the only branch of the criminal justice system with which the vast majority of Americans have any acquaintance.

The earliest police officials in English-speaking jurisdictions are the sheriff and his deputies. The sheriff has numerous duties, including patrolling rural areas, securing the courts, and maintaining the county jail.

The urban police force dates to the early nineteenth century, during which police were concerned with riots of all kinds. Many of these riots were caused by racial tensions.

The federal police organization, or FBI, is the outgrowth of the belief that the federal government needs to investigate such crimes against the United States as treason. The FBI is also based on the notion that much crime has become interstate, so that the jurisdiction of one state cannot deal with such offenses; this view is particularly true of narcotics violations.

The private police began at a time when public policing did not exist or was too weak to protect citizens. Later, private police forces were used by large business interests to serve as strikebreakers.

In the twenty-first century, private and public police cooperate, particularly in the face of the threat of terrorism. The police or law enforcement agencies are only one branch of the criminal justice system. The other branches are the judiciary and corrections. The judiciary begins with the prosecution of those accused of crime. That aspect of the system is the substance of our next chapter.

NOTES

1. Steve Gullion, "Sheriffs in Search of a Role," *New Law Journal* 142, no. 6564 (August 14, 1992): 1156.
2. Edson R. Sunderland, "The Sheriff's Return," *Columbia Law Review* 16, no. 4 (April 1916): 281.
3. "Office of the Sheriff: English Roots," *History of Sussex County*, http://www.sussexcountysheriff.com/History.htm
4. Gullion, "Sheriffs in Search of a Role," 2.
5. Bureau of Justice Statistics, "Jail Statistics," http://www.ojp.usdoj.gov/bjs/jails.htm
6. John Roman, and Aaron Chaflin, "Does It Pay to Invest in Re-entry Programs for Jail Inmates?" *Justice Policy Center*, June 27–28, 2006, 7.
7. Anne Boldue, "Jail Crowding," *Annals of the American Academy of Political and Social Sciences* 478 (March 1985): 47–57.
8. Ibid., 52.
9. Brenda Goodman, "Prisoner Flees Custody in Atlanta but Is Caught," *New York Times*, November 11, 2005, A14.
10. J. T. Lyman, "The Metropolitan Police Act of 1829," *Journal of Criminal Law, Criminology and Police Science*, no 1 (March 1964): 142.
11. George Lankevich, *American Metropolis: A History of New York City* (New York: NYU Press, 1998), 84.
12. Arthur E. Peterson and George W. Edwards, *New York as an Eighteenth Century Municipality* (Port Washington, NY: Friedman, 1967), 324.
13. Allen Steinberg, *The Transformation of Criminal Justice* (Chapel Hill: University of North Carolina Press, 1989), 119.
14. Eric H. Monkkonen, *Police in Urban America* (New York: Cambridge University Press, 1981), 196.

15. Joan Underhill Hannon, "The Generosity of Ante-bellum Poor Relief," *Journal of Economci History* 44 (1984): 1007.

16. Eugene E. Watts, "Police Response to Crime and Disorder in 20th Century St. Louis," *Journal of American History* 70 (1983): 340.

17. Angus Mcleod, "Carnegie Gave Scots a Bad Name," *Times* (London), October 26, 2006, 27.

18. Artemus Stewart, "The Legal Side of the Strike Question," *American Law Register* 42, no. 9 (September 1894): 609.

19. *New York Times*, "The 'Hell's Kitchen' Riots," August 7, 1898, 5.

20. *New York Times*, "Race Riot on West Side," August 16, 1900, 1.

21. *New York Times*, "Negroes Accuse the Police," August 22, 1900, 3.

22. *New York Times*, "Police Accused of Inciting Race Riots," July 20, 1905, 12.

23. *New York Times*, "Race Riots Laid to Lax Police Rule," July 8, 1917, 19.

24. *New York Times*, "Tulsa Race Riot Jury Indicts Police Chief," June 26, 1921, 16.

25. *New York Times*, "Suggests 59 Means to Curb Race Feeling," September 25, 1922, 11.

26. Louis Stark, "Riot Photos Force Police Admission," *New York Times*, July 1, 1937, 5.

27. *New York Times*, "Injured Reach 600," June 22, 1943, 1.

28. Turner Catledge, "St. Louis Combats Race Riot Rumors," *New York Times*, July 11, 1943.

29. *New York Times*, "Makes Race Riot Charges," July 29, 1943.

30. Ibid.

31. *New York Times*, "Police Chief Indicted in Cicero Race Riots," September 19, 1951.

32. *New York Times*, "Rochester Police Battle Race Riot," July 25, 1964.

33. Kenneth B. Noble, "The Endless Rodney King Case," *New York Times*, February 4, 1996, E5.

34. *Philadelphia Inquirer*, "In Cincinnati Blacks Say Racial Inequality Has Been Years in Making," April 15, 2001.

35. FBI, "History of the F.B.I.," http://www.fbi.gov/libref/historic/history/origins.htm

36. William Preston Jr., *Aliens and Dissenters: Federal Suppression of Radicals, 1903–1933* (New York: Cambridge University Press, 1963), 216–19.

37. Frank J. Donner, *Age of Surveillance* (New York: Vintage Books, 1981), 38–39.

38. Five Episcopal Bishops, "An Open Letter," *New York Times*, January 9, 1920, 2.

39. Jerold S. Auerbach, "Patrician as Libertarian: Zechariah Chafee Jr. and Freedom of Speech," *New England Quarterly* 42 (December 1969): 411–531.

40. Donner, *Age of Surveillance*, 120.

41. Stanley Cohen, *A. Mitchell Palmer: Politician* (New York: Columbia University Press, 1963), 196–245.

42. Francis A. J. Ianni, *A Family Business* (New York: Russell Sage Foundation, 1972), 43–54.

43. Dwight C. Smith, *The Mafia Mystique* (New York: Basic Books, 1975), 123–242.

44. President's Commission on Law Enforcement and the Administration of Justice, *Task Force Report: Organized Crime* (Washington, DC: GPO, 1967), 6.

45. Athan G. Theoharis, *J. Edgar Hoover: Sex and Crime; An Historical Antidote* (Chicago: Ivan R. Dee, 1995).

46. David Caute, *The Great Fear: The Anti-Communist Purge under Truman and Eisenhower* (New York: Simon and Schuster, 1978), 25–28.

47. Smith, *The Mafia Mystique*, 177.

48. FBI, "History of the F.B.I.," http://www.fbi.libref.historic/history/text.htm

49. Ibid., 15.

50. Harry Anslinger, "U.S. Finds Heroin Big Narcotic Snag," *New York Times*, May 2, 1951, 17.

51. Harry Anslinger, "Narcotics Rise Laid to China and Cuba," *New York Times*, June 1, 1962, 2.

52. Alexander Cockburn and Jeffrey St. Calir, "The Bi-partisan Origins of the Total War on Drugs," *Counterpunch*, August 21, 2004, 1.

53. "Drug Enforcement Administration," http://www.usdoj.gov/jmd/mps/manual/dea.htm

54. Elizabeth E. Joh, "The Paradox of Private Policing," *Journal of Criminal Law and Criminology* 95 (2004): 55.

55. *New York Times*, "Private Police Equals McAdoo Force in Numbers," January 22, 1905, SM4.

56. David R. Johnson, *Policing the Urban Underworld* (Philadelphia: Temple University Press, 1979), 90–95.

57. *New York Times*, "The Private Detective Abuse," January 25, 1889, 5.

58. A. H. Raskin, "GM Doubles Force to Curb Sabotage," *New York Times*, April 5, 1942, 35.

59. Terrence J. Mangan and Michael G. Shanahan, "Public Law Enforcement / Private Secuity: A New Partnership?" *F.B.I. Law Enforcement Bulletin* (January 1990): 18–21.

Chapter 2

A BRIEF HISTORY OF CRIMINAL PROSECUTION IN THE UNITED STATES

PRIVATE PROSECUTORS

Although the American criminal justice system is largely derived from the British model, this is not true of the role of the prosecutor. Unlike trial by jury, habeas corpus, and the right to counsel, the private prosecutorial function in use in Britain in the eighteenth century, and even continuing in part today, was not adopted in this country. Instead, the United States chose to institute public prosecution for criminal offenses but nevertheless obtained the assistance of private lawyers.

There had been several attempts to introduce public prosecution to Great Britain, but these did not succeed until 1880 when Sir John Maule was appointed the first director of public prosecution with very limited powers and responsibilities. It was not until 1985 that an amendment to the Prosecution of Offences Act finally established the Crown Prosecution Service. This service has the power to charge possible offenders in all but minor cases and has become the public's prosecutor in a manner similar to that already in existence in the United States since the beginning of the American Republic.[1] The U.S. Constitution does not provide for a public prosecutor. Instead, the office developed gradually from the common law based on the colonial experience. The outcome of this evolution is an office that has, according to Supreme Court Justice Robert H. Jackson, "more control over life, liberty, and reputation than any other person in America."[2] In common law, a crime was viewed as an act against the victim but not the state, so that the target of the crime and/or that individual's friends had to prosecute the offender privately. This meant that in Britain, there was no public prosecution until 1879, when the rather weak office of Director of Public Prosecution was created. Yet, even that office was charged with the responsibility to act as a private citizen interested in law and order. The English prosecutor even then was far more limited than has ever been true in the United States. In fact, it has been estimated that the English prosecutors handled only about 8 percent of all complaints. The history of British public prosecution did not really begin until 1879, when Parliament passed the Prosecution of Offences Act—this, despite early criticism of the private prosecution of crimes. In fact, Henry VIII proposed in 1534 that the penal statutes of England be prosecuted by public prosecutors throughout the kingdom and also be enforced by public prosecutors. His suggestion was rejected by Parliament. A director of public prosecution was then appointed, but his limited role meant that the police had the responsibility to deal with most public prosecutions. In 1907, the director became responsible for handling appeals, but the police organization continued in its role as public prosecutor. To do so, the police used local firms of "solicitors," or lawyers, to advise them on prosecutions. Then, in 1978 the Royal Commission on Criminal Procedure was appointed. In 1981, the commission published a report that sought to reform the process by making several recommendations, including the recommendation to Parliament that an independent prosecuting authority be initiated. This led to the passage of the amended Prosecution of Offences Act of 1985, which further expanded the powers and duties of the Public Prosecution Service but did not give the government nearly the power inherent in the American district attorney.[3]

The American form of prosecuting crimes derives in part from the Puritan heritage embodied in the practices of the Massachusetts Bay Colony in the seventeenth century. There, it was believed that the courts and the church were equally responsible for public order and morality. This belief was enforced on Anne Hutchinson (1591–1643), who was banished from the colony for challenging the power of the all-male government, and on Roger Williams (1603–1683), an English cleric who was driven out of Salem, Massachusetts, not only because he sought better treatment of Native Americans but also because he preached the separation of church and state.[4]

The courts in Puritan Massachusetts were empowered to prosecute religious dissent and also adjudicated religious disputes that threatened to become public issues. These powers meant that government became the enforcer of religious doctrines as well as the enforcer of a patriarchy that strictly regulated gender roles.[5]

Nevertheless, the seventeenth-century Massachusetts courts placed far more emphasis on enforcing public order than enforcing religious mandates. David Fisher has listed the crimes prosecuted by magistrates in the Puritan communities of New England in the seventeenth century. These crimes were the same offenses that today are listed as Class 1 offenses by the FBI, namely, murder, rape, assault, theft, arson, and fraud. (The Class 1 offenses listed by the FBI are homicide, rape, assault, robbery, larceny, arson, and auto theft). Next, the Puritans viewed as crimes conduct inimical to order in the court. Such offenses included failure to appear (as juror or witness or party to the offense), vexatious suits, penalty adjustments, appeals, nonreturn of warrants, and abuse of process. Breach of calendar was also a Puritan offense, unknown today. This included breach of the Sabbath, failure to attend a meeting, failure to attend church services, "and the declaration of days of thanksgiving and humiliation." Violating order in the public square was another form of crime in the Puritan communities. This category included drunkenness, violating sumptuary laws, railing, cursing, swearing, and "light carriage." Breach of regulation referred to commercial and economic regulations, including price regulations, extortion, usury, and failure to obey safety rules. Even speech could be punishable in Puritan New England if it offended on religious or political grounds, became slanderous, or involved swearing and cursing. Sexual misconduct was also of concern to the Puritans, whose influence in that arena continues into the twenty-first century. The law prohibited premarital sex, fornication, lewd conduct, bestiality, homosexuality, and "ravishing," which is called rape today. Finally, order of the household concerned offenses involving marriage and the family; it also dealt with relations between masters and servants.[6]

The punishments for the foregoing offenses seem outlandish to twenty-first-century Americans. The punishments included wearing chains, wearing a sign in a public square attesting to bad conduct, or walking about with one's tongue in the cleft of a green stick to punish bad speech.[7]

Bad speech included expounding so-called Antinomianism (against the law), a philosophy that denied the right of government to know the mind of God. Puritan doctrine held that governments could punish failure to obey the will of God and that governments knew that will. Anne Hutchinson was banished from the Massachusetts Bay Colony for just that offense. The Puritans punished speech and divided offensive speech into four categories. The least offensive speech was defamation, which referred to insults of a person. Disorderly speech was considered more offensive and included cursing, swearing, and lying. Heresy and blasphemy were speech insulting to religion, and hence they were considered worse than defamation. It was political speech that was absolutely banned from Puritan communities, since such speech threatened the dominance of the upper class. Questioning the honesty of officials, challenging the government, or questioning the legitimacy of the law were all subject to severe punishments.[8]

Punishments among the Puritans included token fines or orders to account for a defendant's time; orders to pay restitution; humiliation such as public acknowledgment of fault, banishment from office, or spending time in the stocks; physical punishment such as whipping, imprisonment, and indenture; and capital punishment, including death, branding, mutilation, and exile.[9] Punishments among the seventeenth-century Puritans of New England were related to social standing. Despite the rejection of British titles of nobility, "gentlemen" were given special privileges not available to ordinary citizens. No gentleman was whipped as were the common people.

Even domestic relations were a matter of public interest in the Puritan communities. This prurience led to spying on neighbors. There was an offense called an "improper betrothal," which meant that the marriage intentions had not been published three times. The "maid's guardian" had to consent to any marriage. Divorce was also a concern of the Puritan clergy and governments, and so men who lived apart from their wives were ordered to return home.[10]

Adultery, bigamy, and spousal abuse were also of interest to the Puritan community governments. Such cases, prosecuted and adjudicated in magistrate's courts, included wife beating, but they also dealt with assaults committed by women against men. Yet, the relationships of parents to children were seldom dealt with by these courts. In addition, Puritan courts also prosecuted and punished servants who disobeyed their masters or who had sexual relations that their masters did not approve. Likewise, masters were limited in their conduct toward servants, for cruelty and unjust treatment of servants was also prosecuted and punished.

THE ADVENT OF THE PUBLIC PROSECUTOR

In May 1704, over 80 years since the arrival of the Puritans in New England, the Connecticut Assembly passed a law generally recognized as creating the first public prosecutor in an English colony in the Americas.

The law was introduced with these words: "Henceforth there shall be in every countie a sober, discreet, and religious person appointed by the countie courts, to be atturney for the Queen, to prosecute and implead in the lawe all criminals and to doe all other things necessary or convenient as an atturney to suppress vice and immoralities" (original spelling).[11]

In 1711, Virginia initiated county attorneys, followed by numerous other states when in 1789 the U.S. government first functioned under the presidency of George Washington and the meeting of the First Congress. That Congress passed the Judiciary Act, which specified in Section 35, "[A]nd there shall be appointed in each district a meet person learned in the law to act as attorney for the United States in such district, who shall be sworn and affirmed to the faithful execution of his office, whose duty it shall be to prosecute in such district all delinquents for crimes and offenses; cognizable under the authority of the United States."[12]

This Judiciary Act did not please everyone. In fact, Andrew Jackson, seventh president of the United States, was as critical of the judiciary as Thomas Jefferson had been. Jackson is well known for saying that "John Marshall has made his decision; now let him enforce it." This comment referred to the Chief Justice of the U.S. Supreme Court, John Marshall, whose aggrandizement of power was resented by many citizens, so much so that Jackson's election in 1828 was seen by many as a repudiation of the judiciary. Marshall was viewed as a symbol of the centralization of political power and as an antagonist of states' rights. It was for this reason that President Jackson ignored the order of the Supreme Court when Georgia executed a Native American, George Tassels. The Supreme Court had issued a "writ of error" to the effect that Tassels was a Cherokee and not an American and that the laws of Georgia could not extend to Indian territory. President Jackson would not enforce this order. Georgia also convicted another Cherokee, James Graves, who was also executed despite a Supreme Court order to the contrary. Marshall held that Indian territory was completely separate from that of the states and that therefore Georgia law could not apply there.[13]

In view of the hostility many Americans who lived on the frontier felt toward the federal courts, prosecutors soon became independent of the federal attorney general. Like Andrew Jackson, citizens demanded democracy as the country moved away from rule by a small oligarchy of "founding fathers" and embraced Jacksonian democracy, which demanded more elected officials and fewer appointed bureaucrats. Therefore, the position of local judge changed from appointed to elected. In turn, the local prosecutor was also elected.[14]

As a result of the consequent decentralization of power, the attorney general in each state was becoming less and less important and finally lost all supervisory functions over the local prosecutors. All this came about after the election of Andrew Jackson. Prior to that election, during the first 40 years of the American Republic, the appointed status of the local prosecutors would not allow them to make independent decisions without regard to the powers who appointed them.[15]

In some jurisdictions, the prosecutor was called district attorney; in others, county attorney or state's attorney. These public prosecutors had become dominant in most states by 1820. Yet, there were numerous deficiencies inherent in these offices, whatever their name. These deficiencies included lack of funds, poor pay, lack of assistance, inexperience, and incompetence. Moreover, the prosecutors were mostly recent law graduates who held these jobs only long enough to become known in their districts so they could start private law practices.[16] Public prosecutors, then and now, were usually overworked but seldom received any assistance because the counties or states would not allocate the money to appoint any assistant. Furthermore, public prosecutors had too much territory to cover, which led them to travel from county seat to county seat without adequate preparation for upcoming trials. As a result, the public prosecutor was forced to deal with trials without ever having seen the defendant or the witnesses on behalf of the state; thus, numerous loopholes had been created by which criminals escaped regularly. This situation resulted in a great deal of frustration for the victims of crime, who were compelled to hire private attorneys to help prosecute offenses.[17]

A number of trials, particularly those involving murder, were conducted with the assistance of private prosecutors hired by the victims' relatives. Several such nineteenth-century cases can be exhibited, including the famous murder trial of Harvard professor John White Webster, who was accused of killing Dr. George Parkman. The Parkman family hired a prominent lawyer, George Bemis, to assist the attorney general of Massachusetts. Parkman was a member of a powerful and wealthy Brahmin family in Boston. Webster was found guilty of the murder and publicly hanged on August 30, 1850, in Boston's Leverett Square. Because the evidence concerning this murder was based mainly on dental records, this may be the first murder conviction ever obtained by the use of scientific means identifying a burned body. Although such identification of the corpse does not, of course, prove the guilt of the accused, it was at least an effort to find an objective means of dealing with this crime. The wealth and prominence of the survivors made it possible to pay a prominent attorney to conduct the prosecution of a professor who had no such resources.

In fact, George Bemis even edited the record of this trial and used that opportunity to alter the charge that Chief Justice Lemuel Shaw had delivered to the jury so that it no longer appeared as prejudicial against the defendant as it had been spoken in court.[18] In 1871, the family of Alexander Crittenden hired Alexander Campbell to help prosecute Laura D. Fair for the murder of Crittenden, who had been her lover for seven years. The defense argued that Fair had become temporarily insane because she had entered business and therefore had taken on a man's role. This, said the defense, caused Fair to be seized by an irresistible impulse; she would not have killed Crittenden, the defense claimed, had she been sane. The jury nevertheless found Fair guilty, and she was sentenced to death, only to have the conviction overturned by the state supreme court, which ordered a new trial. She was acquitted at her second trial.[19]

On Monday, October 17, 1870, Henry Black found Colonel William McKaig on the street in downtown Crawford, Maryland. Black confronted McKaig and shot him to death in front of 20 witnesses. Evidently, McKaig had been intimate with Black's sister on numerous occasions when McKaig's wife was out of town. Black shouted at McKaig before shooting him, "That's what you get for ruining my sister," and then proceeded to the murder. Tried by a jury, Black was found not guilty because his victim was viewed as a scoundrel—this, although the wealthy family of McKaig had hired a famous lawyer, Milton Whitney, to prosecute Black.[20]

In 1870, Horace Greeley hired Noah Davis to prosecute Daniel McFarland for murdering Albert D. Richardson, a prominent editor. McFarland accused Richardson of cohabiting with McFarland's wife. McFarland was acquitted because the jury thought that Abby McFarland was worse than the killer, since she had violated family values and responsibilities.

There are numerous other cases of murder and lesser crimes in which private lawyers were hired to prosecute offenders alongside public prosecutors. It is noteworthy that the opinions of nineteenth-century Americans were such as to find murderers not guilty if their victims had committed adultery. Such a view is hardly visible in the United States of the twenty-first century. Private prosecution was so common in the nineteenth century that at least 15 state supreme courts held this practice legal and justified on the grounds that the practice was well established.

It was not until 1875 that the supreme courts of Massachusetts and Michigan disapproved of privately paid prosecutors. In *Meister v. People*, the Michigan court prohibited the district attorney in that state to accept private pay or being privately retained in order to "secure impartiality from all persons connected with criminal trials."[21]

Wisconsin was the third state to abolish the practice of hiring private prosecutors on the grounds that they are hired by "parties who from passion, prejudice or even an honest belief in the guilt of the accused, are desirous of procuring his conviction."[22]

In 1911, the Illinois Supreme Court ruled that a trial court was in error when it appointed two young and inexperienced lawyers to represent a criminal defendant while permitting two privately paid, experienced lawyers to participate in the prosecution.[23]

Even as late as 1991, the courts of 30 states still allowed the practice of having private prosecutors, hired for a fee, assist the public prosecutors in criminal cases. The gradual disappearance of privately funded prosecutors was also promoted by the defense's attack on this system in that the defense argued that the prosecutors accepted "blood money" in return for gaining a conviction by any means and no matter what the evidence. Thus, John Graham, who defended Daniel McFarland, claimed that the privately funded prosecutor Noah Davis was motivated by personal gain. Henry S. Ballard paid attorney Edward Sanford to prosecute Amelia Norman in 1844 for the attempted murder of Ballard, who had been Norman's lover. Her lawyer argued that the privately paid prosecutor at that trial was motivated by his fee and not by a pursuit of justice. Such arguments were highly successful and led to numerous acquittals.[24]

In the late twentieth century and in the early twenty-first century, the issue of private prosecution is hardly discussed. In fact, few Americans know that the option of private prosecution exists or has ever existed. In the twenty-first century, private prosecution, though not held illegal, is hardly practiced.

The abuses of private prosecutors have, therefore, been generally ended. However, as the use of DNA evidence has revealed, the American people have, for a long time, been the victims of public prosecutors' abuses that appear to be far more serious than anything objectionable ever conducted by private prosecutors. Yet, both are hardly matched by the vigilante system in use in the western part of the United States for many years.

THE VIGILANTE TRADITION

In an analysis of "why men rebel," Ted Robert Gurr has featured "relative deprivation" as a principal cause of such rebellion. Relative deprivation refers to the belief by any group or individual that his reference group has attained greater rewards than are available to the subject and that these rewards were obtained by illegitimate means.[25]

Relative deprivation is related to a good deal of white-collar crime in that some who have high-prestige occupations and good incomes may nevertheless resort to stealing because their expectations are not achieved relative to those who matter to them. For example, a well-to-do physician nevertheless deals drugs because he compares himself with other physicians who graduated from medical school with him and are earning a good deal more than he is earning.[26]

Likewise, the social context of vigilantism is rooted in the belief that government is incapable of dealing with those who threaten the social order and that the dissidents who believe they are the victims of relative deprivation must be kept in check.[27]

Vigilantism evidently succeeds when it is supported by the population in which it occurs. When vigilantes have the support of the so-called establishment in a community, it generally succeeds. This is so because the government in areas where vigilantism flourishes is not capable of suppressing it any more than it is capable of suppressing the criminal gangs who provoked vigilantism in the first place.

Vigilantism, according to Jon Rosenbaum and Peter Sederberg, may relate to crime control, social group control, or regime control. In the case of the American West after the Civil War, crime control was the undoubted motive for vigilantism.[28] No better example of vigilantism as a means of crime control can be found than the vigilantes who "enforced" the law in the American Southwest after the Civil War (1861–1865). The area was largely underdeveloped and so far removed from the seat of the U.S. government in Washington, D.C., that law enforcement on the federal level was not possible. Even state capitals were far removed from many areas in Texas and other large states. For example, Austin, the capital of Texas, is 600 miles distant from El Paso and equally far from other communities in that state. Evidently, in the nineteenth century such a distance guaranteed that state government could not be effective even in areas at a lesser distance from the state capital. Courts could not be established fast enough to deal with the ever-expanding settlements in the American West, so that citizens felt justified in defending themselves collectively against murder, robbery, theft, and rape. It was claimed by some that the outlaws of the era killed only people of their own kind and that decent citizens were not attacked. The evidence shows otherwise. Many a citizen was wounded or murdered by gangs, either by error or by intent. A well-known proverb summarized the conditions prevalent in the southwestern United States in the nineteenth century: "There is no Sunday west of Newton and no God west of Pueblo."[29]

So much violence and crime existed in Texas shortly after 1865 that it was believed in the eastern states that the population of Texas must be recruited from the worst and most undesirable citizens of the country. The phrase "Gone to Texas" was applied to anyone who was viewed as a drunkard and ruffian; so popular was the phrase that this prejudice against the citizens of Texas was even repeated in England.

Such outlawry was particularly prominent between 1865 and 1885, when the frontier closed with the occupation of California. Frederick Jackson Turner described this significant event in American history: "Up to our own day, American history has been in a large degree the history of the colonization of the Great West."[30]

In 1873, the *San Antonio Daily Express* reported that cattle stealing had become ubiquitous in Texas and that more than 100,000 cattle had been driven from Texas during the 20 years preceding that article.[31] A number of cattle thieves and other criminals disguised themselves as "Indians," or Native Americans, while stealing horses and other animals, and they usually "got away with it" because communication was difficult and methods of identification hardly existed. Moreover, the cattle thieves and other criminals crossed the Rio Grande at will and could not be arrested in Mexico for crimes committed in Texas. The prohibition of entering Indian reservations was equally enforced, and so outlaws could also seek refuge in one of these territories, which were deemed outside the jurisdiction of the state. This meant that Indians, as well as so-called "whites," entered reservations after raiding settlements. The whites were usually disguised as Indians and were discovered to be of European descent only when some were occasionally killed during gun battles between them and the U.S. Army.[32]

There is a great deal of evidence in letters, articles, and books describing the manner in which Mexican bandits crossed into the United States when chased by Mexican police and vice versa.

In many of the small towns established in New Mexico, Texas, and Arizona, a virtual reign of terror developed shortly after the Civil War as such killers as William Antrim or William H. Bonney, known as "Billy the Kid," and others engaged in bloody feuds over the spoils of robbery. Together with Tom O'Foliard, Dave Rudabaugh, and Charles Bowdre, all of these professional criminals died violent deaths.[33] A number of western and southwestern communities shared the title of "wickedest town in the West." Among these communities was Dodge City, which was first laid out in 1872 by the chief engineer of the Atchison, Topeka, and Santa Fe Railway. Like Abilene before then, Dodge became the target of numerous immigrants, among them cattle thieves and hold-up men. "We were entirely without law and order," wrote R. M. Wright, one of Dodge's citizens.[34]

It is, of course, true that the conduct of the few who violated every law and terrorized the decent majority gained the most publicity, so it appeared to some that all southwestern towns were inhabited by gun-slinging killers. The truth was that a considerable majority were interested in living in peace but could not rely on government to defend them against widespread crime. Therefore, citizens sometimes organized secret groups known as vigilantes or vigilante committees. These citizens decided to rid themselves of the aggressors who victimized citizens at random. Consequently, the vigilantes themselves became "outlaws" in that they hanged thieves as well as murderers without consulting any law, of which they were usually ignorant. In short, almost any criminal activity could result in the death penalty imposed by angry citizens.

Examples of vigilante organizations were the Squatters Claim Association of Kansas; the Self Protective Association of Linn County, Kansas; and the Council City Organization, also in Kansas.[35]

Evidently, the vigilante movement often deteriorated into establishment violence. This meant that the innocent had no protection, that punishments were disproportionate to the crimes committed, and that a number of the most aggressive vigilantes were themselves violence-prone individuals who used the vigilante organizations as a means of fostering their own antisocial interests.[36]

Vigilantes, according to Richard Brown, are generally motivated by the belief that the "establishment" is being jeopardized and that this danger must be met by prompt action. Vigilantes see themselves as virtuous, and for that reason they usually attract popular support. Vigilantes seek deterrence by using threats or actual sanctions. These threats and sanctions are generally supported by the public or even the government as long as the threat continues. Once the threat or crime has been eliminated and the offenders "run out of town" or hanged, support dwindles, the vigilantes lose their legitimacy, and normal life returns to its routines.

Prosecutors in the Twentieth Century

The closing of the American frontier at the end of the nineteenth century invalidated the need for vigilantes because the prosecution of crimes became the province of the government attorney on the county, state, and federal levels. Each jurisdiction has its own prosecutors. These government attorneys present the state's case against the defendant in criminal prosecutions.

The use of private prosecutors was abolished in the United States when the U.S. Supreme Court ruled in *Leeke v. Timmerman* that "a private citizen has no judicially cognizable right to prevent state officials from presenting information, through intervention of a state solicitor" or the like. This ruling did not mean that the aid of private lawyers helping prosecutors became illegal, but it nevertheless resulted in the disuse of this resource.[37]

Consequently, by the 1940s, most states had created licensing requirements for the office of prosecutor, so that a person not licensed to practice law cannot be a prosecutor, ending the practice of hiring private prosecutors and increasing the power of the public prosecutor immensely. On the federal level, the U.S. attorney general appoints a

U.S. attorney for each federal district. On the local level, prosecutors are elected. Subject to a great deal of political pressure, the prosecutors are expected to take charge of the investigation of a crime, present the evidence to a grand jury, and question witnesses during a trial. In most states, the prosecutor must present the court with a written statement of the charges against a defendant. This is called an "information." In other states, the prosecutor needs to present the evidence to a grand jury, so called because it consists of 15 members or more, as contrasted with a trial jury of 12 members. The grand jury then decides, based on the evidence presented, whether or not to indict the defendant as required by the Fifth Amendment to the U.S. Constitution.

Although prosecutors have almost limitless discretion as to whom to prosecute, the law prohibits prosecution based on race, religion, ethnic origin, or sex.

Furthermore, a prosecutor may not charge a defendant with additional charges if the conviction in a first trial has been overturned by a court of appeals.[38]

Because the prosecutor must present evidence against the defendant in court, the prosecutor uses police detectives to gain as much evidence as possible against the citizen. Defendants are, of course, at a great disadvantage, as they have no police department to help their case. The law provides that the prosecutor must turn over to the defense any evidence against the defendants and must also inform the defense of any exculpatory evidence in the defendants' favor. This is sometimes not done. Prosecutors occasionally hide or destroy evidence favoring defendants.

Nevertheless, plea bargaining settles more than 90 percent of cases in the American criminal justice system. This means that defendants will frequently plead guilty to an offense lesser than the one being prosecuted. Such a plea gives the overworked prosecutors a conviction and, in case defendants know they are guilty, provides defendants with less punishment than a conviction would have entailed. The few cases that go to trial may be tried only by a judge or by both the judge and a jury. The prosecutor makes an opening statement, presents evidence and testimony, and makes a closing argument. Although the law demands that prosecutors drop the charges if there is a lack of evidence supporting the guilt of a defendant, prosecutors seldom do so because they know that their own reelection depends on the public's belief that the prosecutor has gained large numbers of convictions. Because prosecutors have unlimited power to decide whether to prosecute or discontinue a prosecution once begun, or whether to exonerate the defendant, the cause of justice frequently has not been served. Lord John Dalberg-Acton (1834–1902), a British historian, coined a famous phrase that pertains to many an American prosecutor. Said Acton, "Power tends to corrupt, and absolute power corrupts absolutely."[39]

Added to the evils inherent in plea bargaining is the short-term elected office pitfall, which makes reelection vital for many prosecutors who have long ago relinquished their private law practices and must therefore be reelected to earn their livelihoods. Pressured to gain convictions and anxious to be reelected, many a prosecutor has used his or her office to convict the innocent and make such behavior seem acceptable. Generally, prosecutors have the power to subpoena (Latin for "under penalty") any person deemed to have relevant information and to compel his or her testimony under oath. The purpose of these efforts is to indict the defendant. An accusation delivered by a grand jury with a view of producing a trial concerning the guilt or innocence of the accused, an "indictment" is a statement of probable or possible guilt but is not a conviction. In theory, this would mean that the grand jury can prevent unjustifiable prosecution. In fact, grand juries "rubber stamp" the prosecutor's accusations, and so it has been said that an American prosecutor can "indict a ham sandwich."[40]

Another means by which a prosecutor can deliver a defendant to trial is by "information." An information is the sum of the prosecutor's evidence concerning the alleged crime. Such an information is subject to a preliminary hearing by a magistrate. Nevertheless, it has been used to harass individuals for the purpose of gaining publicity for the prosecutor and thereby enhance the prosecutor's reputation as a means of ensuring reelection. Since prosecutors are immune from civil suits, malicious prosecution, although illegal, is commonly conducted by prosecutors. This tactic seldom affects the prosecutors in any negative manner, although there are a few instances in which prosecutors did not succeed. Such failures are rare because the victims of false accusations and false prosecutions are usually poor and defenseless.[41]

Perhaps the most publicized case of false prosecution ever aired by the media in the United States occurred as the result of a rape accusation against three lacrosse players who were students at Duke University in 2006. Dave Evans, Collin Finnerty, and Reade Seligmann were accused of raping an exotic dancer at a party. The accusation was false, and the district attorney, Mike Nifong, knew this. However, he was running for reelection in 2006 and therefore sought to gain votes by portraying the three students as "a bunch of hooligans" and telling the media that he would not allow "a bunch of lacrosse players from Duke to rape a black girl." There was no rape. Yet, the district attorney indicted the students even as the media displayed "mug shots" of these innocent young men. To make matters worse, the faculty of Duke University denounced the youths as rapists without knowing the facts and were utterly unwilling to hear the evidence. The faculty even provided an advertisement in a local newspaper headlined, "What Does a Social Disease Sound Like?" presuming the lacrosse players' guilt. Because the families of the three students had the money to hire lawyers, the charges against the students were finally dropped and the district attorney, Nifong, was disbarred. This result is so unusual that the case may be the only one of its kind in all the history of criminal justice in the United States.[42]

The disbarment of a former district attorney is indeed unusual. More often, many innocent Americans have been sent to prison and even to their deaths not only because of malicious prosecution but also because of ignorance. Prior to the discovery of the double-helix structure of deoxyribonucleic acid, or DNA, by Rosalind Franklin in 1953, prosecutors relied on eyewitness accounts, on jailhouse confessions, on fingerprints, and on the so-called lie detector to discover the truth about an accusation.[43] Numerous experiments by psychologists have demonstrated that eyewitness accounts of any event are at best dubious, if not total inventions. The courts have taken this into consideration when so-called eyewitness accounts have been introduced as evidence of guilt. It is, of course, possible that a good number of eyewitness accounts reflect the truth. Nevertheless, a number of cases are known to have convicted the wrong person on the grounds of eyewitness evidence. This was particularly true before the end of the twentieth century, when the police and the courts relied on such accounts. An example of false identification by eyewitnesses is the case of Christopher Ballestrero, who was arrested and tried for armed robbery after four eyewitnesses identified him as the robber of an insurance office. The actual offender continued his crime spree after Ballestrero was already in custody. Then, the robber confessed that he, and not Ballestrero, had been the insurance office robber. In fact, the robber had left a handwritten note. This note was compared to Ballestrero's handwriting sample and proved that Balllestrero was not the writer. The use of handwriting samples was, in the mid-twentieth century, one means then available to verify such accounts. In fact, in one case 13 different individuals identified a man as having defrauded a number of victims. Only after he was already jailed was it discovered by means of a handwriting sample that the imprisoned man was innocent.[44] In 2001, the New York State Court of Appeals ruled on the admissibility of eyewitness testimony during criminal trials. In *People v. Anthony Lee*, the court ruled that the reliability of eyewitness accounts could be, but need not be, affirmed by an "expert." The court ruled that the trial court shall decide whether expert testimony of reliability of eyewitnesses should be introduced during trial.[45]

Confessions have been used by prosecutors for centuries. It is assumed by many, including jurors, that one would not confess a crime unless one knew oneself to be guilty. Yet, the evidence teaches us otherwise. There are indeed innocent people who take responsibility for crimes they have nothing to do with and which they never committed. One of the most atrocious such confessions was coerced from two Chicago boys, aged 7 and 8, who were pressured by the police to confess to the murder of an 11-year-old girl. Interrogated without lawyers or their parents, alone and defenseless, the boys told the police what these "law enforcers" wanted to hear. This is, of course, not an isolated or unusual case of false confessions.[46]

Allison Redlich and Gail Goodman conducted a convincing study of the reasons for false confessions. They found that false confessions are related to age, in that young people are more likely to make incriminating statements that are not true, that such confessions are more likely for young children than adolescents, and that adults are less likely, but not immune, to making false confessions.[47] The reason for making such confessions lies first in the need to obey authority. The youngest children are evidently more anxious to do so than would be true of adults. Police often present false evidence to teens or to children—false evidence such as claiming that the target of the interrogation has already been identified by eyewitnesses when this is not true, claiming that the defendant's fingerprints were found at the scene of the crime, or claiming that the defendant had "failed" a lie detector test.

Prosecutors have also promised early release to prison inmates willing to testify in court that their cellmate confessed a crime to them even if that is not true. Or the police interrogate a "suspect" for many hours until sleep deprivation brings the desired results. One such example is the 2006 confession obtained from Ozem Goldwire, who was questioned by six detectives for 17 hours until he confessed to murdering his sister. He spent a year in jail awaiting trial until the false charges had to be dropped.[48]

Much worse in its implication than the Goldwire confession was the confession of Martin Tankleff, who admitted to killing his parents, Seymour and Arlene Tankleff, in 1988. After spending 20 years in prison, Martin Tankleff was released in 2008 because it was evident that his confession had been coerced by the police, who had failed to provide the then-17-year-old with a lawyer and had worn him down with hours of questioning. Innumerable such cases have existed in all the states for years and are only now (2009) coming to light as DNA testing and electronic methods begin to shed some light on the conduct of police and prosecutors.[49]

Prior to the introduction of DNA testing, prosecutors and police used lie detectors, also known as polygraphs, to find the truth of a suspect's testimony. In the 1980s and beyond, the polygraph was credited with discovering lies, and so-called polygraph experts were allowed to testify in criminal trials. This practice has been largely discredited in the twenty-first century not only because many such experts falsely accused defendants so as to keep making money from jobs assigned by the police and prosecutors but also because the belief that blood pressure and other measurements were accurate indicators of telling a falsehood were proved to be wrong. The lie detector is a psychometric device that should meet the scientific standards of reliability and validity. A test using a polygraph includes answering a number of questions posed by the examiner. That examiner then interprets the "autonomic disturbances" a question may reveal in the subject. Such interpretations are highly subjective and are unreliable even if the examiner is not influenced by personal gain.[50]

Because the polygraph appears to be a scientific mechanism and its practitioners scientists, many jurors and judges held utterly innocent people guilty of all kinds of crimes solely because these lie detectors implicated their victims. Polygraphs are so unreliable that the results of these examinations are not admissible in U.S. courts. Nevertheless, police and prosecutors make every effort to persuade suspects to submit to these examinations. As a result, innocent suspects are accused and even convicted while guilty criminals may be able to "beat" the polygraph.

An excellent example of the failure of the polygraph is the manner in which Dennis Donahue passed a lie detector test in the killing of Crystallynn Girard in 1993. Donahue at that time told the polygraph operator that he was not at the scene of the crime, that he did not know who killed Girard, and that he did not kill her. The polygraph operator determined that Donahue was telling the truth. In fact, Donahue was given immunity from prosecution for testifying in court against Lynn Dejac, who was convicted of a murder that Donahue may have committed, unless Crystallynn Girard died of natural causes. In 2007, when Dejac was freed after 13 years in prison, no final determination of the cause of Girard's death was possible.[51]

Lie detectors discover changes in the subject's heart rate, respiratory rate, and a number of other physiological responses. These changes can occur for many reasons but are nevertheless attributed to lying. Likewise, good liars show no such physiological changes. For example, Mark Christie, about 21 years old in 1994, killed 4-year-old Kali Ann Poulton that year. Nevertheless, he passed two lie detector tests.[52]

All the foregoing unreliable means used in criminal investigations could now be discarded because the use of DNA testing is a truly reliable means of determining the presence of an accused at the scene of a crime.

In 1992, two professors of law at Yeshiva University in New York City founded the Innocence Project. Barry Scheck and Peter Neufeld sought to exonerate wrongfully convicted people through DNA testing, thereby reforming the criminal justice system and preventing the further incarceration and killing of innocent victims of prosecutors. Law students, under the supervision of their professors, handle these cases. The project has grown from its founding at the Cardozo School of Law at Yeshiva University to national dimensions as law schools all over the country are now engaged in this effort to help the poorest of the poor who have no other means of defense.[53]

In 1993, Kirk Noble Bloodsworth became the first American to be exonerated through DNA testing, after having been sent to death row and later incarcerated for life in a Maryland prison for a murder committed by another man. Five witnesses had placed Bloodworth at the scene of the crime. Even forensic evidence was introduced by the prosecution to gain a conviction. The death sentence was overturned by the Maryland Court of Appeals because the prosecution had withheld exculpatory evidence. Tried a second time, Bloodworth was found guilty again and sentenced to two life sentences. Finally, the court approved a DNA test of biological material, leading to a full pardon for Bloodsworth.

On May 2, 2008, Levon Jones became the 129th prisoner released from death row since 1973. Jones spent 13 years in prison because a prosecutor was more interested in gaining convictions than administering justice. Jones, like so many of the other innocents sent to prison or death, became the victim of prosecutorial lies and deception and poor representation by defense attorneys. Jones was freed in North Carolina because the American Civil Liberties Union (ACLU) employed DNA testing to prove his innocence and further showed that the witness against him had testified in order to collect $4,000 in reward money from the governor's office.[54] The number and proportion of prisoners jailed for murder is small compared to all 2.2 million prisoners now held in American jails and prisons. Therefore, it is evident that the release of 129 innocent citizens from death row alone demonstrates that far greater numbers of innocent people are now in prison than those innocently on death row. It should also be remembered that only those individuals whose biological material is still available years after conviction can be rescued through DNA testing.

In 2004, law professor Samuel R. Gross of the University of Michigan published a 15-year study of 328 exonerated former prisoners. Of these, 199 had been unjustly convicted of murder, 120 had been convicted of rapes they did not do, and nine cases involved other so-called crimes. In more than half the cases the defendants had been in prison for more than 10 years, and 73 of the murder convictions sent the innocent victims to death row. DNA was successfully used in 88 percent of the false accusations of rape. In murder cases, only 20 percent had DNA evidence available to them. Ninety percent of the falsely accused in rape cases involved misidentification or eyewitness accounts. Black men were most often the victims of false imprisonment, particularly if the prosecution relied on eyewitness testimony from whites who viewed all blacks as looking the same. The leading cause of false convictions for murder is false confession linked to intimidation by police.[55]

Despite the overwhelming evidence that DNA testing is a secure means of determining the presence or absence of someone accused of crime, prosecutors keep fighting the use of DNA evidence. Prosecutors are far more interested in gaining a conviction, however false, than in securing justice. This vindictiveness is particularly visible in Florida, where prosecutors have convinced the legislature not to allow DNA testing.[56] An excellent example of this kind of unjust prosecution is the treatment of Frank Lee Smith, who was sent to death row in Florida in 1985 for the murder of eight-year-old Shandra Whitehead. Smith confessed to this murder after the police pretended that three eyewitnesses had identified him at the murder scene. He recanted this confession, however, and refused to plead guilty. Smith then sought to have a DNA test performed, but the court refused the request. Yet, by the late 1990s, Eddie Lee Moseley confessed to having killed Shandra Whitehead, and a DNA test showed that Moseley was indeed her killer. Smith could have left prison on December 15, 2000, the day DNA proved his innocence, except that he had died in prison 11 months earlier.[57]

In 2008, the recently elected district attorney for Dallas, Texas, Henry Watkins, built a national reputation for freeing wrongfully convicted prisoners who had been railroaded into prison and death row by Henry Wade, his predecessor. Wade had routinely violated the law by ignoring the Supreme Court ruling in *Brady v. Maryland* that prohibited prosecutors from withholding evidence favorable to the defense and boasted about his ability to convict innocent people. By May 2008, Texas paid $8.6 million in compensation to the wrongfully imprisoned, even as more and more such cases were coming to light. Watkins has sought to disbar prosecutors who have intentionally prosecuted the innocent.[58]

It is, of course, evident that all who are in prison are not innocent and that those who commit crimes against citizens must be prosecuted. Such prosecution deals with street crime, including the Class 1 offenses as listed by the FBI and white-collar crime committed by people of high social standing in the course of their daily business.

Summary

The English tradition of conducting private prosecutions was continued in part in the United States despite the enactment of the Judiciary Act of 1789.

In Puritan Massachusetts, prosecution of various offenses was conducted by magistrates who were also clergy. After the American Revolution, public prosecution with the help of private attorneys became common, except in the Southwest, where vigilantes administered justice in the absence of government. As the country was settled and the frontier disappeared, public prosecution became the rule. Public prosecutors have immense power and have frequently misused this power to imprison and even kill innocent people. This practice has been somewhat curtailed by the use of DNA testing, as fostered by the Innocence Project.

Notes

1. Jack M. Kress, "Progress and Prosecution," *Annals of the American Academy of Political and Social Sciences* 423 (January 1976): 99–116.

2. Robert H. Jackson, "The Federal Prosecutor," *Journal of the American Judiciary Society* 24 (1940): 18.

3. "The Crown Prosecution Service," *http://www.cps.gove.uk/about/history.html*

4. Keith Thomas, "Cases of Conscience in Seventeenth Century England," in *Public Duty and Private Conscience in Seventeenth Century England*, ed. J. Morrill, P. Slack, and D. Wolff (New York: Oxford University Press, 1993): 37.

5. Mary Beth Norton, "Gender and Defamation in 17th Century Maryland," *William and Mary Quarterly* 44 (1987): 3–39.

6. David H. Fischer, *Albion's Seed* (New York: Oxford University Press, 1989), 189–96.

7. Gary King, Robert O. Keohane, and Sidney Verba, *Designing Social Inquiry* (Princeton, NJ: Princeton University Press, 1994), 153–55.

8. Roger Thompson, "Holy Watchfulness and Communal Conformism: The Functions of Defamation in Early New England Communities," *New England Quarterly* 56, no. 4 (1983): 504–22.

9. Edwin Powers, *Crime and Punishment in Early Massachusetts, 1620–1692* (Boston: Beacon Press, 1966), 195.

10. D. Kelly Weisberg, "Under Great Temptation Here: Women and Divorce Law in Puritan Massachusetts," in *Women and the Law*, ed. D. K. Weisberg (Cambridge, MA: Schenkman Publishing, 1982), 117–21.

11. Walter M. Pickett, "The Office of the Public Prosecutor in Connecticut," *Journal of Criminal Law and Criminology* 17 (November 1926): 348.

12. Judiciary Act of 1789, Section 35.

13. Richard P. Longaker, "Andrew Jackson and the Judiciary," *Political Science Quarterly* 71, no. 3 (September 1956): 344.

14. Newman Baker, "The Prosecuting Attorney—Provisions of Organizing a Law Office," *Journal of Criminal Law and Criminology* 23 (1932): 926.

15. Thomas P. Abernethy, "Jackson and the Rise of South-Western Democracy," *American Historical Review* 33, no. 1 (October 1927): 64–77.

16. John A. J. Ward, "Private Prosecution: The Entrenched Anomaly," *North Carolina Law Review* 50 (1972): 1171–79.

17. Robert M. Ireland, "Privately Funded Prosecution of Crime in the Nineteenth-Century United States," *American Journal of Legal History* 39, no. 1 (January 1995): 45–46.

18. Robert M. Ireland, "Review of Murder at Harvard," *American Journal of Legal History* 16, no. 4 (1972): 373–76.

19. Holly Streeter, "The Sordid Trial of Laura D. Fair: Victorian Family Values," *Georgetown Law* (July 24, 2003): n.p.

20. Laura James, "The Famous Black-McKaig Trial," *Esquire,* May 11, 2005.

21. *Meister v. People*, Michigan 99, 103–104 (1875).

22. *Biemel v. State*, 71 Wisconsin 444,37 N.W. 244, 245–248 (1888).

23. *People v. Ford*, 19 Illinois 2d 466, 168 N.E. 2d 33 (1960).

24. *New York Herald*, January 17, 1844.

25. Ted Robert Gurr, *Why Men Rebel* (Princeton, NJ: Princeton University Press, 1970), 317–59.

26. Alex Thio, *Sociology* (New York: Longman, 1998), 182.

27. H. Jon Rosenbaum and Peter C. Sederberg, "Vigilantism: An Analysis of Establishment Violence," *Comparative Politics* 6, no. 4 (July 1974): 545.

28. Ibid., 548.

29. Charles M. Harger, "Cattle Trails of the Prairies," *Scribner's Magazine* 11 (1892): 736.

30. Frederick Jackson Turner, "The Significance of the Frontier in American History," *Report of the American Historical Association* (1893): 199–227. Turner's article has been reprinted innumerable times in history books and journals and is regarded as one of the most seminal American history papers ever written.

31. C. C. Rister, "Outlaws and Vigilantes of the Southern Plains," *Mississippi Historical Review* 19, no. 4 (March 1933): 541.

32. Thomas C. Battey, *A Quaker among the Indians* (Boston: Lee and Shepard, 1875): 239 (microfiche).

33. Jon Tuska, *Billy the Kid* (Westport, CT: Greenwood Press, 1986): 67.

34. Robert Marr Wright, *Dodge City* (Wichita, KS: Wichita Eagle Press, 1913): 10 (microform).

35. Rister, "Outlaws and Vigilantes," 551.

36. Richard Maxwell Brown, "Legal and Behavioral Perspectives on American Vigilantism," *Perspectives on American Vigilantism* 5 (1971): 106–16.

37. *Leeke v. Timmerman*, 454 U.S. 83 (1981).

38. *Oyler v. Boles*, 368 U.S. 448, 82 S. Ct. 5017 L Ed.2d 446 (1962).

39. John Dalberg-Acton, in *The New Dictionary of Cultural Literacy*, ed. John Kett, 3rd ed. (2002).

40. Marcia Kramer and Frank Lombardi, "New Top State Judge: Abolish Grand Juries and Let Us Decide," *New York Daily News*, January 31, 1985.

41. *Los Angeles Times*, "Immunity for Prosecutors," April 19, 2008, 3.

42. Ann Blythe, "Claims against Nifong to Be Heard in Civil Court," *News and Observer*, May 28, 2008, 1.

43. Anne Sayre, *Rosalind Franklin and DNA* (New York: Norton, 1975).

44. Ordway Hilton, "Handwriting Identification vs. Eyewitness Identification," *Journal of Criminal Law, Criminology and Police Science* 45, no. 2 (July–August 1954): 207–12.

45. Jill Milller, "Decisions on Expert Testimony Left to Trial Courts," *Rochester (New York) Daily Record*, May 23, 2001.

46. Richard A. Leo and Richard J. Ofshe, "The Consequences of False Confessions," *Journal of Criminal Law, Criminology and Police Science* 88 (1998): 429–96.

47. Allison R. Redlich and Gail S. Goodman, "Taking Responsibility for an Act Not Committed: The Influence of Age and Suggestibility," *Law and Human Behavior* 27, no. 2 (April 2003): 141–56.

48. Jim Dwyer, "Trying to Give Police the Right Answer, Even When It's Wrong," *New York Times*, June 13, 2007, B1.

49. Katherine G. Madigan, "Videotape Interrogations, Confessions," *Albany Times Union*, February 25, 2008, A7.

50. David C. Raskin and John A. Podlesny, "Truth and Deception," *Psychological Bulletin* 86 (1979): 54.

51. Gene Warner, "Donahue's Denial Was Backed by Lie Detector," *Buffalo News*, October 2, 2007, A1.

52. Debra A. Skok Watson, "Polygraph Test Can Do More Harm Than Good," *Buffalo News*, August 23, 2001, B4.

53. Abraham McLaughlin, "Tales of Journey from Death to Freedom," *Christian Science Monitor* 90, no. 246 (November 16, 1996): 1.

54. Mandy Locke, "Death Row Inmate to Go Free," *News and Observer*, May 2, 2008, 1.

55. Adam Liptak, "Study Suspects Thousands of False Convictions," *New York Times*, April 19, 2004, A 15.

56. Adam Liptak, "Prosecutors Fight DNA Use for Exoneration," *New York Times*, August 29, 2003, A1.

57. Betty Fitterman, "Case Story: Post Conviction DNA Testing," National Clearing House for Science, Technology and Law, Stetson University, South Gulfport, Florida, March 2006.

58. Jennifer Emily and Steve McGonigle, "Dallas County Attorney Wants Unethical Prosecutors Punished," *Dallas Morning News*, May 4, 2008, 1.

Chapter 3

PROSECUTING VIOLENT CRIME AND SEX OFFENSES

SOME CRIME STATISTICS

The true extent of violent crime in the United States is unknown. This is so simply because many crimes are unknown to the police or anyone other than the perpetrator and the victim. Several reasons exist for this "dark statistic" of crime: Some crimes, like rape, remain unreported for fear of embarrassment. Other crimes are unreported to the police because the victim himself or herself was involved in a crime. Sometimes such organized crime gangs as La Costa Nostra terrify their victims into keeping quiet. Many victims of crimes—children, old people in nursing homes, the sick, and others—do not know how to access the district attorney or the police and therefore cannot report the crimes committed against them.

Consequently, prosecution of violent offenders is limited, ipso facto, because prosecutors are not called on to deal with the many offenses never brought to their attention. In addition, the offices of district attorneys are usually understaffed and overworked, making it difficult for the attorneys to prosecute all those crimes that do end up as complaints in their offices.

An overview of violent crimes in the United States may be gained from the Uniform Crime Reports issued by the FBI. Those reports generally reflect crimes known to the police two years previous to publication of a report. For example, statistics for 2006 are published in 2008, and these reveal that in 2006 there were 17,034 murders known to the police in the United States. These murders constituted a rate of 5.7 per 100,000 inhabitants of the country, with a population in 2006 of over 299 million. Other violent crimes included 92,455 forcible rapes, 860,853 aggravated assaults, and 447,403 robberies, which are crimes against person and property.[1] In general, violent crime in the United States declined over the 10 years ending in 2007. Between January and December 2007, the violent crime rate in the United States declined by 1.7 percent. Urban areas saw a decline of 2.4 percent for murder alone.

The majority of violent crimes are committed by men aged 16–26. The victims of these offenders are also mainly found in the same age group. The reasons for the 2007 decline are to be found in the decline in the birthrate, which had fallen from 3.6 in 1960 to 2.0 in 2006, and in the rate of abortion, which had increased from 1960 to 2005 from 0.01 per 1,000 women aged 15–44 to 19.41. This increase came about with the legalization of abortion in 1973. By 1981, abortion in the United States was at an all-time high, reaching 29.25 per 1,000 women aged 15–44. The actual number of reported abortions in 2005 was over 1.2 million. Clearly, the decline in the birth rate and the legalization of abortion reduced the violence rate because they resulted in a decrease in the population likely to commit violent crimes—men aged 16–26.[2]

Additional reasons for the decline in violent crime are the increase in incarceration, which reached over 2.2 million in 2006; an increase in community policing; and the decline in the crack cocaine epidemic. Crack was responsible for a large increase in homicides between 1981 and 1995.[3]

There is a considerable difference between white and black rates of violence. According to the Bureau of Justice Statistics, the rate of victimization among whites for all crimes of violence in 2005 was 6.5 per 100,000 inhabitants of the United States. For blacks, that same rate was 13.8. A similar discrepancy may be found in 1973, when whites had a violence victimization rate of 20 per 100,000 and blacks had a violence victimization rate of 37.3. Likewise, all the years between 1973 and 2005 exhibited a black violence victimization rate more or less twice the white rate.

Turning now to gender, it is evident that males commit more violent crimes than females. In 2005, the Bureau of Justice Statistics reported that males had a violence victimization rate of 25.6 and females 16.6 per 100,000. In 1973, these statistics were 66 and 31.4, respectively; in all the years between 1973 and 2005, males had a violence victimization rate nearly twice that of females.[4]

THE PROSECUTION OF MURDER

Evidently, murder or homicide is a crime of violence. There are, however, a number of motives and means by which humans kill each other; and so the word "murder" needs definition if we are to understand who is prosecuted for this offense and who is not prosecuted. According to the U.S. Code, Title 18, "Murder is the unlawful killing of a human being with malice aforethought."

The FBI reported that in 2006 more than 17,000 persons were murdered in the United States. These murders were 1.2 percent of all

violent crimes that year, constituting 5.7 murders per 100,000 inhabitants of the United States.[5] It is, therefore, unlikely and perhaps impossible to prosecute all murderers, or "killers," as the media would have
it. In addition, it is important to emphasize that the prosecution of
homicide is uncertain, not only because the probable offender cannot
always be determined but also because a good number of killers are
never prosecuted; in their stead innocent people are prosecuted.

Among those who are prosecuted and convicted though innocent
are a good number of people accused of murder. It is therefore certain
that for as many years as the American criminal justice system has
existed, innocent people have been put to death by state employees
applying the death penalty, and others have spent years in prison
although they committed no murder or other crime.

Objective observers were always certain that the innocent were often
the victims of false prosecution. The power of American prosecutors or
district attorneys is so great, however, that until DNA testing proved
conclusively that numerous innocent persons were incarcerated or even
murdered by the criminal justice system, few if any prosecutors would
ever admit an error. In fact, some prosecutors even prided themselves
on convincing juries to convict innocent persons. One such prosecutor
was Henry Wade, who was the Dallas, Texas, prosecutor from 1951
until 1987, when he retired. During these years, Wade prided himself
on never losing a case he himself prosecuted. He also bragged that he
was able to convince juries to send innocent people to prison and even
to the "death house," or death row.[6] During his long tenure, Wade
was responsible for the wrongful conviction of hundreds of innocent
citizens. Included were several men who were given the death penalty
only to be exonerated later because DNA testing was available to the
Texas Innocence Project, which took up their cause. Many others for
whom such efforts could not be made continue in prison or were
wrongfully put to death—killed—by the state. Among those exonerated
are Vernon McManus, convicted by Wade of murder in 1977, and
Randall Dale Adams, also falsely accused and convicted in 1977.
Adams, the subject of a movie, *The Thin Blue Line,* was convicted of
killing a Dallas police officer although the prosecutors knew that David
Harris was guilty of the killing. In 1981, Clarence Bradley was wrongfully prosecuted and convicted, but he was exonerated in 1990 when it
was shown that prosecutors suppressed evidence favoring Bradley and
that so-called witnesses had lied in court at the prosecutors' instigation.
Likewise, John C. Skelton was convicted of a murder that took place
800 miles from where Skelton was seen at the time of the killing. Yet
Skelton spent seven years in prison despite his innocence.[7] All these
abuses of the prosecutor's office came to the attention of the public

after Craig Watkins was elected district attorney for Dallas in 2007. Watkins, the first black ever to serve in that capacity, promptly allowed the Texas Innocence Project to review hundreds of Dallas County cases, dating back to 1970, to determine which prisoners should have DNA tests conducted on the grounds that their convictions appeared to have been caused by false prosecutions.[8]

Texas is by no means the only state in which innocent citizens have been convicted of murder. In November 2007, Lynn DeJac of Buffalo, New York, was released from prison after serving 13 years for murdering her daughter. She was freed after DNA evidence implicated her former boyfriend in the murder. That man is Dennis Donahue, who was convicted on May 14, 2008, of having committed several murders in addition to probably having killed DeJac's daughter, Crystalinn Girard, in 1993.[9]

On August 27, 1987, the body of Jacqueline Harrison was discovered in the woods near Pemberton, New Jersey. This discovery led to the arrest of Larry Peterson on the grounds that a neighbor had seen scratches on his arm. Furthermore, a forensic expert claimed in court that the hair on Peterson's arms matched the hairs at the crime scene. Not until 2003 did the Innocence Project, using DNA tests, prove that the hair did not belong to Peterson and that the forensic expert had lied in court. Despite this new evidence, the district attorney, Robert Bernardi, contended that Peterson was still guilty. When Peterson was released on bail, Bernardi wanted to try the case again. A retrial did not occur, however, because Bernardi finally concluded that "there was not enough evidence to persuade a jury beyond a reasonable doubt." Nevertheless, Bernardi still insists on Peterson's guilt.[10]

Another victim of malicious prosecution is Cynthia Sommer, who spent 2.5 years in prison for a murder that never occurred. Her husband, Todd Sommer, died suddenly in 2002 although he appeared in excellent health and was only 23 years old. Prosecutors claimed that Cynthia had poisoned Todd with arsenic because she wanted to collect his $250,000 life insurance. The facts were that Todd Sommer died of a heart ailment and that no arsenic was found in his body. Because Cynthia had sex with several men after Todd's death and also visited bars and other amusements, her behavior was construed as evidence that she had murdered Todd. It was this behavior that was used to influence a jury to convict her.[11]

On January 25, 2005, the Sixth U.S. Court of Appeals overturned the conviction of Kenneth Richey, who had been convicted in Ohio 20 years earlier and sentenced to death. Richey was accused of setting an apartment house fire that killed his ex-girlfriend.

The fact was that no arson had taken place but that the fire was caused by a gasoline-soaked carpet that had been in the open near a gas pump for weeks. Prosecutors argued that Richey had poured gasoline on the carpet and then set it on fire. Richey spent 21 years on death row and at one time came within one hour of execution. Perhaps no case of wrongful prosecution reveals the brutality of some American prosecutors more than this hideous miscarriage of justice.[12]

JURY NULLIFICATION

As depicted in television dramas, the prosecution of murder seems straightforward, even simple. Reality is otherwise, however. Murder is not always provable, and prosecution for this most heinous of crimes is not always successful. One reason for the failure to convict those who kill their fellow human beings is jury nullification. There are those who believe or say they believe that American prisoners convicted of violent crimes are really the victims of racism. This argument would have us believe that the police, the prosecutors, and the courts throughout the country are racists and that therefore an inordinate number of Americans of African heritage are imprisoned.

The Bureau of Justice Statistics reported in 2008 that in 2007 there were 4,618 black males sentenced to prison for violent crimes for every 100,000 black male citizens. This number compares to 1,747 Hispanic males and 773 Euro-American males per 100,000 in the population. Since the African American population is only 13 percent of all Americans and the Hispanic population is just 12 percent of all Americans, there is indeed a great overrepresentation of blacks and Hispanics in our prisons.[13]

The argument that the discrepancy in numbers reflects racism is spurious because the victims of violence are almost always members of the family or community in which the offenders live. Therefore, members of the African American community have every right to demand protection from the violent criminals among them. Failure to incarcerate such criminals would indeed be racism in that such failure would expose defenseless citizens to violence without recourse to the criminal justice system. The practice of jury nullification, which has gained popularity among some jurors, is as much an obstacle to judicial fairness and the perpetuation of the American criminal justice system as the conviction of the innocent.

African American law professor Paul Butler discussed the issue of jury nullification in 1995. Butler argued, "The decision as to what kind of conduct by African Americans ought to be punished is better made by African Americans themselves." Butler regarded the American criminal justice system as an instrument of white supremacy. He claimed that jury nullification should not be used to excuse violent criminals but that black jurors should use their power to excuse other types of offenses. Nevertheless, jury nullification has been applied in cases of murder and other violent crimes.[14]

It was in 1991 that Yankel Rosenbaum, a fundamentalist Jew, was murdered on the streets of Brooklyn, New York, solely because of his religious beliefs. As Rosenbaum was walking on a Brooklyn street, a crowd of African American men, led by Lemrick Nelson, accosted him, shouting "get the Jew" as the crowd punctuated their assault on Rosenbaum with anti-Jewish epithets. Then, Nelson stabbed Rosenbaum four times with a butcher's knife. Rosenbaum fell to the street but remained alive long enough to identify his assailant, Nelson. In turn, Nelson admitted to a detective that he had stabbed Rosenbaum, who died on his way to a hospital.[15]

In 1992, Nelson was tried for murder. The jury, predominantly of African American descent, voted Nelson not guilty. Following this nullification, the lawyer for Nelson sponsored a party for the jury to celebrate the killer, Lemrick Nelson, as a hero. This led the then-governor of New York, Mario Cuomo, to call on federal prosecutors to indict Nelson for violating Rosenbaum's civil rights. A second trial resulted in a hung jury in 1996, and so Nelson was tried a third time, in 2003. By then, 12 years after the murder of Rosenbaum, some witnesses could not be found, and others were no longer certain of what they had seen. As a result, Nelson, though found guilty of violating Rosenbaum's civil rights, served little time in jail. In 2004, Nelson was released from prison.[16]

The most prominent among those individuals tried for murder but found not guilty despite all the evidence to the contrary is Orenthal J. Simpson, usually called "O.J." or "the Juice." Simpson, a famous actor and former football player who had achieved enviable records on the playing field, was accused of killing his wife, Nicole Brown Simpson, and a waiter, Ron Goldman, on the night of June 12, 1994. Both bodies had been found fatally stabbed outside Nicole Brown's condominium. Evidence collected by the police led to the conclusion that Simpson had killed both of them. Because of the double murder, Simpson was not eligible for bail and could have received the death penalty upon conviction had the district attorney sought it. His trial began on January 25, 1995. Simpson, however, had hired six prominent lawyers, who in turn appointed several consultants. His defense cost at least $4 million. Using numerous courtroom dramatics, this defense team succeeded in gaining an acquittal from the jury on October 3, 1995. Because of the trial was televised each day, a vast audience followed the proceedings and became convinced of Simpson's guilt. The evidence included DNA testing, which showed that blood found at the murder scene was O.J.'s. The DNA tests also showed that Nicole Brown's blood was located on Simpson's socks, and that the blood of both murder victims and of Simpson was found in his car and in his bedroom. In addition, a glove found in the driveway of Brown's home included Simpson's blood and Goldman's hair.

This scientific evidence was augmented by Nicole Brown Simpson's complaints to police and family that her husband had beaten her repeatedly and that she separated from him to move to her parents' home with her children. Despite all this evidence, the jury of nine blacks, one Hispanic, and two whites returned a verdict of not guilty.[17]

On February 5, 1997, a civil jury unanimously found that there was a preponderance of evidence that Simpson was liable for damages in the killing of Nicole Brown Simpson and Ron Goldman; consequently, the jury awarded the two families damages. This verdict was affirmed on appeal.[18] It is reasonable to conclude that the jury decided to acquit on the grounds that Simpson is of African descent and that nullification is a legitimate means of exercising minority power within the criminal justice system.

The trial of the actor Robert Blake (Michael James Vincenzo Gubitosi) ended with an acquittal in March 2005. Blake-Gubitosi was accused of shooting his wife. Then, in November 2005, a civil jury decided that based on the preponderance of evidence, he had to pay $30 million to his children, who held him responsible for their mother's death. Many observers believe that he was found not guilty because of his celebrity status.[19]

PROSECUTING MURDER IN THE FAMILY

In 2006, the Uniform Crime Report issued by the FBI revealed that in that year 14,990 murders were committed in the United States. Of these murders, 24 percent victimized relatives of the murderer; acquaintances and friends accounted for 30 percent of all killings. These statistics demonstrate that family and friends are more at risk of being killed than are strangers. In fact, another 25 percent of killings involved victims who were acquaintances of the murderer.[20]

The phenomenon of "murder in the family," so to speak, has been observed for many years. For example, a study conducted in 1989 of 972 homicides occurring between 1916 and 1983 concluded that 21 percent of the victims were related to the killer, that another 21 percent were friends, and that 19 percent were acquaintances.[21]

There are evidently numerous examples of murder within the family. Most such killings are hardly mentioned by the media, who routinely publish news about sensational murders involving very wealthy people or so-called celebrities or those famous for other reasons.

Among sensational killings were the murders of Jose and Kitty Menendez, who, on August 20, 1989, were brutally killed by their own children. On that day, Eric and Lyle Menendez shot their parents, who were watching TV in their living room. The boys, 18 and 21 at the time, shot their mother and father with a 12-gauge shotgun and then added some birdshot to make sure they succeeded. The description of these murders is so heinous that it is difficult to read these reports. The Menendez brothers were tried twice because their first trial ended with a hung jury. They were convicted at their second trial in 1996 and imprisoned for life.[22]

The defense of the Menendez brothers consisted of the argument that both boys had been sexually abused by their father and that their mother had stood by and done nothing about the abuse. This argument holds that abuse, and particularly sexual abuse, is so devastating that hate and murder are quite possible outcomes of such maltreatment. The prosecution refuted this claim, however, and argued that we are all responsible for our own actions and that the Menendez brothers fully understood that they deliberately brought about the death of their parents. The prosecution also relied on a book by Allan Dershowitz, *The Abuse Excuse and Other Cop-Outs: Sob Stories and Evasions of Responsibility*. In this work, Dershowitz argues that failure to hold people responsible for their criminal actions undermines the principle of individual responsibility. Dershowitz believes that too many brutal criminals have used the abuse excuse to be acquitted.[23] Prosecutors also questioned whether sexual abuse had really occurred in the Menendez household, particularly because the boys were consulting a psychotherapist but never mentioned sexual abuse to him. The Menendez brothers argued that they feared for their lives at the hands of their father and that therefore they acted in self-defense. This seems implausible because at the time of the murders, both "boys" were really full-grown adults, aged 18 and 21, and fully capable of defending themselves if needed. The prosecution viewed the efforts of the defense as an attempt to "smear" the parents to such an extent that the jury would believe they deserved to die. Furthermore, the prosecution built its case, in part, on the frivolous spending displayed by the Menendez brothers, together with their callous nature. It was also shown by the prosecutors that the murders took place at a time when the alleged sexual abuse was no longer practiced.[24]

Much earlier, in 1974, Michael Sielski killed his father, Thaddeus Sielski, by stabbing him to death at his place of work in a print shop in Buffalo, New York. Michael stabbed his father 21 times with a knife he carried with him on a bus while traveling to his father's place of work. The father was killed deliberately "with malice aforethought." Michael Sielski's defense was that he suffered from paranoid schizophrenia. He was, consequently, found "innocent by reason of mental defect or disease."

The prosecution claimed that the cold-blooded, deliberate manner in which Michael traveled some miles to kill his father proved that he was fully capable of knowing the difference between right and wrong and that he was in no way impaired. Nevertheless, Michael Sielski was sent to the Buffalo Psychiatric Hospital, from which he was released in 1975. On the day of his release, he killed himself by allowing a freight train to run over him.[25]

MURDER BY ORGANIZED CRIME

So many books, movies, magazine articles, and the like have been expanded to discuss organized crime that exposition of such organized-crime families as La Mafia or La Cosa Nostra has become entrenched in the entertainment industry. It is by no means entertaining, however, to follow the careers of true organized-crime killers. One such murderer was John Gotti, who was convicted of 13 crimes, including several murders, in April 1992, and sentenced to life in prison. His associate, Frank "Frankie Locs" Locascio was also convicted of murder and sentenced to life in prison.[26]

Gotti had been tried on three previous occasions but was never found guilty, for the jurors were intimidated or paid to reach not guilty verdicts. In addition, prosecutors in the earlier trials faced lawyer Bruce Cutler, whose skill as a defense attorney was so impressive that the judge in Gotti's fourth trial refused to let Cutler defend Gotti.[27]

MURDER IN THE WORKPLACE

Murder in the workplace has been recorded repeatedly in this country. Some workplace killers are employees, whereas others are former employees who were dismissed or who left for reasons involving emotional issues. One such killer is Anthony LaCalamita, who returned to an accounting firm in Troy, Michigan, from which he had been dismissed four days earlier. On entering the offices of the firm, he murdered a receptionist and gravely wounded two firm partners on April 9, 2007. The defense argued that LaCalamita was insane and therefore could not be held guilty. "Insanity" is a legal term defined by the Insanity Defense Reform Act of 1984. This law, passed by Congress as the result of the shooting of President Ronald Reagan, whose shooter successfully argued temporary insanity, defines insanity thus: "The defendant, as a result of severe mental disease or defect, [is] unable to appreciate the nature and quality of the wrongfulness of his acts."[28]

This argument did not convince the jury or the judge. LaCalamita was sentenced to life in prison without parole. Michigan has never had the death penalty, which LaCalamita said he wished had been imposed on him. The prosecution successfully argued that LaCalamita was not insane but full of rage because he had lost his job. According to a psychiatrist testifying for the prosecution, LaCalamita "was aware of the wrongfulness of his actions, he knew exactly the nature and quality of his actions and he knew he was wrong." Revenge killings of this kind are also part of the history of crime.

WHAT PROSECUTORS NEED TO KNOW

The reasons for workplace killings are hardly discussed in the media nor much understood by lawyers—that is, by prosecutors whose emphasis is on punishment, not prevention. Nevertheless, some underlying reasons for workplace mass murder shed light on these frightening events.

American society views occupation as the most important criterion of social prestige, so that the unemployed are regarded and regard themselves as having sunk to the bottom of society's prestige barrel. Losing a job, therefore, is much more than a loss of income. It is a loss of dignity and self-worth and impinges on the loser's beliefs concerning his or her standing with others in the proverbial "looking-glass self." Consequently, there have been numerous workplace killings in the United States. So many of these killings have occurred at U.S. post offices that "going postal" has become synonymous with random murder on the job. Such killings can be matched by school shootings, including mass murders at universities as well as high schools and grade schools. Workplace killings usually target supervisors and bosses held responsible for a job loss or for the pressures on the job. Such killings may be likened to slave rebellions inasmuch as a vast number of American workers are so constrained and so pressured at work that some become murderous in their hate of the bosses who employ them.

Workplace bullying is another catalyst for violence on the job, just as it is responsible for school shootings. Although the law appears to protect workers from discrimination based on age, religion, sex, disability, or race, it is very difficult to prove such discrimination in court. Moreover, few workers have the resources to hire a lawyer to represent them. Furthermore, the damage done to the target by offensive bullying based on age or ethnicity is not avoided by the victim's later complaining to a federal agency. The rage such discrimination provokes cannot be alleviated by the possibility of later legal action. Instead, some employees rebel by shooting.

It is unfortunate that America's business culture supports bullying on the job while concentrating exclusively on security.

THE PROSECUTION OF RAPE CRIMES

According to the Bureau of Justice Statistics, 272,350 Americans became victims of rape or first-degree sexual assault in 2006. The crime of first-degree sexual assault is defined as "non-consensual sexual intercourse that is committed by physical force, threat of injury, or other duress." A lack of consent could include the inability of one party to reject sex because of the effect of alcohol or drugs. The victim can be a date or even the offender's spouse. A second kind of rape is called "statutory" rape. This type includes sexual intercourse between an adult and a consenting child. This generally means that the "child" is someone not yet age 18.[29]

Because the victims of this crime are often embarrassed to report the assault to the police, rape is sometimes described as the "hidden crime." Although there has been a rise in the number of rapes reported to the police since the 1970s, most such crimes remain unreported. In fact, it has been estimated that even in the early twenty-first century only 31 percent of rapes are ever reported to the police.[30]

These circumstances make prosecution for rape difficult. Among the difficulties are the attitudes of the police toward the rape victims and the perpetrators. Police are as much the product of their socialization as any other member of a society, so the attitude police personnel have toward rape victims and women in general affects the outcome of complaints against rape perpetrators.[31] Undoubtedly, the patriarchy that has until recently dominated life in the United States has led to the failure of many female rape victims to report this crime. The attitudes of both victims and police, as well as others, with reference to rape are, of course, socially constructed. Thus, gender determines the manner in which each sex responds to the other, the term "gender" being defined as the social outcome and interpretation of sex in various cultures.[32] There are those critics who hold that "gender performance" contributes greatly to sex stereotypes that are difficult to overcome and appear to be self-perpetuating. Gender performance refers to aggressive male behavior, docility among women, and a neat fit between sex and emotional and social characteristics exhibited by either sex.

The gender performance model is, of course, gradually disappearing as more and more women become heads of households, earn advanced degrees, become professionals, and raise their income and their social standing higher than their mothers could have imagined. As a result, traditional patriarchy is no longer as effective as it was a generation ago, although it still exists and must be accounted for with reference to police attitudes concerning rape victims.

Therefore, police treat women who adhere closely to the gender stereotypes expected of them differently than they do complainants who deviate from such gender-driven beliefs. Indeed, the sexual history of a female complainant is often used to decide whether or not the victim should be given credibility.[33]

A number of beliefs about the victims of rape have been current for some years and continue to plague the prosecution of this crime. The first of these beliefs is that only "bad" girls get raped. "Bad" here refers to the sexual conduct of the victim, although smoking, drinking, using prohibited substances, being divorced, and other prejudicial categories are also factors in how victims are judged by the police and by society in general. This belief is augmented by the view that "women ask for it" and the further rapist defense that women use the rape tactic only to cover up that they have been rejected by the alleged offender.[34]

A further myth relates to the view that sexually active women are more likely to be raped, particularly if they wear "provocative" clothing. Women are advised by some believers in these myths not to walk alone at night but assure themselves the company of a man; further, women should also not enter a bar alone nor be visibly inebriated or otherwise impaired. All these behaviors are viewed by American men as unacceptable for women but perfectly fine for men, and thus such behaviors have been used to "blame the victim" of rape.[35] There is one more obstacle to the prosecution of rape, and that is false accusation by some women. Such lies do occur, as best illustrated by the accusations against three students at Duke University in 2006. In March 2006, a woman dancer who had performed at a fraternity house near the campus of Duke University alleged that she had been raped by three lacrosse players who were also students at Duke. This allegation led to the immediate suspension of the lacrosse season at Duke and to protest rallies against the three accused players as well as against the university president, Richard Broadhead, for not acting decisively against this alleged "racist" attack. The accuser, Crystal Mangum, was black; the accused were white.[36]

By May 2006, two DNA tests had been performed showing that the accused students were not involved in the alleged rape. Nevertheless, the then–district attorney of Durham County, North Carolina, indicted Reade Seligmann, Collin Finnerty, and David Evans.[37] In April 2007, an English professor, Houston Baker, and 87 cosigners, all Duke faculty, took out a full-page advertisement in a local newspaper accusing the three indicted athletes of rape, racism, and other offenses and blasting the administration of "pious legalism" and other sins for not at once declaring the accused guilty. Baker and his associates were joined by Jesse Jackson and Al Sharpton, two New York City civil rights leaders, in condemning the accused and worrying about the "fate" of the "victim."[38]

The district attorney, Michael Nifong, was campaigning for reelection and therefore found the indictment and possible conviction of the three accused students a convenient means of gaining the votes of black citizens and the so-called liberals in the community who were eager to see three wealthy whites incarcerated for years to come. Nifong charged the three with first-degree forcible rape, first-degree sexual offense, and kidnapping.[39] The case never came to trial. The parents of the three students hired a number of attorneys and proved that the alleged rape never occurred. The story's fabrication became evident when, in a television interview, one of the dancers told the whole world on television that she was present at all times during the party at the fraternity house and that her associate, Crystal Mangum, had lied. This, together with the results of DNA tests and the fact that one of the accused, Reade Seligmann, was not at the fraternity house at the time of the alleged rape, led to the dismissal of the charges and the removal of Nifong from his position as district attorney. Furthermore, Nifong was deprived of his license to practice law.[40] The false accusations made by Crystal Mangum did not lead to any charges against her, however. Normally, those who make false accusations are charged with making a false report with the possibility of serving jail time. Mangum suffered no such fate.

Mangum is not the only woman who has made false accusations of rape. There are a good number of others who have created serious problems for prosecutors and for true victims of such crimes. On March 18, 2008, Katherine M. Clifton, a Seattle college student, pleaded guilty in King County District Court of making a false report. In June 2007, she accused an unnamed professor of rape. The professor spent nine days in jail and was suspended from his job. The woman whose lies put the professor in jail was incarcerated for only eight days. Prosecutors, as usual, blamed everyone but themselves for the pain and suffering they caused the innocent man falsely accused and jailed.[41]

Billie Joe Eads claimed, in November 2004, that she was raped in Kokomo, Indiana, by a strange man. In this case, the police doubted her story and arrested her for making a false claim. She did not accuse a particular man but nevertheless cost the taxpayer a good deal of money, employing the time of the police and forensic scientists who made medical tests on her.[42]

In October 2002, Kylee McNeal of Toledo, Ohio, told police she was abducted and raped on a dead-end road for seven hours by two men. She said she walked seven miles back to a Toledo hospital. This report led police in Ohio and Michigan to search for the alleged offenders as well as a "Good Samaritan" who gave her a T-shirt, for she was only partially clothed. Two days after making these claims, McNeal told police that all these reports were a lie. She blamed her lies on the use of drugs, which caused her to spend all of her money. She then used the false rape story to explain her absence from home.

Because the police spent a great deal of money and resources to investigate her allegations, McNeal was charged with "false alarms," and Monroe County, Ohio, charged her with "filing a false police report." The outcome of these false reports was that McNeal was prosecuted and not some unknown rapist.[43]

Alberto Ramos spent seven years in prison until a judge ruled in 1992 that prosecutors had failed to give the defense the documents proving his innocence. Instead, the prosecution wrongly accused Ramos of raping a five-year-old girl at a day care center.[44] This occurred in 1984, at a time when hysterical accusations against child care workers were popular and led to innumerable false convictions. The most prominent of these false accusations concerned the McMartin preschool in California, which was operated by Virginia McMartin and her family. Numerous parents complained that their children had been sexually and otherwise abused after the police sent letters to all parents inviting such complaints. Fantastic stories about secret tunnels and hideous orgies were elicited from children interviewed by so-called experts. Years of trials followed, only to end in the ruination of the McMartins. The jury found all defendants innocent. Yet, this injustice led to huge legal bills and unjust suffering imposed by hysterical media reports and vindictive prosecutors.[45]

In 2000, Lee Long was released from prison after serving six years in prison on the false testimony of a police officer and a rape victim who wrongly identified Long as the rapist who had also robbed her. The rape had taken place in Queens, New York, even while Long was visiting his girlfriend in Brooklyn. Evidently, he could not have been in two places at once. That, however, made no difference to the police or the prosecutor.[46]

A most glaring instance of unjust and malicious prosecution took place in Buffalo, New York. Anthony Capozzi was released from prison after having been incarcerated for 22 years for several rapes—this, despite the fact that DNA evidence regarding these crimes was stored in a local hospital but never used. Capozzi was denied parole five times because he refused to admit guilt to crimes he never committed. The prosecutor who sent him to prison has since become a judge based on her record in gaining convictions. In 2007, two "cold case" detectives studied old records of the so-called Bike Path rapist and concluded that the DNA evidence stored at the hospital could not have come from Capozzi. They discovered that the DNA instead belonged to Altemio Sanchez, who had been suspected of being the rapist as early as 1984, though no effort was made to investigate him until 2007.

One consequence of the false imprisonment of Capozzi was the passage of a New York law requiring that compensation for wrongful imprisonment be paid at once after exoneration, so the victims would not have to spend years gaining recompense from those who had injured them.[47]

The foregoing examples indicate that false accusations of rape are quite common. It has been estimated that 41 percent of such accusations are false. This view is based on a study by the U.S. Department of Justice indicating that of 10,000 convictions for sexual assault, about 6,000 were proven by DNA testing, whereas about 4,000 such accusations were false. The report shows that these figures have been true for seven years and seem to be constant.[48]

A study by Eugene Kanin also found that false rape accusations constitute 41 percent of all such complaints. These false allegations may be precipitated by a desire for revenge on a rejecting male, or they may serve to cover up long absences from home or be related to guilt over consensual sex. In some cases, they are extortion scams. In all instances, such false accusations cause considerable suffering for the falsely accused, even if many of the accusations are not followed by further action.[49]

In addition to recognizing forcible rape, the law also recognized statutory rape, defined as sexual intercourse between an adult and a minor who consents to this activity. Statuatory rape is, therefore, not a violent crime but is classified as rape nevertheless.

There are those individuals who claim that children who have been used sexually carry a major psychological burden thereafter and that such activities are damaging to the affected child. It should also be understood, however, that there are "puritans" in this country who dislike sex of any sort and who are more than anxious to employ a sex police wherever this common human interest may be found.

The definitions of "adult" and "minor" vary from state to state, although the differences are small. In Alabama, for example, sexual intercourse between someone aged 16 and someone under 12 is called "first-degree rape" and is punishable by life in prison for between 10 and 999 years' incarceration. In California, punishment for "statutory rape" is less severe. There, a distinction is made between an actor who is not more than three years older than the underage participant and is charged with a misdemeanor, whereas someone over 21 who does the same may be charged with either a misdemeanor or a felony.[50] In New York, the penalties are also based on the age of the participants. There, "third-degree rape" is defined as sexual intercourse between someone 21 years old or older with someone under age 17. "Second-degree rape" is defined as sexual intercourse between someone 18 or older with someone under age 15, and "first-degree rape" is sexual intercourse between a child less than 11 or less than 13 if the actor is 18 or older. Such action carries a penalty of 5 to 25 years in prison.[51] There are a number of well-publicized examples involving women teachers and men teachers accused of introducing one or more of their students to sex. According to a federal Department of Education study, about 40 percent of teachers convicted of having sex with their students are women.[52]

A survey of a database, New York State Newspapers, reveals that there were 130 cases of sexual activity between teachers and students reported in New York State newspapers between 1989 and 2008. Evidently, some of these relationships did not take place in New York. Nevertheless, it is reasonable to assume that the preponderance of such relationships outside New York was not reported in New York newspapers, so the number of such cases is by no means inconsiderable.

Among the most reported and so-called scandalous sexual relationships between a teacher and a student was the pregnancy of Mary Kay Letourneau, whose affair with one of her male students became a cause célèbre in the U.S. media. It should be understood that scandal caused by sex between an older woman and a young boy is a U.S. cultural phenomenon related to our country's Puritan heritage. In France, by contrast, and in many other Latin-speaking countries, such affairs are viewed as love relationships and carry little stigma. This acceptance elsewhere suggests that the problem lies in the belief system prevalent in American culture, which has little difficulty accepting 17,000 murders every year but becomes shocked at sex.

THE PROSECUTION OF FEMALE STATUTORY SEX OFFENDERS

Mary Kay Letourneau was married when she was convicted of having sex with a 13-year-old boy in her class. She bore his child in

Seattle and was, therefore, convicted of statutory rape. Thirty-five years old at the time of the rape, Letourneau already had four children with her husband, Steve, who divorced her after her conviction.

After serving seven years in prison for rape, she was released in 2004. She then married her former student, Vili Fualaau, the father of her child. Subsequently, she had another child with Fualaau.[53]

Sandra Geisel was convicted of having sex with a 16-year-old male student at the exclusive Colonie Catholic High School in Albany, New York. Geisel pleaded guilty to second-degree rape in September 2005. On that occasion, the judge, Stephen W. Herrick, also blamed the 16-year-old boy and his friends for "manipulating" the 42-year-old teacher. This accusation caused Albany County district attorney David Soares to complain that the judge had no cause to call Geisel, the mother of four children, the victim. She was assigned 10 years' probation and an in-house alcohol and mental health treatment course.

Another woman teacher sexually involved with a student is Debra LaFave of Tampa, Florida. She was sentenced to three years' house arrest for having sex with a 14-year-old boy. The boy suffered extreme anxiety, produced not by sex but by the media coverage concerning this event. Because he did not want to testify in Marion County court, the prosecution dropped the charges against LaFave so as to protect the boy. Since LaFave was also convicted in Hillsborough County, however, her house arrest and seven years' probation remained intact. In that county, the 22-year-old teacher pleaded guilty to two counts of lewd and lascivious battery. Here, also for his own protection, the boy was not required to testify. Consequently, LaFave did not serve time in jail.[54]

In 2005, Diane Cherchio West pleaded guilty to sexual assault in Bayonne, New Jersey. West had already been observed kissing and groping a 13-year-old boy 25 years earlier, in 1980, when she supervised an eighth-grade dance in her capacity as guidance counselor at a middle school. Thereafter, she became a guidance counselor at a high school and became pregnant by an 11th-grade student, Stephen West, whom she married in 1985, when she was 31 years old.

In 2000, a friend of Chercio's 15-year-old son moved into her house. By then, West was divorced. She promptly had sex with the 15-year-old, when she was 46. She was arrested and prosecuted, but the judge sentenced her only to probation. A trial was avoided to protect the reputation of the school and the boy involved. Furthermore, many citizens do not view an adolescent boy as a victim.[55]

Marci Stein of Westchester County, New York, was 31 years old in 2001 when she was convicted of engaging in sexual relations with three teenage male students. She was sentenced to 12 years in prison and had already served 3 years at the Albion Prison in New York when the

New York Court of Appeals overturned her conviction on the grounds that the families of the affected boys were suing the state and the school district, a fact not disclosed by the prosecution at trial. At her second trial, Stein pleaded guilty to child endangerment and was then sentenced to a year in jail. This sentence was not carried out because Stein had already served 3 years.[56]

Jennifer Sanchez was obsessed with a 15-year-old student in her social studies class. So that she could continue an affair with him, she moved into the same apartment building in New York where this boy was living with his family. She was 23. Sanchez also had a boyfriend, who discovered this relationship and threatened the youngster with whom Sanchez had sex. Sanchez was then arrested because the boy told his mother, who reportedly was "furious." Consequently, Sanchez was charged with sodomy and rape and on her plea of guilty was sentenced to 10 years' probation.[57]

THE PROSECUTION OF MALE STATUTORY SEX OFFENDERS

The number of male statutory sex offenders is higher than that of females mainly because female offenses are more surreptitious than male offenses and because Western ideas of "chivalry" often allow women to go unpunished. Furthermore, false accusations against men are far more frequent than false accusations against women. Such false accusations are usually believed by the authorities and continue to haunt men so maligned even after the accused have been exonerated. No better example of this kind of cruelty was the unjust allegation that Percy Jones, a Buffalo music teacher, had sex with a 13-year-old girl. The media, relying on the principle "guilty unless proven innocent," at once condemned Jones as soon as he was accused. Following the hysteria created by television, newspapers, and politicians, the public reviled the teacher. Jones was not charged with the crime because the 13-year-old girl failed a polygraph test and then admitted that she had lied. She even went so far as to plant a condom behind a bookcase in Jones's classroom. Jones's ordeal not only involved his fear of losing his professional position but also took a toll on his family, who had to watch the media circus resulting from these allegations.[58] Convicting innocent people in the media is so common that it is difficult to believe that anyone would pay attention to such reports ipso facto.

Examples of male teachers charged with raping girl students are Mark Taussig and Gary Jarvis. Taussig was convicted of having sex with two students in the Albany area. Taussig was charged with having sex in his classroom on two separate occasions. Jarvis was also accused of two rapes, one taking place on school property and the other elsewhere. He was convicted of second-degree assault for having sex with two girls not yet 17 years old.[59] The country's horror of sex is undoubtedly the principal reason for these convictions. Even as pornography is widely disseminated in the United States and sexual unions between the same sex are more and more popular, and even as advertisements, movies, and television do not hesitate to exhibit the most gross sexuality, we condemn and approve the same conduct. It was this conflict concerning sexuality that led Vance Packard in 1968 to write the classic *The Sexual Wilderness*.[60]

PROSECUTING AGGRAVATED ASSAULT

The FBI's Uniform Crime Reports define "aggravated assault" as "an unlawful attack by one person upon another for the purpose of inflicting severe or aggravated bodily injury."[61]

Nationwide there were 860,853 aggravated assaults in 2006. This constitutes a decline of nearly 16 percent since 1997, a decline caused by the decline in the birthrate, the increase in abortion, the increase in the length of prison sentences, and the decline of the crack epidemic, as discussed earlier. In 2006, the rate of aggravated assault in the United States was 287.5 per 100,000 inhabitants, a decline in the rate of aggravated assault since 1997 of 24.8 percent. Of these assaults, firearms were involved in 25 percent of incidents, hands or fists were used in 27 percent, and knives were used in 18 percent; the remaining 30 percent involved all kinds of weapons and even motor vehicles.[62]

Assault can take place in many situations and under a variety of circumstances. One bizarre example of an assault was the beating given to a prisoner in the Chester County Prison in Pennsylvania when two prison guards opened the cell door of one prisoner so another could enter and beat the intended victim. In June 2007, John Hampton and Charles Goodman, both prison guards, were charged by District Attorney Joseph W. Carroll with aggravated assault and criminal conspiracy for allowing Christopher Gilchrist to assault Mario Benegas. The two suspended officers also prepared a false incident report claiming that Benegas had "banged his head against the cell door."[63]

Well-known athletes, including professionals, are frequently charged with violent crimes. One example is Farouq Aminu, a college basketball player regarded in 2008 as one of the highest-ranked college recruits. Aminu is accused of using a BB gun to shoot Rebecca Baltich in the stomach and shatter the back window of her truck. Although only 17 years old, Aminu is being prosecuted in Georgia, where 17-year-olds are prosecuted as adults.[64]

Assault charges against athletes are by no means unusual. In 2003, John "Jumbo" Elliott, an offensive tackle with the Jets football team, was charged with assault when he lifted up a 60-year-old limousine driver, Donald Matinsky, and threw him to the pavement with such force that Matinsky suffered a fractured kneecap. Matinsky was a limousine driver who had been hired to pick up several Jets players from a New York steak house. Elliott became incensed because Matinsky had asked him to leave the cab.[65] Indeed, so many professional football players have been charged with assault and other violent crimes that Jeff Benedict and Don Yaeger have written an entire book about the topic, entitled *Pros and Cons: The Criminals Who Play in the NFL*.[66]

Another form of aggravated assault is found in schools. School violence is so prevalent in the United States that it is routine to have police patrol schools. This surveillance has become a necessity because students assault other students and also teachers. Thus, when Donte Boykin, 17, assaulted his teacher, 60-year-old Frank Burd, he exemplified the violence common in many American schools. Burd reprimanded Boykin for playing with an electronic device while algebra class was in progress. The teacher was followed into the hall by Boykin, who pushed him while his associate James Footman punched the teacher in the face three times. In the course of the attack, Boykin and Foreman broke Burd's neck. Burd spent 11 days in the hospital and 17 days in a rehabilitation center. Subsequently, Footman pleaded guilty to aggravated assault and was sentenced to four years in a juvenile institution.[67]

Yet another category of aggravated assault, hate crimes are crimes based on the intense dislike of ethnic or religious groups or individuals of deviant sexual orientation. In April 2008, four Temple University students assaulted Jordan Blady because he is Jewish. All the attackers were blacks who screamed anti-Jewish epithets during the attack. Blady was punched in the nose and suffered a fractured bone around his eye.[68]

Spouses are frequently the victims of domestic assault. Such conduct is particularly common among police officers, who beat and intimidate their wives but may elude justice. Why? Because prosecutors and judges seldom charge or adjudicate batterers with badges; these individuals are instead given favorable plea deals or their cruelty is excused and ignored by prosecutors. Furthermore, police officers will not act on the complaint of a citizen against a fellow officer. This deliberate exclusion is as true for battered women as for any other citizen. It was therefore a sensation when Boston police officer David Murphy was convicted of punching his wife in a Baltimore bar. A Maryland judge ordered Murphy to serve 18 months' probation. Murphy was briefly suspended from his job as a police lieutenant in Boston but was promptly reinstated by arbitrators who generally side with the police no matter what their crime. Police are thus also unlikely to arrest men engaged in beating women, for they may themselves be involved in such conduct.[69]

Assaults against old parents or against the old in nursing homes are by no means uncommon. In addition, several thousand men are assaulted by women in the course of any one year. Because over 860,000 such assaults are reported in the United States each year, these crimes are too widespread to be presented here. Suffice it to say that assault is related to murder in that the speed of an ambulance may well decide whether a victim lives or dies.

SUMMARY

Violent crime is reported to the FBI by nearly all U.S. police departments and the statistics published as Uniform Crime Reports. These reports indicate a falling violence rate in the United States during the decade ending in 2006.

Among the many persons convicted of crimes of violence are a good number of innocent people who are sometimes exonerated through DNA testing. There are also evidently individuals guilty of a violent crime who are freed through the process of jury nullification.

Murder is the most heinous of all violent crimes. It occurs more often among family, friends, and acquaintances than strangers. This is also true of rape, which the law divides into two categories: forcible rape and statutory rape.

The violent crime known as aggravated assault is related to murder in that the perpetrator commiting assault has the same motives as the murderer, but the assault does not necessarily lead to the death of the victim.

NOTES

1. U.S. Department of Justice, FBI, *Uniform Crime Reports* (Washington, DC: GPO, 2008), Table 1.

2. Robert Johnston, "United States Abortion Rates: 1960–2005," *Johnston's Archives* (February 17, 2008): 1.

3. Steven D. Levitt, "Understanding Why Crime Fell in the 1990s," *Journal of Economic Perspectives* 18, no. 1 (Winter 2004): 177–82.

4. U.S. Department of Justice, Bureau of Justice Statistics, *Violent Victimization Rates* (Washington, DC: GPO, September 10, 2006), n.p.

5. U.S. Department of Justice, FBI, "Murder," *Uniform Crime Reports* (Washington, DC: GPO, 2007), n.p.

6. Grady Abrams, "Quest for Justice Can Take the Longest Road," *Augusta Chronicle*, May 26, 2008.

7. "Innocence Cases," *Death Penalty Information Center*, http://www.deathpenaltyinfo.org/acticle.php?did=2339

8. Sylvia Moreno, "New Prosecutor Revisits Justice in Dallas," *Washington Post*, March 5, 2007, AO4.

9. Donn Esmond, "On Third Try, Justice System Gets Donahue," *Buffalo News*, May 14, 2008, 1.

10. "Falsely Accused: Justice and the Willing Suspension of Belief," *Forensic Examiner* 17, no. 1 (Spring 2008): 82.

11. Tony Perry, "Release of Widow Ends Bizarre Case," *Los Angeles Times*, April 19, 2008, part 8, 1.

12. Steven Henry and Sarah Bruce, "Family Joy as Kenny Richey Heads for Home," *Daily Mail*, December 20, 2007, SC1, 1.

13. U.S. Department of Justice, Bureau of Justice Statistics, *Prison Statistics* (Washington, DC, June 30, 2007).

14. Paul Butler, "Racially Based Jury Nullification: Black Power in the Criminal Justice System," *Yale Law Journal* 105 (1995): 677–725.

15. Robert F. Worth, "Juror in First Crown Heights Trial Remains Bitter about Ordeal," *New York Times*, May 1, 2003, 1.

16. *New York Post*, "New Trial Agony for Yankel Kin," March 28, 2005, 24.

17. David Margolick, "After 474 Days as a Prisoner, He Is Free," *New York Times*, October 4, 1995, A1.

18. Akhill Reed Amar, "A Second Chance at Justice," *New York Times*, February 6, 1997, A25.

19. *New York Times*, "Actor Is Ordered to Pay $30 Million in Killing," November 19, 2005, A12.

20. U.S Department of Justice, FBI, "Expanded Homicide Data," *Uniform Crime Report, 2006* (Washington, DC: GPO, 2007), Table 9.

21. Gerhard Falk. *Murder: An Analysis of Its Forms, Conditions and Causes* (Jefferson, NC: McFarland, 1990), 45.

22. Ann Mulvey, Amelia Fournier, and Teresa Donahue, "Murder in the Family: The Menendez Brothers," *Victims and Offenders* 1 (2006): 221.

23. Alan Dershowitz, *The Abuse Excuse and Other Cop-Outs: Sob Stories and Evasions of Responsibility* (New York: Little Brown, 1995).

24. Mulvey, Fournier, and Donahue, "Murder in the Family," 223.

25. Falk, *Murder*, 10.

26. Laurie Goodstein, "Gotti Convicted of 13 Crimes," *Washington Post*, April 3, 1992, 112, issue 17.

27. John Sullivan, "Cutler, Gotti's Lawyer, Gets Three Months Contempt Sentence," *New York Times*, December 14, 1996, NA.

28. Norman J. Finkel, "The Insanity Defense Reform Act of 1984: Much Ado about Nothing," *Behavioral Science and the Law* 7, no. 3 (1989): 403–19.

29. U.S. Department of Justice, Bureau of Justice Statistics, *Criminal Victimization, Number and Rates, 2006,* by Michael Rand and Shannon Catalano (Washington, DC: GPO, 2007), Table 2.

30. Lauren R. Taylor, "Has Rape Reporting Increased over Time?" *National Institute of Justice Journal,* no. 254 (July 2006): n.p.

31. Laura Fortier, "Women, Sex and Patriarchy," *Family Planning Persepctives* 7, no. 6 (1975): 278–81.

32. Judith Lorber, *Gender and the Social Construction of Illness* (Lanham, MD: Rowman and Littlefield, 2002).

33. James Placek, "Battered Women in the Court Room," *Crime, Law and Social Change* 35 (2001): 363.

34. Marvin Scott and Stanford Lyman, "Accounts," *American Sociological Review* 33, no. 1 (February 1968): 46–62.

35. J. K. Wesely and Edward Gaarder, "The Gendered Nature of the Urban Outdoors: Women Negotiating Fear of Violence," *Gender and Society* 18, no. 5 (2004): 645–63.

36. Viv Bernstein and Joe Drape, "Rape Allegation against Athletes Is Roiling Duke," *New York Times,* March 26, 2007, A1.

37. *New York Times,* "New Duke DNA Tests Are Reportedly Inconclusive," March 13, 2006, A14.

38. Karen W. Arenson, "Duke Grappling with Impact of Scandal on Its Reputation," *New York Times,* April 7, 2006, A 16.

39. Duff Wilson, "New Timeline by Prosecutor in Duke Case," *New York Times,* September 23, 2006, A12.

40. *New York Times,* "Day in Jail for Ex-Duke Prosecutor," September 1, 2007, A9.

41. Peyton Whiteley, "Woman Pleads Guilty to False Rape Report," *Seattle Times,* March 19, 2008, 1.

42. *Indiana News,* "Police: Woman Admits Making False Rape Claim," November 12, 2004, 1.

43. Christina Hall, "Woman Admits Rape Tale Was a Lie," *Toledo Blade,* October 9, 2002, 2.

44. Maria Newman, "Man Freed after Serving Seven Years for Rape," *New York Times,* June 3, 1992.

45. Robert Reinhold, "How Lawyers and Media Turned the McMartin Case into a Tragic Media Circus," *New York Times,* January 25, 1990, 1D.

46. Sarah Kershaw, "New Evidence in Rape Case Frees Man after Six Years," *New York Times,* June 29, 2000, 1.

47. Maki Becker, "Newfound Evidence That Exonerates Capozzi Stored at ECMC All Along," *Buffalo News,* March 29, 2007.

48. Edward Connors, Thomas Lundregan, Neal Miller, and Tom McEwen, *Convicted by Juries, Exonerated by Science* (Washington, DC: Office of Justice Programs, National Institute of Justice, 1996).

49. Eugene Kanin, "False Rape Allegations," *Archives of Sexual Behavior* 23, no. 1 (February 1994): 81.

50. Sandra Norman Eady, Christopher Reinhart, and Peter Martino, "Statutory Rape Laws by State," OLR Research Report, April 14, 2003, 1.

51. Ibid., 9.

52. Kate Zenike, "The Siren Song of Sex with Boys," *New York Times*, December 11, 2005, C3.

53. Michale Ko, "Letourneau Released from Prison Today," *Seattle Times*, August 4, 2004, 1.

54. Mitch Stacy, "Teacher in Sex Case Spared Second Trial," *Buffalo News*, March 22, 2006, A6.

55. David Kocieniewski, "A History of Sex with Students," *New York Times*, October 10, 2006, A1.

56. *New York Times*, "Ex Teacher in Sex Case Freed," February 18, 2005, B10.

57. *New York Post*, "Probation for Woman Perv Teacher," September 27, 2003, 6.

58. Gene Warner, "False Allegations Take Toll on Teacher," *Buffalo News*, June 7, 1996, A1.

59. *New York Times*, "Teacher Arrested in Two Sex Attacks," June 24, 1993.

60. Vance Packard, *The Sexual Wilderness* (New York: D. McKay, 1968).

61. U.S. Department of Justice, Bureau of Justice Statistics, *Crime in the United States, 2006*, Uniform Crime Reports (Washington, DC: GPO, 2007), n.p.

62. Ibid.

63. Kathleen Brady Shea, "2 Jailers Charged in Inmate Attack," *Philadelphia Inquirer*, June 12, 2007, B04.

64. Jim Halley, "All-American 17, out of Jail but Facing Charges," *USA Today*, March 31, 2008, 2C

65. Ken Berger, "Grand Jury Hears Jets vs. Santa Case," *Newsday*, February 11, 2003.

66. Jeff Benedict and Don Yaeger, *Pros and Cons: The Criminals Who Play in the NFL* (New York: Warner Books, 1998).

67. Martha Woodall, "The Assault Broke the Teacher's Neck," *Philadelphia Inquirer*, April 6, 2007, B01.

68. Dwight Ott, "Some Charges Dropped against Temple Students Accused of Hate Crime," *Philadelphia Inquirer*, April 30, 2008, B04.

69. *Boston Globe*, editorial, "Batterers with Badges," December 30, 3007, D8.

Chapter 4

PROSECUTING WHITE-COLLAR CRIME

EDWIN SUTHERLAND (1883–1950)

When Edwin Sutherland was elected president of the American Sociological Association (ASA) in 1939, he delivered to the membership a presidential address entitled "White Collar Criminality." This concept had never been considered before, since the very phrase "white-collar crime" was coined by Sutherland himself. A professor of sociology at the University of Indiana, Sutherland made several major contributions to our understanding of criminal behavior, including the concept of differential association and others.[1]

Although Sutherland's comments occurred 70 years ago, much of what he said then is still applicable to the effort of prosecuting white-collar crime in 2009.

Sutherland begins by showing that "less than 2 percent of persons committed to prison in a year belong to the 'upper' class and were imprisoned for 'business offenses,'" as white-collar crime was called before 1939.

In 2007, more than 2 million Americans were incarcerated for violent or nonviolent crimes, of which the war on drugs led to the incarceration of 249,500 state prisoners and 93,751 federal prisoners. That year, the states held over 1.2 million inmates and the federal government imprisoned 176,258 inmates. Of these, 20 percent of the federal prisoners and 1 percent of state prisoners were incarcerated for white-collar crime.[2] Evidently, the conviction and incarceration of white-collar offenders has increased tenfold since Sutherland first called attention to this kind of offense, though it is highly unlikely that only 20 percent of all offenses are of the business crime nature.

Sutherland goes on to write that it is a mistake to assume that crime is related to poverty and so-called social pathology. He calls the statistical association between these and other indicators of "social disorganization" biased samples because the wealthy and the privileged criminals are not included in studies concerning crime. Sutherland says, "More important crime news may be found on the financial pages of newspapers than on the front pages."[3] Sutherland defined white-collar crime as "crime committed by persons of respectability and high social status in the course of their occupations."[4] This is, of course, not a legal definition, since it assumes that a criminal can be someone not convicted in a court of law but involved in activities that are socially harmful and create many innocent victims. Included in white-collar crime are misrepresentation of financial statements, manipulations on the stock exchanges, commercial bribery, bribery of public officials, misrepresentation in advertising, embezzlement of funds, and tax fraud, among innumerable others.

According to Sutherland, white-collar crime is so often overlooked and not penalized because the social class of white-collar criminals is the same as that of judges, prosecutors, and other court personnel. Furthermore, according to Sutherland, the "corporate culture" is of such a nature as to invite white-collar crime by those in a position to make decisions. Sutherland points to what he calls "differential association," which refers to the manner in which crime is learned by those who associate with persons already availing themselves of illegal income with whom newcomers to the corporate culture then associate in a positive manner. Such association with a reference group leads to viewing criminal behavior in a positive light, so that the offender "neutralizes" his or her conduct because everyone else in the offender's reference group is also engaged in financial crimes.[5] In 2007, the Justice Department reported that in January of that year there were 597 new convictions for white-collar crime in the United States. This figure meant that the number of convictions for this type of crime had increased by more than 11 percent over the previous month. Yet, if such convictions are compared on an annual basis, a decline of 7.6 percent from 2002 has been recorded.

The white-collar crimes prosecuted by the Justice Department include 21 types of fraud and six kinds of antitrust violations.[6]

SCIENTIFIC AND COMMERCIAL WHITE-COLLAR CRIME

Among the other types of white-collar offenses are those to be found in the medical profession, such offenses as the illegal sale of drugs, unnecessary operations, fee splitting, and falsification of medical research.[7] One example of such falsification concerns Dr. John Darsee. Labeled a "brilliant" student, Darsee came to Harvard University after earning degrees from Notre Dame University, Indiana University, and Emory University. Darsee was mainly occupied with testing heart drugs on dogs with a view of eventually helping human cardiac patients. He seemed highly successful, since his results were published in major scientific journals. In less than two years, Darsee published seven papers in such journals, so that his colleagues in the medical profession viewed him as an "all-star" researcher.

Yet, in 1981, three scientists in cardiac research laboratories discovered that Darsee had fabricated his research results, that he had covered up fraud in earlier research results he had published, and that he had used questionable research practices all the way back to his undergraduate days.

As a consequence, Darsee was barred from ever receiving any research grant from the National Institutes of Health. Barred from further research opportunities at any university, Darsee entered the practice of medicine as a critical care specialist. The Brigham and Women's Hospital where Darsee had committed his frauds was forced to repay the National Institutes of Health over $122,000. His former boss was severely criticized for not discovering Darsee's practices sooner. Yet, no legal action was taken against Darsee other than his exclusion from further funded medical research.[8]

From the sociological point of view, Darsee is a criminal. But he was never convicted, and so he is by no means an offender in the legal sense. A quite different outcome awaited Kenneth Lay, Jeff Skilling, and Andrew Fastow, all executives at Enron, at one time the largest and most successful supplier of gas and other commodities in the United States. Convicted of numerous counts of fraud, conspiracy, insider trading, money laundering, and other charges, all three were sentenced to prison terms. Kenneth Lay, Enron's founder and first CEO, was charged with stealing upward of $43.5 million from the company's shareholders. Before he could be sentenced, Lay died of heart failure, leading to the dismissal of Lay's fraud and conspiracy conviction on the grounds that he could not appeal his conviction. This meant that the government could not seize the $43.5 million from Lay's estate. Furthermore, former Enron employees and shareholders could hardly expect to recover some of their losses from Lay's estate because Lay's conviction has been erased from the books and thus legally he did not commit a crime.[9]

Jeff Skilling reported to the federal corrections institute in Waseca, Minnesota, on December 12, 2006. Convicted of fraud and conspiracy charges, Skilling was sentenced to 24 years in prison, indeed an exceedingly long sentence for a business crime. Although this minimum security prison affords prisoners access to basketball courts, ping-pong tables, and a running track, it is nevertheless a prison and a tremendous comedown for a man who lived in a $4.7 million mansion in Houston and was feted by the elite of that city, including leading politicians.[10] Andrew Fastow, also convicted of fraud and conspiracy, was sentenced to six years in a federal prison. Since the federal system has no parole, anyone sentenced to a federal prison must serve all of the sentence. Fastow was the chief financial officer of Enron. Using various accounting tricks, Fastow and the other officers of the company convicted in these schemes ran up billions in debts, which the company could not pay. In view of the inevitable collapse of Enron, which the top executives foresaw, the company's officers sold their stock options at considerable profit to themselves, thereby violating the laws prohibiting insider trading. On the collapse of the company, those former Enron employees who invested all their savings in Enron stock, at the urging of the executives, lost all they had.

Many of the investors lost $75,000 or more when Enron stock became worthless. For these investors, years of savings were lost. Most of these former Enron employees held office jobs and other low-earning positions, so they had to work two jobs or gain help from relatives to survive.

It is not generally known that in addition to Lay, Skilling, and Fastow, three British bankers were also convicted of fraud related to Enron. David Bermingham, Gary Mulgrew, and Giles Darby were sentenced to 37 months in prison for their role in the Enron disaster. They had enriched themselves at the expense of the National Westminster Bank of England, which had a major role in the Enron collapse.[11] The total loss caused by their machinations was estimated at $60 billion in market values, more than $2 billion in pension plans, and the loss of thousands of jobs.[12]

POLITICAL WHITE-COLLAR CRIME AND THE INTERNAL REVENUE SERVICES

Edwin Sutherland also referred to political white-collar crime, which is undoubtedly widespread. Examples include such crimes that violate the oath of office of an elected or appointed official as selling one's vote in a legislature, bribery of all kinds, and outright theft of public funds. There are also numerous crimes committed by agencies of the government who abuse citizens by illegally employing the power inherent in an office or agency. Such abuses are mainly concentrated in law enforcement and tax collection.

No better example of white-collar crime committed against the citizens of the United States can be found than the abuses inflicted on taxpayers by the Internal Revenue Service (IRS). Because the perpetrators of IRS offenses are immune from prosecution, their crimes are not legally recorded. Yet, Sutherland held that such crimes are crimes nevertheless. On July 31, 1996, President Bill Clinton signed the Taxpayer Bill of Rights into law. This law was the product of a number of congressional hearings concerning the illegal manner in which the IRS has abused its power. According to that law, taxpayers can sue the IRS for up to $1 million for "reckless collection," that is, for having been forced to pay what they do not owe.

According to that law, taxpayers can also sue anyone filing false information about wages and interest income. Furthermore, the IRS must prove that its effort to collect taxes is correct, instead of burdening taxpayers with the need to prove that they do not owe more taxes. In addition, the taxpayer can sue the IRS for legal fees up to $110 an hour whenever a taxpayer wins a lawsuit against the IRS. There are a number of additional provisions in the Taxpayer Bill of Rights.[13]

This law is the product of a good deal of testimony before congressional committees concerning the conduct of IRS agents. A good example of such conduct is the experience of a San Diego grandmother, Barbara Hutchinson, who gave a critical talk about the agency to a real estate class. This talk led the IRS to read her mail, tap her telephone, seize her husband's business, and cause her to owe $200,000 in legal fees. "The Gestapo is alive and well," said Hutchinson to the House Ways and Means Committee.

The IRS denies that it has a quota system that automatically brands a segment of tax returns as deficient, whether true or not. However, the executive director of the National Taxpayers Legal Fund testified before the same committee that the IRS has an "abusive" property seizure policy, and a businessman from Arkansas told the committee that the IRS overwhelms honest taxpayers with unfounded demands because individuals cannot usually afford the legal fees needed to defend themselves. Further, the IRS was accused by Michael O'Brien of targeting any lawyers seeking to help taxpayers by auditing them 18 times more often than anyone else.[14]

Despite the Taxpayer Bill of Rights, the IRS appears to continue its abusive practices. This continuation of abuse is the reason for the dismissal of charges against an accounting firm, KPMG, by Judge Lewis A. Kaplan of the U.S. District Court of Manhattan.

The judge found that the IRS told the KPMG management not to pay legal fees for its employees harassed by the IRS and not to furnish the defense with documents needed by the defendants. The IRS pretended that 16 former KPMG executives invented fraudulent tax shelters so as to deprive the IRS of its income. Yet, the judge told the IRS lawyers, "Their deliberate interference with the defendants' rights was outrageous and shocking in the constitutional sense because it was fundamentally at odds with two of our most basic constitutional values—the right to counsel and the right to fair criminal proceedings."[15]

Because IRS agents are immune from prosecution and cannot be convicted, they and the agency are never criminal in the legal sense. However, Professor Sutherland wrote, "conviction in a criminal court[,] which is sometimes suggested as the criterion, is not adequate because a large proportion of those who commit crimes are not convicted in criminal courts."[16] In 1997, six veteran IRS employees testified before a Senate committee to the effect that IRS managers routinely cover up abuses of taxpayers by IRS agents, punish internal whistle blowers, and protect senior agency officials from investigation. The employees were shielded by a screen and their voices distorted electronically to shield them from retribution by IRS management. According to the employees' testimony, a "culture of arrogance" exists at the IRS "where ordinary citizens are treated as criminals."[17]

Confronted with such accusations, the IRS management generally seeks to defend its conduct by saying that Congress, not the IRS, determines how much tax must be paid by the voters and citizens. That, however, is no defense, since the manner in which taxes are collected by the IRS, together with the organization's illegal activities, forms the crux of the complaints about that agency. The IRS imposes taxes that are never legal. The IRS destroys the lives of innocent citizens by demanding huge sums never owed. The IRS ignores the constitutional rights of citizens and exercises a reign of terror in the land of the free and the home of the not so brave.

In December 1997, the IRS admitted that taxpayers' rights had been abused by illegal tactics and claimed that new policies would prevent such abuse thereafter. As we have seen, this was not so and the abuses continue.

POLITICAL CRIME AND THE POLICE

There are those critics who believe that the police can get away with anything because their crimes are never prosecuted. This is not so. The evidence is that some outstandingly brutal crimes by police are indeed prosecuted and lead to prison time for the convicted offenders. It is also true, however, that a vast majority of crimes committed by the police are ignored by prosecutors mainly because the police will protect even the most outrageous conduct by fellow police officers, maintaining a "wall of silence" that holds that the interests of the police outweigh the interests of the public the police claim to serve.

No more hideous crime, short of murder, has been committed by a police officer against a citizen than the torture of Abner Louima, a Haitian immigrant, by Justin Volpe, a New York City police officer convicted and sentenced to 30 years in prison on December 15, 1999. This sentence came about after Volpe admitted sodomizing Abner Louima with a broom handle as the victim was handcuffed. Volpe also threatened to kill Louima. All this violence was precipitated by Volpe's belief that Louima had struck him, a claim later shown to be false. In addition to Volpe, five other New York City police officers were also convicted in this case. One is Charles Schwarz, who was sentenced to 14 years in prison for participating in the Louima atrocity by holding the victim down during Volpe's attack. In March 2002, the New York Court of Appeals threw out this conviction. Thereafter, Schwarz was tried and convicted a second time and sentenced to five years in prison. Schwarz was finally released on May 4, 2007.

Also convicted in that case were Thomas Bruder and Thomas Wiese, who were charged with obstruction of justice for covering up Volpe's crimes. Their convictions were also overturned by the court. In 2001, Abner Louima was paid $8.75 million by the city and the police union, who were accused and convicted of a cover-up. His lawyers were paid one-third of that sum.

The beating of Rodney King by Los Angeles police officers on March 3, 1991, became a major event in U.S. urban history. That beating, recorded on videotape by a nearby citizen, led to the acquittal of the officers involved and subsequently to three days of riots, costing 55 lives and untold injury and damage to the city of Los Angeles and its citizens. Four police officers were tried for assault and acquitted by a jury on April 29, 1992. After the riots, two of the officers, Stacey Koon and Lawrence Powell, were prosecuted on federal civil rights charges and convicted. They were sentenced to 30 months in a federal prison.[18] In December 1995, Koon and Powell were released from prison and began two years of supervised release.

Evidently, police are not immune from prosecution. Of course, the assaults on Louima and King were widely publicized, so it would have been almost impossible to avoid some action in both cases. It needs to be emphasized that both foregoing assaults committed by police were white-collar crimes according to Sutherland's definition.

According to that definition, murder can also be a white-collar crime if committed by those individuals enjoying respectability, having high social standing, and yet committing crimes in the course of their occupation. In this category, the murder of Arthur McDuffie by the Miami police in 1980 stands out as the kind of white-collar crime that usually goes unpunished. Indeed, the police officers involved in the killing were prosecuted, but the jury acquitted them despite the overwhelming evidence that McDuffie had been beaten to death for speeding. His skull was cracked as he was beaten with flashlights and batons. Several officers held him down while others kicked him. He was then sent to a hospital, where he died.

The police, seeking to cover up their crime, drove over McDuffie's motor bike with a squad car, gouged the road with a tire iron, and threw the victim's watch down a gutter. This was done to make the murder look like an accident. Nevertheless, these efforts failed to convince investigators, who were told by eyewitnesses that "they looked like a pack of wild dogs attacking a piece of meat." When the killers were acquitted, Miami suffered a major riot in the streets, leading to the deaths of 18 people and $100 million in property damage.[19] Police criminal conduct toward ordinary citizens is widespread and seldom prosecuted. Even then, police are usually exonerated by judges and juries, so it is not unreasonable to comment that police white-collar crime is normally tolerated.

WHITE-COLLAR CRIME BY ELECTED OFFICIALS

An "indictment" is an accusation by a grand jury to the effect that there is cause to believe that a defendant may have committed a crime. An indictment is not proof of guilt but a statement of probable cause to prosecute and try accused persons for the charges against them. Many people indicted by a grand jury are later found innocent. On July 30, 2008, Senator Ted Stevens of Alaska was accused by a federal grand jury of concealing on financial disclosure forms lucrative gifts in excess of $250,000 from executives of companies doing business with the federal government. Evidently, Stevens used his office to promote the business interests of Bill J. Allen of the Veco Corporation in obtaining profitable deals in Russia and Pakistan. Stevens, at age 84, was the longest-serving Republican senator. He was chairman of the Appropriations Committee of the Senate and oversaw $900 billion in spending by the government. Having been in the Senate for 40 years, Stevens became the target of FBI investigations after Representative Dan Young, also a Republican from Alaska, came under FBI scrutiny.[20]

Senator Stevens is not alone in having been convicted of taking bribes. Over many years, a number of elected officials have likewise been prosecuted and convicted of various offenses. Most spectacular among these cases were the convictions of one U.S. senator and four representatives in the so-called Abscam scandal of the 1980s. These convictions came about because the FBI deliberately created the crimes that then entrapped the politicians.

There can be no doubt that none of the five members of Congress sent to prison in the Abscam scheme had any intention of committing any crime or taking any bribe, so the normal requirement of mens rea, or a guilty mind, was absent in these cases. Undoubtedly, the Abscam trials and convictions were the most serious attacks by the government on the freedoms guaranteed U.S. citizens by the Constitution and marked the beginning of a police state mentality that, 30 years later, has become commonplace. In 1978, the FBI created a front called Abdul Enterprises. Using a well-known confidence man not directly employed by the FBI, the bureau set up its trap. This "agent" posed as an Arab sheik in New Jersey, where he offered elected officials money in exchange for special favors, including the obtaining of gambling licenses normally not accessible to foreigners. Five members of Congress, including Senator Harrison Williams of New Jersey, agreed to sell their offices and were subsequently convicted of bribery and conspiracy. Williams was fined $50,000 and imprisoned for three years.[21]

Also convicted in this entrapment scheme was Representative Frank Thompson of New Jersey. He had served in the House for 26 years until he was sent to prison for 2 years on bribery and conspiracy charges. The same charges led to the conviction of Representative John M. Murphy of Staten Island, New York, and Representative Richard Kelly of Florida. Also involved was John W. Jenrette, a representative from South Carolina who was convicted of taking $50,000 in bribes.[22]

In addition to the five politicians jailed as a result of Abscam, numerous other politicians and their associates have been convicted of theft, bribery, embezzlement, and conspiracy over the years. It is for that reason that many Americans equate the word "politician" with "crook," so that public service is in low repute in this country and elsewhere.

It is not possible to list here all the indictments, convictions, and imprisonments of elected officials occurring almost daily in the United States. Therefore, a perusal of a sample of such proceedings must suffice to outline the extent of this conduct. On June 28, 2008, two aides to New York City councilman Kendall Stewart of Brooklyn were indicted for embezzling $45,000 from a nonprofit program designed to tutor public school children.[23]

In July 2008, 19 people were indicted for accepting and paying bribes in connection with New York City housing. Included in the indictment was Joba Cottoreal, the New York City housing supervisor, who was charged with 26 counts of receiving bribes and falsifying business records.[24]

Also in 2008, the U.S. Supreme Court announced it would not hear an appeal by the former governor of Illinois, George Ryan, who was convicted and imprisoned for using taxpayers' money to cover campaign expenses, lying to federal agents, and handing out public contracts to friends in exchange for gifts for himself and his family.[25] In 2007, Alan Hevesi, the New York State comptroller, was sentenced for defrauding the government by using state employees as drivers and personal assistants for his wife. He was fined $5,000 and forced to resign his $151,500-a-year job. In addition, he repaid the state $206,000 for use of the employees.[26]

It was the same Alan Hevesi who uncovered similar fraud among other state politicians. For example, an auditor for Hevesi's office found that the court clerk in the village of Perry, New York, Ruth Milks, added $35 to every traffic ticket paid in Perry and then pocketed the difference, amounting to tens of thousands of dollars. Likewise, Joseph Trudden, former mayor of Farmingdale, New York, was convicted in 2005 of concealing that he had used his village credit card to pay for meals and drinks and other personal expenses. In addition, the Hevesi audits revealed numerous other cases of minor and major fraud by elected officials.[27]

It was the conviction of Congressman Randy Cunningham in 2006 on bribery charges that prosecutors called "unprecedented in depth, breadth and length." Cunningham was sentenced to eight years and four months in a federal prison for taking $2.4 million in bribes from military contractors. Cunningham had been a "top gun" pilot ace in the Vietnam War, and this allowed him to promote a political career. Evidently, Cunningham demanded cash payments as well as such gifts as a sport utility vehicle, a Tiffany statue, rugs, and adornments, depending on the size of the favor he was expected to deliver. Cunnigham had developed an entire menu of bribes to be paid him for various favors. For example, he offered a businessman a $16 million government contract in exchange for the title to a boat. He also listed how much more government money in the form of contracts could be bought for every $50,000 paid to him.

Cunningham was also ordered to pay over $1.8 million in back taxes, penalties, and interest and was also ordered to pay more than $1.8 million in addition based on profits from his crimes. Since bribes are not only collected but also paid, prosecutors succeeded in gaining the conviction of Mitchell Wade, a military contractor, former president of MZM Inc. of Washington. He pleaded guilty of giving Randy Cunningham $1 million in bribes.[28]

In June 2008, Justice Robert C. McCann of the New York State Supreme Court in Brooklyn sentenced Diane M. Gordon to two to six years in prison for offering to help a developer acquire city land if he would build her a house free. The judge called her action "an outrageous breach of trust."

Gordon was a four-term Democratic state assemblywoman. The prosecutors were most incensed because Gordon won another term in the New York Assembly after having been indicted on these charges.[29] Roger L. Green, a New York assemblyman, was convicted in 2004 on two counts of petty larceny for billing the New York Assembly for travel expenses he did not incur. Subsequently, Green resigned his seat but won the next election and returned to his old seat.[30]

THE WATERGATE SCANDAL AND THE RESIGNATION OF PRESIDENT RICHARD NIXON

No politically motivated crime became so prominent in the history of the United States as the series of offenses associated with the resignation of President Richard Nixon from his office on August 10, 1974. There can be little doubt that Nixon was eligible for prosecution despite his resignation had he not been pardoned by his successor, President Gerald Ford. According to a memorandum by Leon Jaworski, special prosecutor: "It cannot be sufficient retribution for criminal offenses merely to surrender the public office and trust which has been demonstrably abused. A person should not be permitted to trade in the abused office in return for immunity."[31] The crimes associated with the phrase "Watergate" referred first to the building in which several burglars broke into the offices of the Democratic National Committee on June 7, 1972. A security guard in the Watergate building at the time, Frank Wills, discovered this break-in and arrested several men inside the offices of the Democratic Party.

The men arrested were Bernard Barker, James McCord, Frank Sturgis, Eugenio Martinez, and Vigilio Gonzalez. Because these men had stolen nothing but had eavesdropping equipment in their possession, it became apparent that the purpose of the break-in was political. Therefore, the FBI questioned G. Gordon Liddy, a lawyer for the Committee to Re-elect the President (Nixon). When Liddy refused to answer any questions by the FBI, the attorney general, John M. Mitchell, dismissed him.[32]

On September 18, 1972, a grand jury returned an indictment against the five men arrested in the break-in and against Gordon Liddy and E. Howard Hunt, who were both in the Watergate building during the break-in. The indictment accused all seven of tapping telephones, planting electronic eavesdropping devices, and stealing documents. Despite this, President Richard Nixon told a news conference that no one on the White House staff was involved, and Attorney General Mitchell also claimed to have had no knowledge of the break-in.

When Bernard Barker admitted his role in the break-in without implicating others, Democrats filed an amended complaint against several White House operatives for political espionage. They accused these men of violating the Federal Election Campaign Act. Included in the complaint was Maurice Stans, the finance chairman of the Committee to Re-elect the President. Evidently, Stans had approved the transfer of $100,000 in campaign funds to Mexico to conceal the identity of the donors.[33]

It was then revealed that the president had authorized a secret campaign fund used to pay Donald Segretti to sabotage the Democratic campaign. Early in January 1973, four of the burglars, Barker, Sturgis, Martinez, and Gonzalez, pleaded guilty, as did Liddy and McCord. Liddy was then sentenced to spend up to 20 years in prison. He was released in 1977. Twenty-six Watergate defendants went to prison for their involvements in numerous crimes, including burglary, espionage, forgery, and covering up these and other crimes. John Mitchell, erstwhile attorney general of the United States and therefore the country's highest law enforcement officer, was also jailed. Mitchell was convicted in January 1975 of conspiracy, obstruction of justice, and perjury; he stayed imprisoned until January 1979.[34]

As the media reported on these many crimes, the president, Richard Nixon, publicly denied that he knew anything about the break-ins, cover-ups, and financial trickery. Yet, Nixon had already ordered a break-in at the Brookings Institution and demanded from his subordinates that burglars steal tax records concerning Leslie Gelb and Morton Halpern, who worked there and wrote a study opposing the Vietnam War. Nixon also had the FBI wiretap Halpern's house.

President Nixon also ordered a burglary at the offices of Dr. Lewis Fielding. Fielding, a psychiatrist, was seeing Daniel Ellsberg, a Columbia University professor and erstwhile Defense Department analyst. Ellsberg had given *The New York Times* and *The Washington Post* evidence that the president had lied about U.S. successes in Vietnam. When that evidence, known to history as the Pentagon Papers, was published, Nixon sought to revenge himself on Ellsberg by sending burglars to the psychiatrist's office in the hope of finding material in the doctor's files that would be detrimental to Ellsberg.

All this subterfuge and more led the Senate to hold hearings that revealed President Nixon's involvement in the numerous crimes surrounding his effort at reelection in 1972. Nixon did, in fact, do very well, winning 570 electoral votes to the Democrat McGovern's 17. Then in 1974, the House of Representatives held impeachment proceedings. In turn, Richard Nixon resigned his office on August 9, 1974. Nixon was the only president ever to resign from the presidency. This made Gerald Ford the 38th president, although he was never elected to the vice president's office nor to the office of the president.[35]

Volumes have been written about the Watergate scandal, the greatest white-collar crime in U.S. history. For the U.S. government, Watergate has had many consequences, of which the principal lesson is that Americans will not allow any president to become a dictator or to deprive the American people of their rights and privileges.

PROSECUTING HEALTH CARE FRAUD

An online service called Lexis Nexis records newspaper stories. Included are those stories concerning health care fraud. The record reveals that in New York State newspapers alone, there were 999 instances of such fraud known to law enforcement during the years 1997–2007. Evidently, the number of such white-collar crimes is far too large to record here and also much too great for the limited resources of prosecutors entrusted to stop such conduct. Examples include the conviction of a physician and three business owners who operated a Miami, Florida, medical equipment company. Dr. Ana Caos and three business associates were found guilty by a jury of defrauding the U.S. government, making false claims to Medicare, soliciting and receiving kickbacks, and conspiring to commit health care fraud. All four were convicted on March 28, 2008, through the efforts of the Medicare Fraud Strike Force, which has operated since March 2007.[36]

Caos falsely diagnosed patients with diseases they did not suffer and then prescribed unnecessary medications. In addition to billing Medicare for false prescriptions costing taxpayers $487,000, the four defendants also billed Medicare $1.6 million in medical equipment supplied by a medical equipment company owned by the three businessmen involved in the scheme. Patients of Dr. Caos testified that they were paid cash kickbacks to accept delivery of unnecessary medication. When the patients received the medication, they threw it in the garbage.[37]

In a related effort to defraud the taxpayer, Alsa Perera was sentenced to 30 months in prison for her role in an $11 million scheme to steal from the Medicaid program. Perera was also sentenced by Judge Frederico Moreno to three years' probation. Further, Perera was ordered to pay back over $8.2 million to the U.S. government.

Perera had pleaded guilty to one count of health care fraud in her role as administrator of Saint Jude Rehabilitation Center. This health care center claimed to help HIV patients. Instead, Perera and Carlo, Jose, and Luis Benitez submitted $11.3 million in fraudulent claims to the Medicare program for HIV infusions never provided or unnecessary. Medicare had already paid more than $8.3 million before the fraud was discovered. The four co-conspirators paid "patients" $100 to $150 in cash kickbacks and then hired a medical billing specialist to make the bills sent to Medicare appear legitimate.

In addition, Rita Campos-Ramirez also pleaded guilty of defrauding Medicare of approximately $170 million in false claims, of which Medicare had already paid $105 million before this fraud was discovered. Ramirez was also connected to the Saint Jude scheme. Prosecutors succeeded in convicting Ramirez, who was then sentenced to 12 years in prison.

On June 12, 2007, Dr. Orestes Alvarez Jacinto was convicted of participating in the Saint Jude health care fraud. Alvarez was charged with approving a drug called WinRho, which the Saint Jude patients did not need and which could actually harm them. He signed bills misrepresenting the amount of the drug actually administered and also signed for treatments never given or medically unnecessary. Alvarez was sentenced to 18 months in prison.[38] The foregoing individual was among the 82 defendants indicted by the Medicare Fraud Section Strike Force, which discovered that these 82 individuals had fraudulently billed Medicare $492 million.[39]

The Medicare Fraud Section Strike Force was organized to deal with the ever-increasing fraud victimizing U.S. taxpayers at a cost of more than $60 billion each year. The strike force has investigated as many as 2,400 such cases each year with some success. The strike force has not only convicted numerous individuals and recovered large sums for the taxpayer but also succeeded in dealing with large companies guilty of such fraud. For example, a corporation called Tenethealthcare returned more than $900 million to Medicare in 2006.

This disturbing state of health care led deputy assistant director of the FBI Salvador Hernandez to warn consumers to make certain they read the explanations offered by health care providers and to make certain the government is not billed for care never received.[40]

Health care fraud can cost a state a great deal. For example, New York has numerous unneeded hospitals. Closing these hospitals would cost the state millions in federal aid unless the state recovers at least $215 million a year of fraudulent claims paid by Medicaid. To that end, James Sheehan was appointed Medicaid inspector general in 2007 with the assignment to prevent the loss of $700 million annually charged to New York Medicaid by frauds. To that end, New York has introduced a new law called the False Claims Act, which includes a whistle blower provision and an increase in Sheehan's staff to 300 from only 100 the previous year.[41]

The American people spend $2 trillion on health care each year. Fraud wastes about 3 to 10 percent of this sum, the amount depending on the state in which Medicare is available. As a measure to fight such waste, United Health Group has introduced software that helps detect fraud. An example of success with such software was the detection of claims from a psychiatrist who seemed to be seeing 63 patients a day. An investigation found that a former patient had stolen the doctor's billing identity and set up a counseling service and then billed Blue Cross $1 million before being detected.[42]

Health care fraud is common and spread across the country from Los Angeles to New York and the all cities and states between. It has become one of the most expensive white-collar crimes and continues to plague Medicare and taxpayers because, as of 2008, no adequate defense against this crime has been found.

THE WAR ON DRUGS

The prohibition of the sale, distribution, and use of alcohol in the United States began when the Eighteenth Amendment to the U.S. Constitution was ratified by the states in 1918; the Volstead Act served to enforce this law as of 1920. The Eighteenth Amendment was repealed in 1933. Before repeal, Americans drank alcohol in ever-increasing numbers as organized crime made a great deal of money by furnishing so many drinkers with the alcohol they craved. Prohibition of alcohol was a failure. Not only did Americans drink as much as or more than before, but Prohibition also launched organized crime in the United States on a large-scale basis. Likewise, the prohibition of drugs other than alcohol has not been effective, as is visible in the failed efforts to prosecute such offenses.

The U.S. war on drugs began as soon as Prohibition was repealed. The reason for the antidrug war was the ambition of Harry Anslinger, who had been appointed chief of the Bureau of Narcotics and who sought to increase his power, his income, and his prestige by claiming that marijuana, which had been in use for thousands of years, was a dangerous drug. Anslinger was supported in this propaganda by the alcohol industry, which did not want to compete with other drugs for the vast amount of money the American public is willing to spend on alcohol each year. Anslinger was a racist who threatened the white majority with stories of "Negro violence" under the influence of marijuana and other drugs. He also claimed that marijuana users of all races would become violent on using the substance and that you would "kill your brother" under its influence.[43] As more and more Mexicans and other foreigners came to the United States in the 1920s, drug prohibition became more and more popular, since drug use was attributed to South Americans in particular. Therefore, in 1914 Congress passed the Harrison Act, which sought to eliminate marijuana and, later, other drugs associated with Hispanics and other foreigners. The Federal Bureau of Narcotics in the Treasury Department was established in 1930 and the Marijuana Tax Act passed in 1937. In 1951, the Boggs Amendment to the Harrison Act increased drug use penalties by four times; and in 1970, Congress passed the Controlled Substance Abuse Act.[44]

Armed with these laws, the Bureau of Narcotics, the FBI, and other state and federal agencies have attempted for years to put an end to the use of narcotics and other drugs in the United States and to prevent the importation of these drugs into this country.

At the outset of the twenty-first century, about 25 percent of U.S. citizens, or 75 million Americans, have at one time or another used illegal substances. One expensive consequence of the war on drugs has been the incarceration of a million Americans for drug abuse, drug use, drug selling, and drug importation. Since it costs about $18,000 a year to imprison one citizen in a federal or state institution, this policy costs the taxpayer an enormous sum without leading to any visible results. In fact, the use of marijuana and other drugs has increased since this policy has been applied. This increase is, in part, a consequence of the decrease in the budgets of federal prosecutors, with the result that prosecutions have shrunk significantly. An example of this decline is the office of the Washington, D.C., U.S. attorney, whose prosecutions have declined by 40 percent in only one year.[45]

The magnitude of drug imports into the United States is evident by the arrest of 16-year-old Anthony Cruz at New York's Kennedy Airport. On his apprehension, in October 2007, Cruz, of the Dominican Republic, was called a "drug mule" by law enforcement officials. Cruz had ingested a kilo of drugs worth $500,000, risking fatal injuries. He had swallowed a number of balloons containing heroin. Had they burst, he would have died.[46]

In December 2007, Akhil Bansai, an MBA student at Temple University in Philadelphia, was sentenced for smuggling 11 million prescription pills from India and distributing them to 60,000 Americans. Bansai supplied dozens of illegal pharmacies without prescriptions. Bansai and his family who participated in the scheme netted $8 million in profits. Bansai was sentenced to 20 years in prison, which is the minimum mandatory sentence for this drug offense. The FBI said that they seized bank accounts in 11 countries involved in this network.[47]

Efforts to control the importation, distribution, and use of drugs other than alcohol have gone on so long in the United States that reasonable people have to conclude that the prohibition of illegal drugs has suffered the same fate as the effort to suppress the sale of alcohol. Neither prohibition has worked to stem the use of illegal substance; instead, both prohibitions have given organized crime considerable income and power. However destructive illegal drugs may be, it is highly recommended that use of all drugs be regulated by the medical profession; at least then the drugs may be used to alleviate the cravings of users and reduce the danger to the general public.

IDENTITY THEFT

On August 6, 2008, 11 people, including a U.S. Secret Service informant (not an agent), were charged by the Justice Department with hacking and identity theft. Three of those charged were U.S. citizens; the others were foreigners. They used computing techniques that allowed them to gather huge quantities of personal and financial information from retailers and their customers. This information was then sold to others or used by the hackers themselves. By installing so-called sniffer programs, the hackers succeeded in identifying credit card and debit card numbers, leading to the storage of more than 25 million numbers in Latvia and Ukraine.[48]

A yet more malicious white-collar crime is the installation of electronic devices at gasoline pumps, which then produce credit and debit card information for the thieves. In San Jose, California, for example, thieves installed such a device at an ARCO station and succeeded in stealing more than $200,000 from 180 victims. Such devices have also been installed at ATM machines.

In Pierce County, Washington, thieves cleaned out 120 bank accounts after having installed and left a device at a gas pump for 11 months. Similar devices were found in Pennsylvania, Delaware, and Nevada.[49]

SUMMARY

Professor Edwin Sutherland, erstwhile president of the American Sociological Association, was first to identity white-collar crime. Sutherland used sociological definitions, rather than legal definitions, in identifying crimes of persons with high social standing conducted in the course of their daily business. White-collar crimes are committed in the scientific community, among business people, and by police, politicians, and health care providers.

Prosecution of white-collar crime is difficult not only because legislatures seldom allot adequate resources to prosecutors but also because many Americans do not view white-collar crime as real crime in the way Sutherland described it. According to Sutherland, white-collar criminality is real criminality and is in all cases a violation of the law. As evident in this chapter, crime is not necessarily the outcome of poverty or psychopathic personality or sociopathic conditions. Crime is learned, said Sutherland, and white-collar crime proves it.

NOTES

1. Edwin Sutherland, "White Collar Criminality," *American Sociological Review* 5, no. 1 (February 1940): 1–12.

2. U.S. Department of Justice, Bureau of Justice Statistics, *Prisoners in 2006: Drug War Facts*, by William J. Sabol, Heather Couture, and Page M. Harrison (Washington, DC: GPO, December 2007), 1.

3. Sutherland, "White Collar Criminality," 2.

4. Edwin H. Sutherland, Donald R. Cressey, and David F. Luckenbill, *Principles of Criminology* (Dix Hills, NY: General Hall, 1992), 62.

5. Alex Thio, *Sociology*, 5th ed. (New York: Longman, 1998), 100.

6. "White Collar Crime Convictions for January 2007," *Tracereports* (2007): 1–2.

7. Sutherland, "White Collar Criminality," 3.

8. Eugene Braunwald, "Cardiolgy: The John Darsee Experience," in *Research Fraud in the Biomedical and Behavioral Sciences*, ed. David S. Miller and Michael Herson (New York: Wiley, 1992), 55–79.

9. Kate Murphy, "Judge Throws Out Kenneth Lay's Conviction," *New York Times*, Octobr 18, 2006, C3.

10. *Albany Times Union*, "Former Enron CEO Skilling Begins Prison Sentence," December 12, 2006, E2.

11. Kate Murphy, "Fraud Case Tied to Enron Ends in Prison for Three Men," *New York Times*, February 23, 2008, C2.

12. Juan Lozano, "Enron Victims to Speak Out," *Albany Times Union*, September 23, 2006, B11.

13. *Albany Times Union*, "Clinton Signs Popular Taxpayers' Rights Bill," July 31, 1996, A2.

14. Bill Billiter, "Horror Stories about IRS Told to Congress Panel," *Los Angeles Times*, October 7, 1980, B3.

15. Richard Rahn, "Stopping IRS Misconduct," *Washington Times*, July 25, 2007, A17.

16. Sutherland, "White Collar Criminality," 5.

17. Robert A. Rankin, "More IRS Abuses Revealed on Final Day of Senate Hearings," *Buffalo News*, September 26, 1997, A10.

18. *Albany Times Union*, "2 Officers in King Case Go to Prison," October 13, 1993, A5.

19. Matt Melzer, "The Arthur McDuffie Riots of 1980," *Miami Beach News*, August 12, 2007.

20. Carrie Johnson and Paul Kane, "Sen. Stevens Indicted on 7 Corruption Counts," *Washington Post*, July 30, 2008, A01.

21. *New York Times*, "Senator Williams Exits Unrepentant,"March 14, 1982, E1.

22. Jospeh P. Fried, "Frank Thompson: Career in Congress Ended with Abscam," *New York Times*, July 24, 1989.

23. Russ Buettner, "New Charges for Two Accused of Embezzling Council Funds," *New York Times*, June 25, 2008, B.

24. *New York Times*, "Graft Rap for Housing Big," July 11, 2008, 17.

25. Monica Davey, "Ex-governor, Now in Prison, Sees Case End," *New York Times*, May 28, 2008, A15.

26. Mark Johnson, "As Hevesi Is Sentenced, Fight Rages over His Successor," *Buffalo News*, Febraury 10, 2007, A5.

27. Michale Cooper, "Hevesi's Investigation Unit Builds Prosecutable Cases," *New York Times*, December 27, 2005, B8.

28. Randal C. Archibold, "Ex-Congressman Gets 8 Year Term in Bribery Case," *New York Times*, March 4, 2006, A1.

29. Kareem Fahim, "Ex-legislator Is Sentenced to 2 to 6 Years," *New York Times*, June 13, 2008, B1.

30. Jonathan P. Hicks, "From Conviction to Re-election," *New York Times*, December 9, 2005, B10.

31. U.S. Department of Justice, Watergate Special Prosecution Force, "Jaworski Memorandum on Prosecuting Nixon," by Carl M. Feldbaum and Peter M. Kreindler, August 9, 1974.

32. *New York Times*, "A Chronology of Events in the Watergate Case, an Election Scheme that Backfired," May 1, 1973, 33.

33. Ibid., 34.

34. *New York Times*, "John M. Mitchell Dies at 75; Major Figure in Watergate," November 10, 1988, D25.

35. "Watergate: The Scandal That Brought Down Richard Nxion," http://www.watergate.info.

36. *Drug Week*, "Miami Jury Convicts Physician and Three Business Owners of Medicare Fraud," March 28, 2008, 2782.

37. Ibid., 2783.

38. *Drug Week*, "HIV Infusion Clinic Administrator Sentence to 30 Months in Prison for Health Care Fraud," July 25, 2008, 2370.

39. Ibid., 2371.

40. Carrie Johnson, "U.S. Targets Health Care Fraud, Abuse," *Washington Post*, July 19, 2007, DO1.

41. Gale Scott, "Top Cop Targets Health Care Fraud," *Crain's New York Business*, June 25, 2007, 2.

42. Julie Appleby, "Medical Claims 'Mined' to Find Fraud," *USA Today*, November 7, 2008, 1B.

43. Richard J. Bonnie and Charles Whitebread, "The Forbidden Fruit and the Tree of Knowledge," *Virginia Law Review* 56, no. 6 (October 1970).

44. *DrugWarrant*, "Why Is Marijuana Illegal?" February 13, 2008.

45. Carol D. Leoning, "D.C. Sees Sharp Drop in Federal Prosecutions," *Washington Post*, October 21, 2007, AO1.

46. *Daily News*, "Teen Drug Mule's Gut Full of Heroin," October 27, 2007, 10.

47. John Schiffman, "Long Sentence in Vast Pill Selling Case," *Philadelphia Inquirer*, December 10, 2007, BO4.

48. Rodrique Ngowi and Anne D'Innocenzio, "11 Charged in What May Be the Biggest ID Theft Case Ever," Associated Press, August 6, 2008, n.p.

49. Katharine Lackey, "Thieves Skim Credit Card Date at Fuel Pumps," *USA Today*, August 6, 2008, 1.

Chapter 5

DEFENDING THE ACCUSED

DEFENDING THE INDIGENT

Public defenders are common in almost all U.S. jurisdictions at the beginning of the twenty-first century. Such has not always been the case. In 1932, in *Powell v. Alabama*, the U.S. Supreme Court interpreted the Sixth Amendment to the U.S. Constitution to guarantee a right to counsel, that is, a lawyer, to anyone accused of a crime. Whereas those able to pay for a lawyer were always represented by counsel if they so wished, the poor who could not afford a lawyer had to face the prosecution alone.[1] It was not until Clara Foltz (1849–1943), California's first female lawyer, spoke at the Chicago World's Fair in 1893 that the very idea of providing lawyers for the poor who could not afford legal representation was ever considered. Foltz spoke on the abuses then existing and on the rights of the accused.[2] The actual appointments of public defenders came about slowly. In fact, not until the case of *Gideon v. Wainwright*, which the Supreme Court decided in 1963, was every criminal court in the country finally required to provide free counsel to indigent defendants. The lawyers appointed and paid by the court are called "public defenders."[3]

The American Bar Association report in 2004 concerning the representation of indigent defendants in criminal proceedings concluded that many thousands of poor people are convicted every year either without any legal representation at all or with a lawyer who represents the defendant inadequately. The report warned of the erosion of the integrity of the criminal justice system.[4] An example of the inadequacy of a public defense is the case of Ronald Rompilla. He was convicted of murder and given the death penalty. On appeal to the Supreme Court, five justices found the defense inadequate because the public defenders never told the jury that the defendant had a horrendous childhood, that he was an alcoholic, and that he had been diagnosed as suffering from mental illness.[5]

Numerous examples of similar cases are recorded in the annals of American jurisprudence. Not only are there numerous defendants whose life history is withheld from the jury in capital cases, but there are a good number of utterly innocent defendants wrongfully convicted because they are poorly defended, if defended at all.

It is evident that the power of U.S. prosecutors invites misconduct on the part of district attorneys. Prosecutors seek convictions at any cost because their reappointment or reelection depends on favorable statistics showing that they have sent large numbers of citizens to prison. To address the problem, an adequate public defender can place a considerable check on prosecutorial misconduct and ensure fairness in court.

A number of decisions by the Supreme Court defeated prosecutorial misconduct, a behavior that was most severely criticized in *Berger v. United States*, which dealt specifically with the higher duty of the prosecutor.[6]

It needs to be understood that poor defendants once convicted cannot appeal even though the right to appeal is based on the Sixth Amendment to the Constitution. An appeal is very expensive. The appellant has to hire an appeals specialist lawyer, pay for the transcript of his or her trial, secure the help of investigators, and so on. Poor people simply cannot afford to appeal a wrongful conviction.

More than a century after Clara Foltz first demanded that the poor be given adequate counsel at public expense, the poor remain without adequate defense in most U.S. jurisdictions. An example of this situation was reported in a *San Jose Mercury News* article that describes how the local prosecutors continue to violate the rights of defendants in order to "uphold a friendly police in its frequent blunders . . . the vanity of winning cases . . . the unfortunate belief, engendered by the office itself . . . that the accused is always guilty."[7]

Public defenders may be court-appointed lawyers who bill by the hour, or they may be salaried employees. Both types of lawyers are paid by the government. Until recently, it was believed by people that both types of lawyers achieved equally and that the poor were as well defended by those lawyers paid by the hour as by those on salary. Yet, a recent study shows that salaried lawyers do much more for their clients than those working by the hour.

The reasons for the discrepancy of results lie in the better training of salaried lawyers as compared with the training of those who work by the hour. Furthermore, the salaried defenders have more interaction with prosecutors and can therefore anticipate how the prosecutor will approach a case. Salaried lawyers are also more experienced and tend to have superior credentials.

An example of a poor defense was the defense of Jukawana Holland, accused of drug violations. Holland was represented by her court-appointed attorney, Henry Zerella, who failed to check his witness list. He did not, therefore, uncover a conflict, delaying the trial. Zerella was assessed a $500 sanction because he failed to recognize that the evidence officer of the Vineland, New Jersey, police department was also on his witness list.[8] Defendants represented by court-appointed attorneys receive sentences about eight months longer than those represented by salaried public defenders. Furthermore, court-appointed lawyers take about 20 days longer to resolve cases by plea bargains than is true of salaried defenders. Also, appointed lawyers cost the taxpayer $5,800 more for each case handled than is true of salaried defenders.[9]

A study of public defenders made in Denver, Colorado, found that the average sentence for clients of public defenders was almost three years longer than those of individuals defended by private lawyers. This finding suggests that the public defender does a better job than lawyers who charge private clients a considerable fee. The Colorado study also revealed that the chances of involving a private lawyer increase as the seriousness of the charges against the defendant also increases. This finding demonstrates that a good number of marginal indigents have such hidden resources as family and friends, which they will use only if the charges against them are most serious. In that case, defendants do not like to be defended by a publicly appointed lawyer. The Colorado study also found that defendants who chose public defenders are more likely to be guilty than those who use private lawyers. The finding means that innocent people charged with a crime will be far more willing to exhaust all their resources to defend themselves than is true of guilty defendants.[10]

DEFENDING ORGANIZED CRIME

No better example of a defense against accusations of organized racketeering and murder by a Mafioso may be found than the defense of John Gotti by lawyer Bruce Cutler, on three occasions. John Gotti was acquitted three times through Cutler's efforts. Gotti's final conviction occurred after the trial judge at Gotti's fourth trial disqualified attorney Cutler, and so Gotti had to hire a different lawyer.

John Gotti was born in 1940. His mother and father had 13 children. Educated in the Brooklyn, New York, public schools, Gotti dropped out of high school in 1956 and joined the Fulton-Rockaway street gang. One year later, in 1957, Gotti was arrested after a street fight. He was not convicted, but in 1958 he was given probation for committing a burglary. In 1959, he was convicted as an adult of gambling and was given a 60-day suspended sentence.

Then in 1962, John Gotti married Victoria DiGiorgio. That did not prevent him from stealing a car and, on conviction, being jailed for 20 days. In 1965, Gotti was arrested again and charged with bookmaking, breaking and entering, and petty larceny. One year later, in 1966, Gotti was again arrested for breaking and entering and in that same year joined the Carlo Gambino crime family. The next year, in 1967, Gotti was arrested by the FBI for hijacking at Kennedy Airport. He was also arrested on hijacking charges in 1968 but was not given jail time. Finally, in 1969, Gotti was jailed for hijacking again and was imprisoned for three years. Released from Lewisburg Federal Penitentiary in 1972, Gotti became involved in a murder. Indicted in 1973, Gotti was charged with conspiracy to murder after Ralph Galione was convicted of shooting and killing James McBratney. In 1975, however, Gotti was arrested for the murder of McBratney and incarcerated in Green Haven State Prison. When he was released two years later, in 1977, Gotti was inducted into the Gambino crime family.

Thereafter, Gotti was not arrested until 1984, when he was picked up on assault and robbery charges; he was then again arrested on federal racketeering charges in 1985, the same year in which the boss of the Gambino crime family, Paul Castellano, was murdered outside Sparks Steak House in Manhattan. In addition to Castellano, Thomas Bilotti was also murdered outside that restaurant while getting out of a car with Castellano. Then, in 1986, Gotti was charged and tried in federal court on a murder indictment but was acquitted by the jury. In 1989, he was again arrested on conspiracy to murder one John O'Connor. The next year, in 1990, Gotti was tried on murder charges dealing with the conspiracy to murder John O'Connor, a union official. O'Connor and associates had vandalized a Gotti-owned restaurant because it was being built with nonunion labor. Although Gotti did indeed order the killing of O'Connor, jurors told the media that they did not convict Gotti despite their belief in his guilt because "he had a great haircut and looked successful."[11]

In sum, Gotti had beaten the law three times. In 1986, he was adjudicated not guilty on all counts. In 1987, he was indicted for racketeering but was found not guilty on all counts. In 1990, he was tried for the shooting of John O'Connor and was again declared not guilty on all counts. It took two more years and a jury willing to convict before any of Gotti's crimes were given credence. Gotti was finally sent to the penitentiary for life without parole, where he died in 2002 at the age of 62.[12]

The list of crimes committed by John Gotti over his lifetime is so long that some people may wonder why any lawyer would want to defend a professional criminal like Gotti. The reason is, of course, that everyone is entitled to a defense on being accused of a crime and that criminals like Gotti make a great deal of money and can pay for the best legal talent in the country. After Bruce Cutler was disqualified by Judge Leo Glasser from defending Gotti in his fourth trial, Gotti hired Albert Krieger, also a specialist in defending professional criminals. Krieger used courtroom tactics commonly employed by lawyers who must defend those defendants with long criminal histories. The methods of such lawyers consist of impugning the witnesses against their client, ridiculing prosecutors, and "slashing" cross-examinations. The methods work well enough when employed on witnesses who can easily be intimidated.[13]

Another well-known lawyer who defends so-called Mafiosi is David Breitbart. Breitbart defended Joseph C. Massino in 2004 when Massino was charged with seven murders, loan sharking, arson, illegal gambling, money laundering, and conspiracy.

On the advice of Breitbart, Massino turned state's evidence against his former associates and thereby avoided the death penalty. He was convicted of all charges against him, including seven murders, and sentenced to life in prison in 2005.[14] Massino was the boss of the Bonanno crime family, having succeeded Phil Rastelli, Massino's mentor. Masssino was accused of killing Dominick Nepolitano, an underboss in the Rastelli organization, because Nepolitano did not know that a federal agent had infiltrated his organization, leading to the conviction of several members of the Bonanno mob. Massino also murdered Vito Borelli on orders of the former "capo di tutti capi," that is, boss of all the bosses, Paul Castellano. Acquitted on charges of truck hijacking, Massino rose to prominence in the organized-crime families of New York, particularly after he murdered Joseph Pastore and Carmine Galante, both of whom were rivals in his rise to power.

Massino was involved in several other killings, all having to do with rivalries among "made" members of the New York Cosa Nostra ("Our Thing"), as the members called their organization. Each time Massino went on trial, he was defended by Breitbart and somehow acquitted until he went to prison for life in 2004.[15]

Breitbart has made his reputation by defending numerous defendants accused of organized crime, including the former "deadly drug lord" Leroy Barnes, who, like Gotti after him, seemed invincible until he was finally convicted in 1977.[16] Breitbart also defended Vitaly Ivanitsky and Marat Krivoi, two Ukrainian immigrants who were tried together in 2007 on charges of murder, extortion, burglary, robbery, and narcotics trafficking. Both were sentenced to 25 years to life in prison.[17]

Not all criminal defense lawyers are connected to organized crime. There are those trial lawyers, like Lawrence Wolf, who advertise that they can and will defend people accused of serious crime although not connected to a Mafia-style organization. Wolf calls himself an "aggressive attorney" and promises "to defend your rights."[18]

Valerie Amsterdam represented numerous organized-crime figures during her career as a New York attorney. She also represented Muslim terrorists accused of the February 1993 World Trade Center bombing, in which six people died.

Amsterdam was known as a dramatic and vigorous defender of her unpopular clients. In 1995, she defended Sheik Abdel Rahman, accused of organizing the bombing of the World Trade Center garage, plotting to blow up the Holland and Lincoln tunnels, and conspiring to destroy the George Washington Bridge. Later, she also defended other terrorists who had been involved in the 2001 destruction of the World Trade Center.[19]

Amsterdam also defended numerous clients belonging to Italian crime families. She defended Thomas Carbonaro, for example, in 2003 on charges of seeking to kill ex-Mafioso Sammy "the Bull" Gravano. Gravano had been instrumental in the conviction of his erstwhile friend and confidant John Gotti. Now, the government charged that Carbonaro sought to revenge the conviction of Gotti by killing Gravano.[20]

Nothing so infuriates government lawyers as the defense of citizens they accuse of various crimes. It is therefore not surprising that the prosecutors in New York made every effort to eliminate Valerie Amsterdam from her profession. In this endeavor, they did indeed succeed.

In April 2006, Valerie Amsterdam surrendered her law license after pleading guilty to money laundering, defrauding the federal government, and witness tampering. She was sentenced to six months in prison and the forfeiture of $374,000. Amsterdam's offenses were probably trivial. Yet, her willingness to defend clients regarded as despicable by the public made her a target for federal prosecutors. No doubt any lawyers willing to undertake the defense of unpopular clients risk prosecution themselves.[21]

So-called mob lawyers are also viewed as suspect by government prosecutors. The dilemma faced by the U.S. criminal justice system lies in the possibility that defense lawyers for professional criminals may become entangled in planning more crimes by allowing their clients to use their offices and facilities to plan more offenses.

Nevertheless, lawyers must enjoy the right to defend anyone while being protected by lawyer-client privilege. Some defense attorneys believe that prosecutors, who usually earn much less than private defense attorneys, are vindictive because they cannot afford the lifestyle of the mob-related lawyers. Such vindictiveness has led some prosecutors to induce judges to seize the assets of accused crime bosses to prevent them from hiring expensive lawyers. This tactic is denounced by the American Civil Liberties Union and others because it can easily lead to depriving all Americans of the right to counsel.[22]

The California-based Criminal Defense Group practices nationwide and includes lawyers from all states. The organization's lawyers are available 24 hours a day, seven days a week. According to advertisements, the group's lawyers have proven the innocence of many accused individuals and even succeeded in bringing about a reversal of a death sentence by the U.S. Supreme Court. These lawyers deal only with felony charges but include white-collar defendants in their efforts.

DEFENDING DOMESTIC VIOLENCE OFFENDERS

The use of violence in the home has become an important issue in the legal and social work communities not only because such violence is so common but also because neither profession has yet found a means of reducing this conduct. Several efforts have so far been made to deal with domestic violence. One of these methods is mediation. This works in some situations but by no means in all, since not all domestic violence is the same. Shared parenting has also been used as a means of dealing with domestic violence, although this is not always a good solution to the problem. There are legal and social work professionals who believe that children living with their mother should avoid contact with their father. There are, however, a good number of women who want their children to know their father. The courts can sometimes help resolve domestic violence, which is usually attributed to men. Yet, there are women who perpetrate domestic violence.[23]

One major reason for the failure of the legal and social work communities to reduce domestic violence in this country has been a long-standing difference of opinion as to how professionals should proceed in connection with this serious problem. As is the case in so many areas of practice, there are those lawyers and social workers who are wedded to one view while disregarding other views. The result can be a feud among professionals leading to a stalemate and consequently to a lack of service to those who need help.[24]

It should be understood, therefore, that all cases of domestic violence are not the same. Yet, some professionals are so convinced that women are always the victims and never the aggressors that much that could be done is not done to reduce violence in the home. Those individuals who subscribe to this view rely on the law and on strong punitive action to address domestic violence issues. They overlook the possibility that in some instances, women use the accusation of domestic violence to gain an advantage in divorce proceedings. According to the feminist view of domestic violence, women must always be given the benefit of the doubt, even at the risk of false accusations. Yet, research and experience have shown that women are equally responsible as men for aggressive behavior designed to exercise control over adults and children. The methods used to gain such control may not be physical, but they are demeaning to the victims just the same. Nevertheless, the physical consequences of violence are greater for women than for men.[25] Lawyers involved in the defense of aggressors and victims of domestic violence may well defend the "victim" one day and the "aggressor" another day. The reason is that the difference can sometimes be difficult to discern. For example, a California law firm specializes in defending those individuals accused of domestic violence. When someone is arrested for domestic assault, the firm tries to discern "what really happened," for both sides are likely to make emotionally laden accusations and overlook many facets of domestic violence. In short, domestic violence lawyers try to get beyond the "he said, she said" dispute.

Of course, some domestic violence leads to murder, as in the case of Barbara Sheehan. Married for 18 years to a police officer, she suffered horrible abuse before killing him in 2008 by shooting him 11 times with his own gun. Sheehan was arrested in her New York home and sent to the Ryker's Island Prison. Her lawyer, Michael Dowd, described in detail how much Barbara was abused and tortured by her husband. Yet, the murder victim's colleagues on the New York City police force called him a "nice guy," a devoted family man, and a church supporter. His colleagues claimed that the stress of his job may have made him irritable sometimes.

Likewise, Donna Cobb stabbed her husband, Kevin Cobb, to death after she had been subjected to years of beatings related to Kevin's crack addiction. Donna claimed that she was sleeping when Kevin came home, beat her, and choked her. She defended herself by hitting him with a ceramic statue and then stabbing him.[26] The police had no record of any complaint by Mrs. Cobb, which her lawyer explained by claiming that "the cops" do not make records of wife-beating on the part of one of their own. According to Donna Cobb's lawyer, her husband tried to kill her, her children, and even her parents.

According to sociology professor Mangai Natarajan of John Jay College of Criminal Justice, long-abused women seldom threaten. Instead, they take sudden, drastic action when they feel that they can no longer suffer the abuse that may threaten their lives.[27]

Women who kill their abusers may have believed with good reason that the law would not protect them from abuse, including beatings and other violence. A good example of the tendency of courts to side with powerful abusers is the manner in which a high-powered New York lawyer was supported by the prosecutors and the court despite his abuse of his wife.

Ira Schachter, a partner at a high-priced New York law firm, was not prosecuted despite photos showing him abusing his wife outside their home in Manhattan. Not only was he not prosecuted, but the judge would not even issue an order of protection for Mrs. Schachter because her husband was surrounded in court by an entourage of prominent lawyers. This result occurred despite the evidence that Schachter had choked his wife, beat her on the head, and otherwise assaulted her. He claimed self-defense and was set free.[28]

The Schachter case is not an isolated event. A study by Voices of Women concludes that the New York courts are biased against those who need the protection the most. The Voices of Women report claims that court personnel violate their own procedures in favor of men, and that children are endangered by the failure of the courts to recognize domestic abuse as a serious problem. The report also charges that preferential treatment is accorded the rich and prominent in family courts.[29]

In 2007, a 52-year-old jewelry designer, Bette Marcheck, complained that she was held prisoner by a millionaire on his estate. William Strauss was charged with assault and harassment in Westchester County Court, New York, in connection with an alleged attack on Marcheck using a lobster trap. Strauss's lawyer, Donald Yanella, denied all these accusations on behalf of his client. Marcheck also complained that Strauss, her boyfriend, had left her without food while he ate dinner at his parents' house. Marcheck also accused Strauss of threatening to kill her if she left him.[30]

An aspect of spousal abuse and domestic violence that seldom comes to the public's attention because it does not involve the civil courts is the killing of and assault on wives of military personnel. In 2002, *The New York Times* published a story dealing with the murder of four wives at Fort Bragg. That so many women were killed in only six weeks at the same base appears to be related to the stress the soldiers experienced in Iraq and Afghanistan.

It has been reported that domestic violence is two to five times more common among the military than the civilian population. The most common explanation for this unusual rate of murder has been that soldiers stationed overseas are frequently suspicious that their wives are having extramarital affairs. Because domestic violence has been a problem among the military for some time, in 1966 Congress passed a law that prohibited police and military personnel convicted of domestic violence from buying or possessing a gun.

Examples of spouse killings are the murder of Teresa Nieves by Rigoberto Nieves two days after his return from Afghanistan; the killing of Jennifer Wright by Master Sergeant William Wright one month after his return from Afghanistan; the shooting of Andrea Floyd by her husband Brandon Floyd, who killed himself after murdering his wife; and the slaughter of David Shannon, whose wife killed him while he slept. Shannon had been a U.S. Special Forces major.[31]

No case of wife abuse and murder has agitated the U.S. media more than the conviction of Scott Peterson in November 2004 for the alleged murder of his wife, Laci, and his unborn son, Connor. The arguments for the conviction of Peterson and the further imposition of the death penalty were influenced by so much media hysteria and a lynch mob mentality that it is not possible to determine whether Peterson actually killed his wife or was simply declared "guilty by suspicion."

On December 14, 2004, the same jury that convicted Peterson recommended to Judge Alfred A. Delucchi that he sentence Peterson to death. During the jury deliberations, a lynch mob assembled in front of the court house. The mob threatened to kill any juror who would not vote for the death penalty and also threatened the judge. Consequently, the jurors and the judge sent Peterson to his death rather than risk their own lives at the hands of the lynch mob.[32]

Peterson was defended by Mark Geragos, a well-known California attorney. He showed that the police made no effort to discover who murdered Laci Peterson because they assumed Scott Peterson's guilt and then collected whatever evidence they could muster to fit their theory. This type of tactic is quite common in cases of murder involving a married person. The police find it far more profitable to assume the guilt of the spouse than to spend time and money on an investigation while the media scream for the blood of the spouse. The problems with Peterson's conviction are numerous. First, the police claimed that a strand of Laci's hair in Scott's fishing boat proved that he abducted Laci and killed her. Yet, innumerable hairs of the other party are found on any couple living together. Normally, a motive for a crime is presented in court. No such motive was presented in the Peterson trial. Tapes were shown the jury that indicated that Peterson had had an affair. These tapes were used to make the jury hate Peterson for being unfaithful. Juries are, of course, easily influenced into believing that adultery is sufficient cause to assume murder. Few juries act on the basis of facts presented to them, however. Juries usually act on the emotion of the moment.

Because several other women in Modesto, California, where the Petersons lived, were also murdered, it may well have been possible that Laci Peterson was the victim of the same killers who murdered other women in and around Modesto. The police refused to consider this possibility and would not investigate such a scenario. In addition, Laci Peterson was seen walking her dog after the time of her alleged murder. Yet the jury, inflamed by anger and hate, paid no attention to these facts but rushed to judgment so as to save their own skin.[33]

In sum, it is possible that Scott Peterson murdered his wife and unborn child. It is also possible that he is innocent of this crime. The real answer cannot be determined as of 2009 because no effort was ever made to determine the truth of the matter.

DEFENDING SEX OFFENDERS

When O. J. Simpson, a former football hero, was acquitted of the double murder of his former wife and her friend, he became the beneficiary of jury negation, which means that the jury voted that Simpson was not guilty because too many minority members are already in prison and more should not be added. Nevertheless, a judgment of wrongful death was affirmed by the California Court of Appeals after that judgment was decided by a civil jury in 1997. This verdict shows that even a double murder can be ignored by a jury influenced by jury negation.[34]

Contrast the verdict and the subsequent freedom enjoyed by Simpson with the treatment of alleged sex offenders. Those persons who have been so convicted, but even those who are merely the victims of accusations of sex offense, are treated far worse than proven murderers. Among these is O. J. Simpson because a civil jury found him guilty of causing two wrongful deaths in 1997.

Sex offenders and those so accused are by no means as lucky as Simpson and others convicted of killing their victims. While murderers are usually accorded all the protection of the Constitution, such is not the case for individuals convicted or merely suspected of sex offenses.

During the decade ending in 2008, numerous municipalities and counties have enacted legislation making it illegal for a sex offender released from prison to live within their jurisdiction.[35] In some of these restricted areas, sex offenders must register for years; in others, for life. In all 50 states, the law requires community notification that a sex offender is present. Notification of murderers is not required. Lawyers who seek to defend sex offenders have argued that it is evident that laws restricting the residence of a convicted sex offender violate Article 1 of the Constitution, which holds that no law may be made that punishes deeds not illegal when they were done. Further, the Constitution prohibits imposing a penalty greater than the one in force at the time of the offense. Such laws are ex post facto, or after the fact, laws.[36]

Defenders of individuals convicted of sexual aggression show that laws dealing with sex offenses also violate the Fifth Amendment to the Constitution. The Fifth Amendment holds that no one may be tried for the same crime twice. Yet, restricting the residence of an ex-convict for sex crimes already punished by incarceration violates the phrase that no individual can be "twice put in jeopardy of life and limb" for a single offense. A good defense of sexual aggressors is the Eighth Amendment to the Constitution. That amendment is also violated by residency laws, since those laws constitute cruel and unusual punishment, which is prohibited under the Eighth Amendment. Individuals who have served a sentence in prison for a sex offense are therefore punished a second time without even a chance to defend themselves because as sex offenders, they may be sent to a state mental institution without their consent. It is also feared that anyone ever convicted of any offense may subsequently be incarcerated on the grounds of being mentally ill. There is now a Sex Offender Registry in the United States. This registry is the product of the Wetterling Crimes against Children and Sexually Violent Offender Registration Act. According to that law, sex offenders must reveal all kinds of private information, including DNA test results, fingerprints, and blood test results. The law was amended with Megan's Law, requiring all states to notify communities that a sex offender lives among them. One of the outcomes of that law is that vigilantes have, in some instances, murdered sex offenders on discovering the offender's residence.[37] Some states attempted to force their sex offenders to live in another state. This requirement, however, was held unconstitutional by the Supreme Court.[38]

The Fourteenth Amendment to the Constitution requires that all citizens be treated equally. Since offenders who were convicted not of sex crimes but of some other crime are not required to register or to live outside specified areas, enacting restrictive laws for only sex offenders clearly violates the Constitution. Here again, lawyers have a powerful argument. It is also important to understand that the most common form of sexual abuse against children is abuse conducted by family members. Such abuse is seldom reported to the police by the victim or other family members. Therefore, the laws restricting the movements of erstwhile convicts are unlikely to make a difference in the number of sex offenses or the number of victims.[39]

A good defense against accusations of sexual deviance is the view that whether or not an action is a sex offense partly depends on the culture in which an action is defined. The definition of the situation determines, in large part, that an act or conduct of any kind is offensive. Because the United States is a country founded on Puritan ethics, a limited number of sex-related acts are penalized severely. Sex is a taboo form of conduct in the United States, and any deviation from prescribed sexual expression is greeted with hysterical reactions. This hysteria is not true of murder or assault or any other crime.[40] Derived from biblical teachings, this Puritanism concerning sexual behavior is incorporated into U.S. law. Such acts as rape, pedophilia, abortion, homosexuality, pimping, pornography, adultery, masturbation, miscegenation, polygamy, and voyeurism were all at one time sex offenses, although some of these behaviors are no longer considered so. The failure to enforce the prohibition against homosexuality is explained by the change in public opinion concerning such sexuality, as is the abolition of miscegenation laws. Social culture changes over time, and so does opinion concerning sex. Thus, there is no sex act that is inherently offensive. Any sexuality can be offensive if so defined; no sex act is offensive if not so defined. This notion is, of course, true of all crimes. In short, nothing is a crime unless the definition of the situation so prescribes.

DEFENDING DRUG USERS

Lawyers who defend drug users and dealers generally seek a court ruling "to suppress." This turn-of-phrase refers to the argument that the court should suppress the complaint of the police and the prosecutors to the effect that the search and the seizure as carried out by the police was unconstitutional. The argument to suppress is based on the Fourth Amendment to the Constitution, which holds, "The right of the people to be secure in their persons, houses, papers and effects, against unreasonable searches and seizures, shall not be violated, and no Warrants shall issue, but upon probable cause, supported by Oath or affirmation, and particularly describing the place to be searched, and the persons or things to be seized."[41] The Fourth Amendment is rooted in English experience and was included in the Bill of Rights because the colonists, mainly of English birth or descent, knew of the *Semayne* case of 1603. In that case, the British courts ruled that a homeowner had the right to defend his home against any intruder, including agents of the king. In addition, in the English case of *Entick v. Carrington*, the British high court ruled that government agents had illegally broken into Entick's house, searched his papers and boxes, desks, and other property to discover whether Entick was a sympathizer with those who had printed pamphlets denouncing the king.[42]

In the United States, the requirement that a warrant must be issued by a court and that the warrant must be based on probable cause has gradually been eroded. In the 1970s, the Supreme Court still held that warrantless searches were unreasonable and hence illegal. By 1992, the court held that exceptions to the requirement that a warrant must be issued by a court are permissible. The court went so far as to uphold warrantless searchers of automobile junkyards and allowed police to decide whether an officer had reasonable reason to believe that a search needed to be conducted without a warrant. The purpose of this amendment is evident. Nevertheless, the protection this amendment seeks to offer citizens of the United States is seldom effective. The police appear to hold the Constitution in contempt and seem to care nothing about the Fourth Amendment or any amendment. The Bill of Rights is viewed by law enforcement as an antiquated nuisance.

The police have little regard for the rights of citizens and therefore raid any home at any time as if the Constitution did not exist. Judges routinely uphold illegal searches and seizure and accept as evidence anything the police show them. The constitutional role of a judge is to restrain government power. Nevertheless, few judges will do so. Instead, judges generally uphold illegal searches for fear of losing their own position in the next election. Moreover, the police invent justification for illegal searches ex post facto, fabricating reasons for a search or even planting drugs where none were found.

Defense lawyers must use cross-examination to show that the police acted illegally and thereby demonstrate to the judge that the evidence needs to be suppressed. Since judges will usually side with the police, it takes exceptional skill on the part of defense lawyers to demonstrate the illegality of police searches contrary to the Fourth Amendment to the Constitution. The defense will try to show that the government, namely, the police, failed to show that the substance seized was a controlled substance, that the drugs did not belong to the defendant, that the drugs were for personal use and not for sale, and that the drugs were not seized within 1,000 feet of a school zone.

An example of the successful defense of a man charged with drug dealing is the acquittal of Peter Gatien, a prominent nightclub owner in Manhattan. Gatien was charged by the government with having used his nightclub as "a drug supermarket." Yet, the jury would not convict him largely because his lawyer showed that the witnesses against him were themselves drug dealers who were promised lighter sentences if convicted.

The government prosecutors had spent two and one-half years on this case but were unable to convince the jury that Gatien was a drug dealer. The jurors also rejected the government's argument that promotional material found on the premises of the Tunnel and Limelight Club were distributed by Gatien and that he made a profit from this material when distributed by someone else. Gatien's lawyer was Benjamin Bratman, a well-known defense attorney who led the jury to feel "reasonable doubt" as to Gatien's guilt.[43]

DEFENDING WHITE-COLLAR CRIME

Any defense of white-collar criminals depends foremost on an understanding of its nature. Susan Shapiro has shown that white-collar crime is an abuse of trust rather than an attribute of the offenders. She shows that business crimes are difficult to detect because the offenders may have used an agent to conduct their business so as to conceal any criminal intent or conduct of the "principal" who appointed the agent to conduct the business.

The violation of trust, according to Shapiro, may take several forms. It may consist of lying about charitable contributions or making misrepresentations involving pictures, exhibits, or sound. Shapiro refers to the Houston Zoo, which exhibited a "deadly snake" for four and one-half years until it was discovered that the snake was really only a rubber mock-up.[44]

Stealing is another form of white-collar crime. Stealing can be a white-collar crime when someone is allowed to manipulate assets belonging to someone else. Stealing can include misappropriation, which refers to the embezzlement of funds entrusted to a "trustee."

Self-dealing is another aspect of the same offense in that bankers and others can use the money entrusted to them to promote their own interests. For example, a banker can give a relative or friend a loan at lower-than-established bank interest rates, or a legislator can introduce a bill that lowers taxes on his or her property or business. Corporate executives can refuse to pay a dividend, or journalists and their friends can publish an article they know will increase or decrease the value of a stock they own. There are other forms of trust violations, all of which amount to theft.[45]

The defense against accusations stemming from such crimes as these relies, in part, on the diffuse nature of these offenses. Thus, it is often difficult to discover who, in a large corporation or enterprise, was directly responsible for the crimes alleged. Another defense is to claim that the accused knew nothing about the theft because as CEO of the company, he had to be told what was going on below him, since he did not work directly with the thieves. A further defense is to argue that what appears as a theft is only an accounting error in a complex bookkeeping system.

All these defenses are investigated by the FBI, the U.S. Postal Service, the Treasury Department, the IRS, the Bureau of Citizenship and Immigration, and the Securities and Exchange Commission (SEC). Individuals investigated by any of these bureaucracies are advised not to tell investigators anything without the presence of a lawyer. The reason for such caution is that investigators will use anything the target says as self-incriminating evidence. Common defenses against such accusations are insanity, intoxication, duress, and incapacity.[46]

The foregoing defense arguments served attorneys well in the past but have, in recent years, done little to defend several CEOs of large corporations accused of financial infidelity. Dennis Kozlowski, the former CEO of Tyco International, was convicted of falsifying business records, committing securities fraud, and being guilty of a number of other charges. He was sentenced to 8.3 to 25 years in prison. This length of time in prison resembles sentences handed to killers, rapists, and assaulters. Evidently, such sentences reflect a revenge motive on the part of prosecutors and judges. Kozlowski spent a large amount of money on luxuries, including a $2 million birthday party for his wife, gold shower curtains, and other extravaganzas. These excesses were reported in the media, leading to envy and disgust on the part of prosecutors and judges as well as juries, who could not come close to spending so much money.[47]

A similar fate befell Leona Helmsley, the wife of a billionaire hotel owner. Having been labeled "the queen of mean" by the media, she was accused of tax fraud. This accusation by government prosecutors rested on dubious evidence. Nevertheless, she was easily convicted, not because her guilt could be proved, but because the prosecutors and the judge used every legal technique to frame Helmsley on the grounds that she was greedy. The government included as witnesses accountants who lied on the stand to please the prosecutors and to escape prosecution for crimes they themselves committed. Undoubtedly, Helmsley was the victim of envy. Moreover, the media had given her a bad reputation, and so prosecutors recognized they could easily find a jury already prejudiced against her. Conviction in the media is frequently a forerunner to conviction in court.[48]

In 2007, Conrad Black was convicted of fraud and obstruction of justice. "Obstruction of justice" is a vague term used by prosecutors to charge anyone unwilling to tell them what they want to hear. That charge is often used to force witnesses to lie in court against someone accused. Prosecutors threaten such witnesses with prosecution for obstruction unless they comply and claim to have witnessed events they never saw.

Black was sentenced to 61.5 years in a Florida prison. Black was the CEO of Hollinger International, which owned a number of newspapers and other media. The judge, incensed at Black for being wealthy, instructed the jury to consider Black guilty despite the fact that he knew nothing of the fraud others committed in his company. He was convicted on the grounds that "he should have known" of the fraud. This argument was used against Black after the government could not prove that Black had anything to do with the fraud committed by the audit committee of the company.[49]

A most recent effort to defend those individuals accused of white-collar crime was the passage by Congress of the Preserving United States Attorney Independence Act of 2007. In view of the many unjustified investigations and unconstitutional interference of government prosecutors in the client-lawyer relationship, Congress passed, and the president signed, this law. It prohibits prosecutors from ordering companies to turn over to the government privileged documents as a condition of a cooperating agreement. The bill also allows companies to pay the legal fees of accused employees, a practice judges heretofore would not allow.[50]

SUMMARY

Public defenders for the indigent were unknown in the United States until the twentieth century. Prosecutors therefore sent many innocent people to prison because the accused could not afford a lawyer. Defense of organized crime is generally done by well-paid private attorneys who specialize in such work. This is best seen in the defense of John Gotti and others by such attorneys as Bruce Cutler and Valerie Amsterdam.

Defending drug sellers depends largely on questioning the evidence, asserting the rights of the defendant, and persuading the judge to suppress the government's assertions.

Domestic violence is common in the United States. Defense lawyers often claim that the probable victim is making false accusations in order to influence divorce proceedings in her favor. Sex offenders are defended by asserting that the offense was minor, that it was committed by someone in need of psychiatric help, or that the offender was insane.

NOTES

1. U.S. Constitution, Sixth Amendment.
2. Barbara Allen Babcock, "Inventing the Public Defender," *American Criminal Law Review* 43, no. 4 (Fall 2006): 1267.
3. *Gideon v. Wainwright*, 372 U.S. 335 (1963).

4. Barbara Allen Babcock, "Duty to Defend," *Yale Law Journal* 1489 (2005): 1489.

5. *Rompilla v. Beard*, 545 U.S. 374 (2005).

6. *Berger v. United States*, 295 U.S. 78 89 (1935).

7. Frederic M. Tulsky, "Last Chance, Little Help," *San Jose Mercury News*, January 26, 2006, A1.

8. Mary Pat Gallagher, "Criminal Lawyer Draws $500 Fine," *New Jersey Law Journal* (July 10, 2008): n.p.

9. Adam Liptak, "Public Defenders Get Better Marks on Salary," *New York Times*, July 14, 2007, A1.

10. Morris B. Hoffman, "Free Market Justice," *New York Times*, January 8, 2007, A 19.

11. *Washington Post*, "Reputed Crime Boss Gotti Acquitted in Conspiracy Trial," February 10, 1990, A5.

12. George Lardner Jr. "John Gotti, Modern Godfather," *Washington Post*, May 28, 1990, 9.

13. Laurie Goodstein, "Gotti's Lawyer Lambastes Government's Star Witness," *Washington Post*, February 14, 1992, A2.

14. William Glaberson, "An Archetypal Mob Trial: It's Just Like in the Movies," *New York Times*, May 23, 2004, N27.

15. Selwyn Raab, "A Mafia Family's Second Wind," *New York Times*, April 29, 2000, B1.

16. Ibid., N27.

17. Michale Brick, "Defendant Is Convicted for His Role in 2 Killings," *New York Times*, August 10, 2007, B3.

18. Lawrence Wolf, "California Mob Crime Defense Attorneys," LW, http://www.youareinnocent.com/articles.

19. Joseph P. Fried, "Top Informant Denies Faking Conspiracy for Bombings," *New York Times*, April 4, 1995, 1.

20. William Glaberson, "Gravano, Ever a Showman, Takes Stand Again," *New York Times*, October 18, 2003, 1.

21. Michael Scholl, "Ex-lawyer Loses $30,000 in Bond for Brief Journey," *New York Law Journal* (August 1, 2006).

22. Michael S. Serrill, "The 'Mob' Lawyer: Life Support for Crime," *Time*, March 25, 1985.

23. Peter Salem and Billie-Lee Dunford-Jackson, "Beyond Politics and Positions," *Family Court Review*, 46 (July 2008): 437.

24. Ibid., 437.

25. K. L. Anderson, "Perpetrator or Victim? Relationship between Intimate Partners and Well Being," *Journal of Marriage and Family* 64 (2002): 851–63.

26. Derek Rose and Jimmy Vielkind, "Wife's Attorney in Slay: He Had It Coming," *Daily News*, November 13, 2006, 5.

27. Patrice O'Shaughnessy, "Ex-cop Terrorized Her, Afraid She'd Die," *Daily News*, February 25, 2008, 16.

28. Barbara Ross and Dave Goldiner, "Who Will Protect Me Now?" *Daily News*, May 7, 2008, 20.

29. Albor Ruiz, "Court System Is Another Abuser," *Daily News*, May 15, 2009, 27.

30. Dorian Block, "Wild Torture Tale: I Was Beaten and Starved by Rich Guy, She Claims," *Daily News*, November 17, 2007, 7.

31. Fox Butterfield, "Wife Killing at Fort Reflect Growing Problem," *New York Times*, July 29, 2002.

32. "Jury Recommends Death for Peterson," *Law Center* (December 14, 2004): 1.

33. J. Neil Schulman, "Convicted by Suspicion: Why Scott Peterson May Be Innocent," *Hollywood Investigator*, November 30, 2004, 1.

34. Walter Goodman, "Bronco to Verdict: In Case You Were Out," *New York Times*, December 20, 1995, C20.

35. Stephanie Sandoval, "Local Officials Seek State 'Safe Zone' Law," *Dallas Morning News*, August 18, 2006, B1.

36. U.S. Constitution, Article 1.

37. *Bangor Daily News*, "Keeping Track of Sex Offenders," May 1, 2006, A1.

38. *People v. Baum*, 231 N.W. 95, 96 (Mich. 1930).

39. Mark Agee, "No Room for Sex Offenders," *Fort Worth Star-Telegram*, September 28, 2006, A1.

40. Donal E. H. McNamara, "Sex Offenses and Sex Offenders," *Annals of the American Academy of Political and Social Sciences* 376 (March 1968): 148.

41. U.S. Constitution, Fourth Amendment.

42. *Wiles v. Wood*, 98 Eng. 489 (C.P. 1763).

43. Joseph P. Fried, "Limelight Owner Is Acquitted after Long Fight in Drug Case," *New York Times*, February 12, 1998, 1.

44. Susan P. Shapiro, "Collaring the Crime, Not the Criminal," *American Sociological Review* (June 1990): 346–65.

45. Ibid., 353.

46. Sherrie Bennet, "Defending White Collar Crime Allegations," *Lawyers. com* (no date).

47. *New York Post*, "Jailhouse Divorce for Koz," July 18, 2008.

48. Paul Craig Robert, "Guilty of Being Rich: Victimization of Hotel Magnate Leona Helsmley," *National Review* (November 15, 1993): 1.

49. *Toronto Star*, "U.S. Appeals Court Refuses to Reconsider Black Case," August 22, 2008.

50. Carl Hulse, "Congress: On Prosecutors and the War," *New York Times*, March 19, 2007, 1.

Chapter 6

THE AMERICAN JURY

THE ENGLISH ORIGIN

The American jury is the product of the English jury because the founding fathers of the Republic were English subjects before they became Americans. Therefore, Article 3 of the U.S. Constitution guarantees the right of trial by jury, but meaning "jury" in the English sense. The English jury was first established in the thirteenth century (1201–1300). Prior to that century, English law required three forms of proof before anyone could be held guilty of a crime. All three proofs were not applied together. Instead, any one of the three proofs sufficed. These proofs were "wager of law or compurgation," the ordeal, and trial by combat.[1]

Compurgation is related to "purification" and refers to the medieval practice of asking the accused to swear an oath that he or she did not commit the offense charged. The accused was also obliged to produce a number of "oath helpers." These were people who backed the accused's denial by also swearing an oath. It was assumed that no one would risk his or her "eternal soul" by perjury and that therefore such oaths were secure.

Evidently, individuals who had been caught in the act or had confessed could not avail themselves of compurgation. Foreigners were also excluded from the use of this proof.[2]

Prior to the development of the grand jury, a "jury of presentment" investigated alleged crimes and reported the findings to the judges. The members of this jury of presentment were representatives of the county.[3]

Because compurgation fell into disuse in the twelfth century and because not everyone was entitled to use this method of proving innocence, King Henry II ordered that anyone adversely affected by a report of the jury of presentment should have to undergo the ordeal of cold water or hot irons. These ordeals appear so bizarre to Americans of the twenty-first century that it is difficult to understand how anyone could have taken such performances as evidence of guilt. It needs to be understood, therefore, that prior to the nineteenth century, Europeans believed that God intervened directly in the affairs of humankind and that guilt or innocence could be determined by the outcome of these ordeals in which the deity reputedly took a personal interest.

Accordingly, the accused was lowered into cold water in a pond or lake that had been blessed by the clergy. If the accused sank, then he or she was adjudicated innocent. It was possible, of course, and frequent, that the accused, unable to swim, drowned before he or she could be rescued. If the accused did not sink, however, because he or she could swim, then the result was a verdict of guilty of the present accusation.

Likewise, the ordeal of hot irons consisted of handing the accused an iron that had been blessed and then heated. The accused was forced to hold the hot iron while walking a number of paces. This iron, of course, burned the accused's hand. A few days later, a priest inspected the hand. If it was infected, then God had decided against the accused, who was therefore guilty of the crime charged.[4]

The method of finding guilt or innocence by ordeal was abandoned when, in 1215, the Fourth Lateran Council of the Roman Catholic Church prohibited priests from participating in the judicial process, for it became doctrine that humans had no right to test the will of God (the Lateran Council was so called because it convened in a palace owned in Roman times by the Laterani family). Trial by battle was yet another means of finding innocence or guilt in the medieval view. These battles between the accused and the accuser continued until evening. If the accused survived until the stars appeared, he was innocent. Women and disabled or old men accused of a crime could ask a knight to fight for them. The rules were the same: the knight representing the accused would "prove" the innocence of his client if he defeated the accuser or his surrogate or if he lasted until the appearance of the stars. Sir Walter Scott describes trial by battle in his novel *Ivanhoe*, named for a knight who fights another knight on behalf of a woman accused of witchcraft in the twelfth century.[5]

Since the stronger party always prevailed in trial by combat, it became evident by the fifteenth century that this method of determining innocence merely allowed physically strong criminals to escape punishment. Consequently, trial by jury was substituted by the judges for trial by combat. The jury, which had heretofore only investigated alleged crimes, now came to determine guilt or innocence. Thus, the investigative function led to the development of our grand jury, and the deterministic function led to our trial jury. These juries consisted of 32 people drawn from medieval subdivisions of a county known as a "hundred." The people employed as jurors were "hundredors." There were 12 subdivisions in each county and therefore 12 hundreds. This then led to the institution of the 12-person jury in our own day.[6]

The Constitution of the United States does not prescribe any jury size. The number 12 is, therefore, only customary and expected; it was not legally binding until the Supreme Court ruled in 1898 in *Thompson v. Utah* that a 12-person jury is required in federal criminal cases. A year later, the Supreme Court ruled in *Capital Traction Co. v. Hof* that a 12-member jury is also required in federal civil cases. Yet, the same court held in 1900 in *Maxwell v. Dow* that an 8-member jury is constitutional in state cases.[7] It is important to remember that originally, the jury brought the accusation and then also adjudicated the trial. This had to mean that conviction was far more likely than in our own day, when a grand jury of up to 23 citizens brings the accusation, and then a totally different jury decides the outcome of the trial.

This procedure was used because there was no full-time police force in England or the colonies and later United States before the last half of the nineteenth century. Therefore, the average trial lasted only 30 minutes, since the jury had decided in advance to consider the case before them, a case they themselves investigated.[8]

The English courts did not require jury unanimity until 1367. Before that, a majority could convict or hold innocent the defendant before them. Moreover, judges decided issues of admissibility in the presence of the jury. Today, the jury is excused while such issues are debated by the lawyers and the judge. The lawyers were, of course, paid by the victim, since the state had no prosecutors. Even the requirement that the defendant had to be guilty "beyond a reasonable doubt" did not exist until the end of the eighteenth century. In the seventeenth century, the English had determined that juries should be composed of one's neighbors, a view that first appeared in English law in the *Bushel* case. This case concerned William Penn, who was accused of "unlawful assembly" for preaching to Quakers outdoors. No proof was offered the jury by either the prosecution or the defense because jurors were deemed to have sufficient knowledge to try a case without evidence. Furthermore, the jury was empowered to decide the case in direct opposition to the evidence.[9]

In the seventeenth century, the jury was a self-informing group. The jury members investigated alleged crimes. Therefore, juries usually had more information than did the judges, who could hardly disagree with a jury that knew more about the case than did the judge.[10] Before the end of the fourteenth century, friends and relatives of the accused were allowed to sit on the jury to determine the case, a practice abolished at the end of that century. Until the eighteenth century, jurors were also allowed to gather information provided them outside court.[11]

The English practice of choosing jurors from the neighborhood where the alleged crime occurred was continued in the new world. This approach was practiced because it was believed that jurors who had knowledge of a crime should not be challenged or questioned by the judge. Furthermore, based on the jurors' community values, traditions, and customs, juries were entitled to nullify a case.[12]

In view of the foregoing brief history of the English jury, it is evident that American juries were similarly constituted and employed because early America was an English colony and the inhabitants were English men and women.

THE AMERICAN JURY

The English influence is reflected in Article 2, Section 2, of the body of the Constitution and in the Sixth Amendment. All state constitutions also include the right to a jury trial. The purpose of these guarantees is to prevent oppression by the government, whose agents in England had brought unfounded criminal charges so as to eliminate political or other enemies. The political motive has also been true in the United States, where prosecutors and judges have used their power to imprison and even kill innocent citizens.

In eighteenth-century colonial America, the grand jury as well as the trial jury were, of course, formed by English tradition so that that tradition entered into U.S. law. Nevertheless, it is possible for a defendant to waive the right to a jury trial and be tried by a judge alone. Failure to waive that right infuriates some judges, who thereupon punish citizens who invoked their rights by handing them an extra stiff sentence if convicted.[13]

THE GRAND JURY

A grand jury is so called because it is larger than a trial jury. The word "grand" is French for "large." The grand jury in the twenty-first-century United States is a powerful investigative body with hardly any checks on its conduct. So great is the power of the grand jury that it is no exaggeration to say that the First Amendment rights of citizens do not apply to those suspects forced to appear before a grand jury, where prosecutors rule and defendants are at a distinct disadvantage. The grand jury has been used for years by government to intrude in areas that the Constitution seeks to protect from such involvement.[14]

The Fifth Amendment to the Constitution guarantees that no citizen shall be held to answer to the government for a crime allegedly committed unless a jury of his fellow citizens has concluded that there is sufficient evidence to hold the defendant for trial.[15] In England, the function of the grand jury grew out of the need of every community to preserve the peace. In Norman times, that is, after William the Conqueror invaded England in 1066, grand juries were used to enforce the criminal law. The ancient grand juries were also charged with investigating possible law violations and to do so in secrecy. These features of grand jury activities are still with us in the United States of the twenty-first century. The secrecy provision has made it possible for grand juries to resist government pressure to indict.[16]

In the United States, the grand jury was at first seen as a means of resisting government intrusion and as an instrument of investigation into alleged offenses. These beliefs have given grand juries almost uncontrolled power. Such power became evident in the case of *Hale v. Henkle*. In that case, a witness was held in contempt for his refusal to answer questions by the grand jury, particularly because he asked to know the specific charges against the accused.[17]

Whereas trial juries, or "petit juries," may not hear evidence seized illegally, this is not true of grand juries. In fact, the grand jury has been given the right to use rumors, hearsay, or any means to obtain information. The reason the courts have given grand juries such powers is that the grand jury procedure is not an adversary trial seeking to determine guilt or innocence. Instead, the grand jury examines whether or not a crime has been committed. The grand jury cannot find guilt or innocence.[18]

A witness before a grand jury may not have a lawyer on the grounds that the grand jury procedure is not a trial and the witness is only being asked to help the grand jury, short of self-incrimination. The right against self-incrimination is protected by the Fifth Amendment and is valid even during a grand jury hearing unless the prosecutor offers the witness immunity from punishment. The trouble with such "immunity" is that prosecutors later argue that the immunity covers only a limited, narrow area of conduct. Such an interpretation allows prosecutors to indict a witness despite so-called immunity by simply inventing some other charge on which to indict the "immunized" witness.[19]

In *Branzburg v. Hayes*, the Supreme Court decided that newspaper reporters are not protected from inquiry by a grand jury concerning their confidential sources of information. The Court wrote, "Neither the First Amendment nor any other constitutional provision protects the average citizen from disclosing to a grand jury information that he has received in confidence."[20] Based on that decision, the grand jury system has defeated the First Amendment to the U.S. Constitution. The most outstanding example of the manner in which the First

Amendment is threatened and even destroyed by grand jury action was the jailing of Judith Miller in July 2005. Miller, a *New York Times* reporter, had refused to reveal her sources concerning the name of a CIA operative. Prosecutor Patrick Fitzgerald and Judge Thomas F. Hogan, both determined opponents of the First Amendment, jailed Miller for her refusal to reveal the sources of her notes and publications concerning Valerie Plame. At issue was the First Amendment guarantee of a free press alongside freedom of religion and freedom of speech. Miller went to jail from July until October to protect her sources, an "offense" so heinous that the prosecutor and the judge were more than willing to overturn the First Amendment.[21]

The First Amendment begins by guaranteeing freedom of religion. Yet, this freedom is also under attack by the judiciary by both lower courts and the courts of appeal. Thus, religious workers have been forced to testify to grand juries even if such testimony violates their conscience and religious beliefs. In *People v. Woodruff*, the New York Appellate Court denied a claim of privilege by a member of a religious minority who told the court that the compulsion to testify would do violence to her religious principles.[22]

It is remarkable that those who seek to deprive the American people of the rights enshrined in the Constitution claim to act on behalf of "the people," whom they seek to deprive of these rights.

THE PETIT JURY

While juries were easily assembled in earlier centuries, the twentieth and twenty-first centuries have seen a considerable decline in Americans' willingness to serve on juries. In fact, only 46 percent of people summoned to jury duty appear willingly, according to the National Center for State Courts. This situation has led judges to use advertisements and even threats of contempt proceedings to increase the potential jury pools needed to conduct trials. In Lee County, North Carolina, a judge sent deputy sheriffs to deliver jury summonses at random in parking lots because trials could not begin for lack of jurors. In Los Angeles, "no-shows"—that is, those who have received a summons for jury duty but fail to report—are visited by sheriff's deputies at home with orders to appear in court and explain their failure to report for jury duty. Even posters showing movie stars encouraging jury duty are used in some jurisdictions to encourage participation.[23]

Another means of creating greater willingness to serve on juries has been the development of the anonymous jury. Such a jury has been used in only a limited number of cases. Normally, the names, addresses, and other personal information of jurors have been available to the public because such information is elicited during jury selection. The place of employment of jurors is also a matter of public information, as are the names of spouses and children of jurors. The anonymous jury numbers each juror and no name is used. The approach seeks to prevent threats against jurors or jury tampering in the form of bribes. Accordingly, anonymous juries are seated if the defendant has previously engaged in dangerous conduct, if the defendant has threatened someone in the past, and if there has been a great deal of pretrial publicity exposing jurors to possible retaliation.[24] An example of jury tampering occurred in September 2004 during the murder trial of Daniel Pelosi, accused of killing Theodore R. Ammon in Suffolk County, New York. The prosecutor, Janet Albertson, announced in open court that Pelosi had made plans to intimidate and assault witnesses and threaten the jury members and their children. The accusations came from numerous hours of tape recording Pelosi. Evidently, Pelosi was involved in an affair with Ammon's wife.[25]

How Juries Reach a Verdict

Several methods have been used by researchers who seek to understand how juries reach a verdict. The most effective method is the archival method, which investigates what juries have done. The conclusions reached by juries are analyzed statistically to discover trends. The method records what has been done by a jury but does not tell researchers how the jury arrived at its conclusion. Interviewing jurors after the trial has concluded is also a means of gaining information concerning the deliberation process, although many jurors are unlikely to discuss the erstwhile deliberations. The approach leaves a skewed result. Finally, there are "mock" trials in which anyone may be a participant. There is a relationship between a mock trial and a real trial, though some real differences have been observed between the outcome of a mock trial and a real trial. One result of research into the outcomes is that many jurors form opinions concerning the verdict before hearing the judge's instructions and before there are any deliberations. In short, many jurors vote their prejudices.[26]

Post-trial interviews have been used by several researchers to assess the weight of each ballot taken by jurors during their deliberations. The research reveals that with very few exceptions, the first ballot decides the verdict.[27] Research on jury deliberations also indicates that the "beyond a reasonable doubt" standard needed in criminal cases results in more acquittals than the "preponderance of the evidence" standard used in civil actions. That result is to be expected, since it is evidently more difficult to be sure "beyond a reasonable doubt" than to consider only the "preponderance of the evidence."[28]

Because American juries are selected at random, juries may include numerous members whose reading and writing ability is severely limited. Because in at least half the states jurors cannot take notes, many are unable to remember testimony or comprehend the evidence. Jurors who are allowed to take notes are evidently in a far better position to make a rational judgment than those who must rely on memory alone. There is also a suggestion that jurors be allowed to ask questions of witnesses, though that is not now in effect.[29]

The decisions jurors make depend, in part, on social class. The Chicago Jury Project has shown that status—that is, the sum of one's rights and privileges—affects the influence a juror has on other jurors. Traditionally, wealthy white men had more influence on jury decisions than did women or minorities. Hence, class, race, and gender were most important in jury deliberations in the mid-twentieth century. Then, men spoke more than women, and whites spoke more than blacks. Because the Chicago Jury Project had to be discontinued when Congress accused the researchers of "jury tampering," it has become most difficult to attain reliable research results concerning jury conduct.[30]

Long experience has shown that juries are far more likely than judges to make decisions based on their perception of a defendant's character than on the evidence. This is true in both criminal and civil trials.[31] An excellent example of the manner in which juries ignore the law and make decisions based on their interpretation of the defendant's character was the conviction of O. J. Simpson on numerous charges arising from his effort to retrieve memorabilia stolen from him. Simpson and his friends attempted to recover his property from a Las Vegas dealer by entering a hotel suite in 2007.

Subsequently, it was alleged that Simpson had robbed the dealer at the point of a gun and that he had also "kidnapped" the dealer. The evidence to support the charges, as well as the exonerating evidence presented by the defense, was hardly noticed by the jury. Instead, the all-white jury convicted Simpson in order to "get even" for his acquittal in 1995, 13 years earlier, on charges of having murdered his wife, Nicole Simpson, and a waiter, Ronald Goldman. In that case, it was believed by many observers that the black jurors acquitted Simpson despite the evidence against him because of solidarity with a black man, a tactic known as jury negation. Those concerned with the rule of law no doubt recognize that both jury negation and revenge are hardly consistent with fair and impartial verdicts, and thus both strategies on the part of jurors undermine the American system of criminal justice.[32]

Research has revealed that jurors with higher education participate more in jury deliberations than those with less education. The finding is also related to income, since those individuals with more education generally earn more than those with less education.[33]

The most important change in jury deliberations over the past 50 years has been the entrance of women and minorities into the jury room. The change has led to an ever-increasing influence by both groups on the decisions made there. The indications are that women and racial minorities are as influential as white men concerning the verdicts reached. It is social class that makes a difference, not gender or race. Class can be an achieved status, whereas gender and race are always ascribed. An achieved high status may involve the ability to speak in public, to reason logically, and to exhibit leadership qualities.

Despite the gradual elimination of racial bias in decisions made by juries, Louisiana, more than any other state, continues to permit race to be a factor in promoting the conviction of blacks. Louisiana's state of affairs is best illustrated by the 2008 decision of the U.S. Supreme Court to reverse the death penalty imposed on Allen Snyder, who had been convicted of killing his wife. The prosecutor, Jim Williams, who prides himself on achieving a death penalty verdict against as many defendants as possible, prevented blacks from participating in the jury that convicted Snyder. Using preemptory strikes, Williams obtained an all-white jury. The Supreme Court reversed the death penalty by a vote of 7–2, with only Clarence Thomas and Anthony Scalia dissenting.[34]

THE MEDIA AND THE AMERICAN JURY

Because the U.S. Constitution calls for public trials with an impartial jury, there are those individuals who believe that the names of jurors should be made available to the media so the public can be assured that the jurors are indeed impartial. Some newspapers have even printed the names and addresses of jurors as well as their occupations.

When the *Connecticut Post* ran a front-page story giving the names and other details of jurors in a death penalty case, the editor defended the decision to do so. Some jurors, however, sought to be excused from the jury for fear of retaliation by the defendant and his friends. The editor's decision to publish such information was condemned by some journalists and lawyers; but providing details about jurors is not illegal, and therefore the practice will undoubtedly continue.[35]

Anyone who watches television, reads a newspaper, or accesses the Internet will find that these information instruments expend an extraordinary amount of space and time depicting police activities and court trials as well as prison life. Of course, the preoccupation with the U.S. criminal justice system distorts the reality associated with that system because the overwhelming majority of Americans never enter a courtroom, are rarely accosted by the police, and know next to nothing about the prison industry. Furthermore, the media exhibit mostly such sensational crimes as the accusations against the football hero O. J. Simpson or the alleged murder of Laci Peterson by her husband. Moreover, TV stories seldom exceed two minutes, so viewers cannot possibly be informed of the whole story but are exposed only to a segment of the whole, and this undoubtedly distorts reality.[36] The media also present viewers and readers with the opinion that crime is the product of individual psychopathology. The notion is true in only a few instances. Criminologists know that crime is far more the product of the social structure and is normal behavior in American society and not dependent on psychiatric abnormalities or pathological conditions. In fact, crime is a definition of a situation and not an act in itself. None of this is explained by the media, for any explanation would be far too lengthy and difficult as compared with the usual explanation derived from popular psychology.[37]

Highlights of such controversial trials as the Simpson trial are the mainstay of television crime-reporting. Such trials are rare, and their depiction does not in any way reflect the daily proceedings found in actual courts. Coverage of ordinary trials or pleas would bore the viewers and is therefore avoided, leaving media followers with the mistaken notion that "courtroom dramas" are the everyday experience of trial lawyers, prosecutors, or defense attorneys. It is notable that dramatic reenactments or fictional accounts of action in the criminal justice system are mainly concerned with police activities, not jury trials or courthouse antics. Fictional accounts of policing usually show wild auto chases, shootouts, and other violence that holds the attention of media consumers. Further, the media generally depict the people apprehended by the police as guilty of the alleged crimes, despite the legal assumption that those arrested or charged are nevertheless innocent unless proved guilty in a court of law. The media give the opposite impression, that is, that all accused persons are guilty unless proved innocent.

Even those media events that purport to exhibit courtroom proceedings are unreliable reflections of reality. For years, the television show *Perry Mason* depicted a so-called lawyer who always seemed to get the better of the district attorney or prosecutor because week after week, the "real" criminal was discovered sitting in the spectators' section of the courtroom.

Plea bargaining, arraignment, indictment, trial, and sentencing are seldom shown on television and only briefly covered in newspapers.

Consequently, few members of the media audience know anything about those real-life procedures. As a result of the noted media distortions, most Americans have a view of the criminal justice system unrelated to the facts. Such readers and viewers are particularly ignorant of the jury and its responsibilities.[38] The media have severely limited the rights of defendants because so many cases are tried in the media before they are tried in court. It is almost impossible for a jury to remain objective concerning a defendant whose whole life has been exposed by the media and whose "guilt" has been widely disseminated by TV broadcasts and newspaper accounts. It is true that judges often instruct the media not to prejudice the jury by writing or broadcasting sensational stories concerning the defendant. The instructions are seldom followed, however, and have little effect on the media.[39]

JURY SELECTION

The selection of a jury from a jury panel may well determine the outcome of a trial. Jury trials are, of course, rare, in that only 5 percent of accused offenders choose to be tried by a jury. Most of the other defendants decide to plea bargain or are tried by a judge alone. An example of jury selection is evident in prosecutors' efforts to find a jury competent to try Cesar Rodriguez, who had beaten a seven-year-old child to death in New York City. This murder is indeed one of the most notorious murders in New York City history. Because the vast majority of murders are the outcome of adult disputes settled by the use of guns, knives, and other means of killing, juries are generally not acquainted with the kinds of circumstances leading to murder. Most jurors have never been involved in gun violence. But beating children is very common, and jurors are far more likely to have been involved in so-called disciplining of a child than in a shooting. Many adults were themselves, as children, the victims of beatings by their parents. The same people have, in turn, probably beaten their own children, since violence begets violence; so parents who beat children will find that these children, once adults, will do the same thing.

Understanding how widespread the physical disciplining of children might be among potential jurors, lawyers on both sides of the Rodriguez trial sought to seat jurors who would accommodate their theory of the killing attributed to the defendant. The prosecutors sought to seat jurors who could see a clear line between discipline and abuse. The defense, on the other hand, sought to find jurors who viewed this child murder as the unintentional outcome of normal discipline.

As a result of the different interpretations, hundreds of prospective jurors were questioned before a jury was finally seated.[40] Rodriguez was convicted of first-degree manslaughter but acquitted of second-degree murder. The verdict reflects the difficulty jurors have in reaching agreement concerning the role of parents as disciplinarians. While child beating is anathema to educated Americans, a large segment of the population continues to believe that assaulting children is justifiable.

"EYEWITNESSES" AND THEIR EFFECT ON JURIES

It is hardly news to learn that eyewitnesses to a crime are often wrong and that accounts of events reported by such eyewitnesses are not necessarily trustworthy. Yet, juries convict innumerable innocent suspects of crimes committed by others solely because a so-called eyewitness testifies that he or she had seen the defendant commit the alleged crime. An example of such conduct is evident in the conviction of Steven Titus. Titus had been identified by the victim of a rape in Washington state. The woman in question had accepted a ride in the vicinity of Seattle, only to become the victim of an assailant who drove her to a secluded area and raped her. Subsequently, the police arrested Titus, who was convicted by a jury that heard the victim identify her assailant as Steven Titus. Some months after Titus was sent to jail, the eyewitness recognized that another suspect had to be the real rapist, since he was arrested for a series of rapes in the Seattle area. The eyewitness then realized her error and became instrumental in securing Titus's release.[41]

While unjust imprisonment is always a nightmare for the victim, the Titus case is unusual in that the so-called eyewitness admitted the error and freed him. Most of the people unjustly convicted are never released, and many have been railroaded into death row and executed, or murdered, by the state, as we shall see later in this book. Wrongful convictions are frequent. In 2002, over 1 million adults were convicted of a felony in the United States. Of these, about 5 percent, or 1 in 20, are wrongful convictions mainly caused by false eyewitness accounts or malicious prosecution.[42] About 5,000 innocent people are convicted each year, although DNA samples indicate that the number of innocent citizens convicted is much higher. At least 27 percent of those undergoing DNA testing were exonerated during the years from 2000 to 2007.[43]

Juries seldom make decisions based on the facts. Instead, jury decisions are largely based on the emotion of the moment and on the appearance of the defendant. Juries are often far more interested in how a defendant looks than in the actual evidence, particularly when the juries are to decide whether to impose a life sentence or the death penalty. Thus, defendants who are perceived to be sorry for the murder of which they are convicted are more likely to be given a life sentence. Defendants who appear bored or look frightening are much more likely to be given the death penalty. The findings demonstrate that the outcome of a trial is related not only to the legal facts but also to extralegal issues.[44]

Experienced lawyers can tell when a jury has decided how to evaluate the evidence. According to such lawyers, almost every case heard by a jury includes an event that either moves juries in their client's favor or against him or her. An example of such a trial is found in a magazine called *Trial*, which relates the negligence conviction of an anesthesiologist who allowed a baby to be injured at birth because he failed to respond to two calls to take the mother to the operating room for a necessary C-section birth. When the anesthesiologist finally responded to a third call, it was too late and the baby was born with permanent brain damage. It was revealed that the anesthesiologist heard the calls but did not answer because he was busy with his mistress in a locked hospital room.[45]

A study conducted in El Paso County, Texas, sought to discover the relationship between ethnicity and conviction rates in that county. The study discovered that regardless of the type of crime attributed to the defendant, ethnicity was associated not with conviction rates but with the length of sentence rendered by juries. The study concluded that sentences for Anglo defendants were usually twice as long as sentences handed Hispanic defendants. In fact, as the number of Hispanics on a jury increased, Anglo defendants' sentences also increased.[46]

Social psychologists have studied in-group bias and concluded that one way in which we can view ourselves positively is to behave more favorably toward members of our own group than toward those we see as outsiders. Conversely, we are more likely to behave negatively toward out-group members. Such distinctions are labeled "in-group bias."[47]

The interaction between juries and defendants has been explained by "similarity leniency" and the "black sheep" effect. These terms mean that a well-liked defendant will receive more leniency than someone not liked. This phenomenon also holds for defendants whose social characteristics are similar to those of the jury.

The exception to the similarity rule is that sometimes an in-group member is viewed negatively by a jury of peers and is therefore considered a disgrace to the group. That perception then makes the individual a "black sheep," leading to a far more negative perception of such a defendant than even an out-group member would elicit.[48]

Texas permits a jury to take into consideration "sudden passion" with respect to a defense of homicide. Accordingly, a Texas jury may find a defendant guilty of murder but may introduce the mitigating circumstance of "the immediate influence of sudden passion." Such a finding would allow the jury to fix the penalty from probation to life in prison. An example of this kind of jury decision and verdict is to be found in the case of Dr. Clara Harris, who was sentenced to 20 years in prison on the recommendation of the jury who found her guilty of killing her husband by driving her Mercedes into him. The jury found that Harris had intentionally and repeatedly run her car over her husband, Dr. David Harris, a 44-year-old orthodontist. Evidently, David Harris was a "philandering husband"—he was dating Gail Bridges. Shortly before Clara Harris killed her husband, she had seen him holding hands with Gail Bridges in a hotel lobby. There, Clara Harris had rushed at Gail Bridges and attacked her. As the two women tore at each other and screamed epithets, David Harris tried to separate them. Subsequently, he walked Bridges to her Lincoln in the hotel's parking lot. Meanwhile, Clara Harris had entered her car together with her step-daughter Lindsay. As David Harris was standing on the driver's side of the Lincoln, Clara Harris "stomped on the accelerator" and deliberately drove into David Harris so that his body was thrown about 25 feet by the impact. His daughter Lindsay screamed at her stepmother to stop. Clara Harris nevertheless drove over David Harris as he was lying on the parking lot ground.[49]

Sociologists call the murder of David Harris "victim-precipitated homicide." This concept refers to a killing in which the victim is a major contributor to his or her own murder. Hans von Hentig, in his book *The Criminal and His Victim*, discusses this phenomenon in a chapter entitled "The Contribution of the Victim to the Genesis of Crime." Likewise, Tarde, Garofalo, and DeQuincey have recognized the phenomenon of victim-precipitated killing.[50] All these authors agree that at least three prerequisites must exist to provide a jury with the justification for a verdict of sudden passion. These are that (1) there must have been adequate provocation; (2) the killing must have been in the heat of passion; and (3) the killing must have come immediately after provocation, so the passion had not cooled. All these elements were present at the Harris trial. Nevertheless, the jury voted to imprison Clara Harris for 20 years. The Harris murder follows a well-recognized pattern in that the victims of such slayings are much more often husbands than wives. For example, Marvin Wolfgang found that of 33 victim-precipitated murders, only 5 victims were wives and 28 were husbands. This discrepancy is attributable to the far greater tendency of husbands to commit adultery and to beat or otherwise assault wives.[51]

FURMAN V. GEORGIA

In 1972, the U.S. Supreme Court handed down a decision that was to remedy the racial bias evident in jury decisions concerning capital punishment cases. The Supreme Court decision was made in the case of *Furman v. Georgia*.[52] The decision consisted of nine separate statements reflecting the views of each of the justices at that time. Of these, two justices, Thurgood Marshall and William J. Brennan, held the death penalty unconstitutional per se. The other justices considered the death penalty arbitrary and discriminatory and unfair to minorities as then administered. The majority did not reject the death penalty ipso facto. The Court held that juries in Georgia and elsewhere had no clear guidance as to when the death penalty could be applied. The Court held that race, class, and origin were unconstitutionally considered by juries in death penalty cases and that defendants were often singled out because of race, class, or ethnic origin. The Court also sought to mitigate the influence of social change on jury decisions in that juries attributed unwelcome social changes to disadvantaged persons. The unwanted social changes, the Court wrote, led juries to impose the death penalty whether or not warranted. Such an invasion of the legal system by popular opinion concerning social change was seen by the Court as originating in the prosecutor's elected office. Thus, the Court suggested, because prosecutors needed to support public opinion to be reelected, they were willing to bring capital charges in the first place.[53] The findings by the Supreme Court did not abolish the death penalty in the United States but did commute the sentences of all 629 death row inmates at that time. It took the states four years to return to the death penalty because the Supreme Court ruled in *Gregg v. Georgia* that Georgia's newly revised death penalty law was constitutional. Since then, the state-sanctioned killing of prisoners has resumed, and 1,099 persons have been executed by the various states since 1976.[54] The remedy the Supreme Court sought to impose was the formulation of clear standards guiding juries in sentencing, procedures removing jury decisions from outside influences, and provisions that would subject jury decisions to oversight.[55]

THE DEATH-QUALIFIED JURY

Because 36 states of the United States have laws that allow the imposition of the death penalty, juries in such states are faced with a task that few citizens must ever confront. That is whether or not to send a defendant to death. According to several polls conducted over a number of years,

63 percent of Americans favor the death penalty if no other alternative is available. If a sentence of life in prison without parole is made available, then only 43 percent favor the death penalty. It is, of course, far easier to tell a surveyor that one favors killing another human than to actually participate in a jury deliberation and vote for death. Very few Americans are ever confronted with such a task. Among those who are impaneled to appear for jury duty are always some who may theoretically consider themselves able to mete out the death penalty but who cannot actually bring themselves to send others to their deaths. Therefore, a number of states have instituted the practice of allowing only those potential jurors to be seated who say in advance of any trial that they are capable of imposing the death penalty if the defendant is found guilty of murder. Composed of such jurors, a jury that excludes anyone unwilling to impose the death penalty is "death-qualified." In 1968, in *Witherspoon v. Illinois*, the U.S. Supreme Court ruled that elimination of potential jurors on the grounds that they would not vote for the death penalty is unconstitutional. The justices cited the Sixth Amendment, guaranteeing an "impartial" jury.[56] In June 2007, the Supreme Court reversed the *Witherspoon* decision and voted 5–4 that prosecutors could exclude from a jury people who expressed reservations about the death penalty. This means that those jurors who remain after death penalty opponents have been removed are more likely to find a defendant guilty than a jury representing all opinions concerning the death penalty.[57] The decision allows judges to exclude from the jury all potential jurors who would normally vote for life in prison without parole, were that alternative available. Thirty-nine percent of Americans have a moral objection to the death penalty. Those citizens can, therefore, be excluded from juries hearing a potential death penalty case. It appears that the ruling will increase the number of false convictions and the execution of innocent prisoners. Although the Supreme Court has evidently made it easier to convict someone eligible for the death penalty, that same court has recently barred the use of the death penalty for the mentally retarded, juveniles, and defendants subject to racial bias. According to Brooks Butler of the University of Southern Florida, jurors eligible to serve on capital cases are most likely to be white males with some education. She also noted, after interviewing over 2,000 jurors, that eligible jurors are mostly conservative Republicans and Christians who earn a middle income of about $40,000 a year.[58]

TEEN COURT JURORS

Although the rate of juvenile crime has consistently declined since 1994, legislators in several states have passed laws treating adolescent offenders as adults. The new laws lower the age at which this can be done.[59] Even as the effort to send adolescent offenders to adult courts has increased, more than 1,000 teen courts operate in 48 states. Also known as youth courts or peer courts, these courts are used to adjudicate nonviolent offenders and use juries of adolescents.[60] Youth courts and youth juries are as much influenced by societal values current at any one time as adult juries. Therefore, such juries will make decisions in accord with the justice pendulum that has, in recent years, swung from rehabilitation to punishment, with the expectation that it will soon move once more in the other direction.[61]

Edith Greene and Kasey Weber made an extensive study of "teen juries" and their deliberations. Their study shows that juries of teens are even less interested in the facts of a case than are juries of adults and that they are much more inclined to consider age, gender, looks, remorse, ethnic origin, and all kinds of other indicators rather than deal with the evidence, which they largely ignore.[62]

SUMMARY

The American jury system originated in England, as did the entire American criminal justice system. A brief history of the English system reveals a medieval reliance on supernatural beliefs, later altered as science replaced religion as the principal means of identifying the relationship of humans to one another. The Constitution of the United States is the foundation of American justice; it guarantees a good deal of protection to the individual against the overreaching efforts of government.

The American jury system includes the grand jury, also derived from the English experience. Grand juries are seen as a distinct threat to citizens' constitutional rights.

Juries reach verdicts mainly based on the appearance and ethnicity of a defendant and not on the facts of the case. They tend to do so because the media generally create a false impression concerning the guilt or innocence of defendants even as the media distort the entire American criminal justice system. Such distortions are also the product of so-called eyewitness accounts because many people believe they saw something they did not really see. Such unreliability has led to the conviction of many innocent defendants because juries rely on eyewitnesses. Because the death penalty continues to exist in most American states and is also used in federal proceedings, juries facing such a choice have been limited to death-qualified jurors, that is, those capable of meting out the death sentence.

NOTES

The author is indebted to Professor Sanjeev Anand of the *University of Alberta Law Review* for a detailed presentation of the history of English jurisprudence.

1. Robert Bartlett, *Trial by Fire and Water* (New York: Clarendon Press, 1986), 31–32.

2. Thomas Andrew Green, *Verdict according to Conscience* (Chicago: University of Chicago Press, 1985), 8.

3. Naomi D. Hurnard, "The Jury of Presentment and the Assize of Clarendon," *English Historical Review* 56, no. 374 (1941): 391–92.

4. Margaret Kerr, Richard D. Forsyth, and Michael J. Pliely, "Cold Water and Hot Iron: Trial by Ordeal in England," *Journal of Interdisciplinary History* 22 (1992): 573.

5. Sir Walter Scott, *Ivanhoe* (New York: Heritage Press, 1950).

6. Roger D. Groot, "The Jury Presentment before 1215," *American Journal of Legal History* 26 (1982): 1.

7. Robert T. Roper, "Jury Size and Verdict Consistency," *Law and Society Review* 14, no. 4 (Summer 1980): 977.

8. J. M. Beattie, *Crime and the Courts in England* (Princeton, NJ: Princeton University Press, 1986), 397.

9. Lynda S. Myrciades, "Grand Juries, Legal Machines and the Common Man Jury," *College Literature* 53, no. 3 (Summer 2008): 160.

10. Sanjeez Anand, "The Origins, Early History and Evolution of the English Criminal Trial Jury," *Alberta Law Review* 43 (2005): 413–22.

11. Ibid., 427.

12. Lawrence M. Freeman, *Crime and Punishment in American History* (New York: Basic Books, 1992), 27.

13. *State v. Funicello*, 60 NJ 60, 286 A2d 55 (1971).

14. U.S. Constitution, First Amendment.

15. U.S Constitution, Second Amendment.

16. George J. Edwards, *The Grand Jury* (Philadelphia: G. T. Bisel, 1906), 28–29.

17. *Hale v. Henkel*, 201 U.S. 43, 65.

18. *U.S. v. Smyth*, 104 F. Supp. 283, 298.

19. *Branzburg v. Hays*, 408 U.S. 665.

20. Ibid.

21. Katherine Q. Seelye, "Freed Reporter Says She Upheld Principles," *New York Times*, October 4, 2005, A20.

22. *People v. Woodruff*, 272 N.Y.S. 2ns 286.

23. *New York Times*, "Great Lengths Taken to Fill the Jury Box," July 29, 2007, national edition.

24. J. L. Frost, "Anonymous Juries," *Journal of Contemporary Legal Issues* 2 (1992): 263–97.

25. Patrick Healy, "Jury Tampering Claim Halts L.I. Murder Trial," *New York Times*, September 30, 2004, B1.

26. Robert J. McCoun, "Experimental Research on Jury Decision Making," *Science*, new series 244, no. 4908 (June 2, 1989): 1047.

27. Harry Kalven and Hans Zeisel, *American Jury* (Boston: Little Brown, 1966), 488.

28. Reid Hastie, *Inside the Jury* (Cambridge, MA: Harvard University Press, 1983).

29. Alan Greenblatt, "Thinking inside the Jury Box," *Governing Magazine*, March 2005, 18.

30. Rita M. James, "Status and Competence of Juries," *American Journal of Sociology* 64 (1959): 563–70.

31. James W. McElhaney, "Character Matters," *ABA Journal* 94, no. 2 (August 2008): 28.

32. Steve Friess, "Many Stark Contrasts as Simpson Is Convicted," *New York Times*, October 4, 2008, A1.

33. Reid Hastie, Steven D. Penrod, and Nancy Pennington, *Inside the Jury* (Cambridge, MA: Harvard University Press, 1983).

34. 128 S. Ct. 1203 (2008); *Snyder v. Louisiana*, no. 06–10119.

35. Desiree J. Hanford, "A Newpaper Defends Naming Jurors," *New York Times*, September 17, 2007, 17.

36. J. V. Roberts and A. N. Doob, "News Media Influence on Public Views of Sentencing," *Law and Human Behavior* 40 (1990): 451–68.

37. Robert Winslow and Sheldon Zhang, *Criminology* (New York: Pearson, Prentice Hall, 2008), chap. 1.

38. David Slater and William Elliott, "Television Influence on Social Reality," *Quarterly Journal of Speech* 68 (1982): 69–79.

39. G. P. Kramer, N. L. Kerr, and J. S. Carroll, "Pretrial Publicity, Judicial Remedies and Jury Bias," *Law and Human Behavior* 14 (1990): 409.

40. Andy Newman, "Seating Jurors for Child Murder Case Raises Questions That All Parents Face," *New York Times*, January 12, 2008, A4.

41. Daniel Goleman, "Studies Point to Flaws in Lineup of Suspects," *New York Times*, January 17, 1995, C1.

42. U.S. Department of Justice, Bureau of Justice Statistics, *Criminal Sentencing Statistics* (Washington, DC: GPO, May 24, 2007).

43. Gary L. Wells and Elizabeth Olson, "Eye Witness Testimony," *Annual Review of Psychology* 54 (2003): 277–78.

44. Michael Antonio, "Arbitrariness and the Death Penalty," *Behavioral Sciences and the Law* 24 (2006): 215–34.

45. Kevin G. Burke, "A Nurse's Dramatic Story," *Trial* 44, no. 3 (July 2008): 44.

46. Howard Daudistel et al. "Effects of Defendants' Ethnicity on Juries' Dispositions of Felony Cases," *Journal of Applied Social Psychology* 29 (1999): 317–36.

47. Henry Tajfel and John Turner, "The Social Identity Theory and Intergroup Behavior," in *Psychology of Intergroup Relations*, ed. Stewart Worchel and W. G. Austin (Chicago: Nelson Hall), 7–24.

48. J. M. Marqes, "The Black Sheep Effect: Outgroup Homogeneity in a Social Comparison Setting," in *Social Identity Theory*, ed. D. Abrams and M. Hogg (London: Harvester Weatsheaf, 1990), 131–51.

49. Nick Madigan, "Woman Who Killed Spouse with Car Is Guilty of Murder," *New York Times*, February 14, 2003, A 20.

50. Stephen Schafer, *Victimology: The Victim and His Criminal* (Reston 1977); Anthony Walsh and Lee Ellis, *Criminology* (Newbury Park, CA: Sage 2006), 243.

51. Marvin E. Wolfgang, "Victim Precipitate Homicide," *Journal of Criminal Law, Criminology and Police Science* 48, no. 1 (May–June 1957): 1–11.

52. 498 U.S. 238 (1972).

53. William C. Bowers, "The Pervasiveness of Arbitrariness and Discrimination under Post-Furman Capital Statutes," *Journal of Criminal Law and Criminology* 74, no. 3 (1967): 1068.

54. Rachel King, "Three Decades Later: Why We Need a Temporary Halt on Executions," ACLU Capital Punishment Project (Washington, DC, 2005), 1.

55. Ibid., 1068.

56. *Whitherspoon v. Illinois*, 391 U.S. 510 (1968).

57. Adam Liptak, "Court Ruling Expected to Spur Convictions in Capital Cases," *New York Times*, June 9, 2007, A4.

58. Ibid.

59. Randall Salekin, "Juvenile Transfer to Adult Court," in *Children and the Law*, ed. B. Bottoms (Cambridge: Cambridge University Press, 2002), 203–32.

60. Michelle E. Heward, "The Operation and Organization of Teen Courts in the United States: A Comparative Analysis of Legislation," *Juvenile and Family Court Journal* 53 (2002): 19–35.

61. Helmut Kury, "Public Opinion and Punitivity," *International Journal of Law and Psychiatry* 22 (1990): 373–92.

62. Edith Green and Kasey Weber, "Teen Court Jurors' Sentencing Decisions," *Criminal Justice Review* 33, no. 3 (September 2008): 361.

Chapter 7

COURTS AND JUDGES

THE SUPREME COURT

A rticle 3 of the U.S. Constitution declares in two sections how the judicial power in the United States shall be exercised. The first section of that article establishes a Supreme Court as well as "such inferior courts as the Congress may from time to time ordain and establish."[1]

Note that there is no mention in this article of any qualifications a Supreme Court judge ought to have except that the judges shall hold their offices "during good behavior." Evidently, it is not necessary to be a lawyer to be a Supreme Court judge, nor does the Constitution call these judges "Justice," as in Mr. Justice Alito. That label was attached to the members of the U.S. Supreme Court by the Judiciary Act of 1789, which established the judiciary courts of the United States.[2]

The law passed by Congress on September 24, 1789, enacts that "the Supreme Court of the United States shall consist of a chief justice and five associate justices." That means that the Supreme Court originally had only six members. In 1807, Congress increased the Supreme Court to seven members because of the population growth in such western states as Kentucky, Tennessee, and Ohio. In 1837, the Court was increased to 9 judges and in 1860, to 10 because there were then 10 circuit courts in the federal system. In 1866, Congress reduced the membership on the Supreme Court to eight and then in 1869 increased the court to nine once more. Since then, the Court has had nine members overseeing 13 courts of appeal and 94 district courts in 50 states.[3]

The Judiciary Act of 1789 also provides for the appointment of district judges and consists of 35 sections describing the judiciary of the United States in detail.

American judges have attributed to themselves a role hardly commensurate with our democracy. Not only do they demand to be called "Your Honor," but they also force all those present in a courtroom to rise whenever they enter or leave. Moreover, judges have the power to jail anyone who has an opinion contrary to their own by calling almost any remark not to their liking "contempt of court." Because federal judges keep their office for life, whereas state judges are reelected time and time again, many federal judges know of no reason for treating those who come before them with respect. Yet, they are most anxious to be so regarded and use ancient British customs to enforce what they have not earned.

As early as 1890, the *Virginia Law Review* discussed the use of judicial gowns and the appellation "Your Honor." The unknown author of that article agreed that the gowns and titles were seen by many Americans as the effete customs of European monarchies. Nevertheless, the writer supported the customs on the grounds that the robes and other paraphernalia of judges enhanced the "majesty of the law." The author called upon "the dignity" of the court and wrote that the form of address does not imply that the judge is more honorable than other citizens.[4]

The judges of the Supreme Court are independent of the other two branches of the U.S. government, that is, of the office of the executive and of the legislature. As the highest judges in the land, the Supreme Court justices interpret the Constitution of the United States and in doing so function as an appellate court. In addition, the Court has original jurisdiction as defined by Article 3, Section 2, of the Constitution, which refers to "all cases affecting ambassadors, other public ministers and consuls and those in which a State shall be a party, the Supreme Court shall have original jurisdiction."[5]

Although the judges of the Supreme Court are nominated by the president of the United States and confirmed by the Senate, those judges so confirmed are independent of the executive and the legislative branches of government.

As of 2009, the members of the Supreme Court are Samuel A. Alito, Stephen Breyer, Ruth Bader Ginsburg, Anthony Kennedy, John G. Roberts (Chief Justice), Antonin Scalia, David H. Souter, John Paul Stevens, and Clarence Thomas.

HISTORY OF THE SUPREME COURT

Although the Supreme Court of the United States is highly regarded at the beginning of the twenty-first century, this was not so at the outset of the American Republic. In fact, the Court was regarded with suspicion by early U.S. presidents and legislators, who looked upon the Court as an outsider interfering with legitimate government. This view was held true because the Constitution does not clearly define the role of the Court. Furthermore, the Court had no home before 1937, when it moved into the present building.

Because the Court's jurisdiction was ill defined, in 1794 Congress passed the Eleventh Amendment, prohibiting the Supreme Court from a hearing in which a citizen of one state sues another state. This amendment limited the jurisdiction of the Supreme Court.[6]

In *Marbury v. Madison*, however, the Supreme Court under Chief Justice Marshall declared the Court to be the supreme decision maker concerning the meaning of the Constitution, with the result that the Court attained at least as much power as the other two branches of government. In *Chisholm v. Georgia*, the Supreme Court sided with the executor of Robert Farquhar's estate, Alexander Chisholm. Chisholm sought payment from Georgia for goods sold to that state during the Revolutionary War. Georgia refused to pay, but the Supreme Court sided with Chisholm. Thereupon Congress overturned that ruling by passing the Eleventh Amendment to the Constitution prohibiting the Court from hearing cases involving a citizen of one state suing another state.[7]

One consequence of that congressional action was the assertion by the so-called Marshall court (John Marshall, 1801–1835), which declared in *Marbury v. Madison* that the Supreme Court is the final arbiter of all disputes and the authentic interpreter of the Constitution. It was the Marshall court that ended the British practice of each justice issuing a separate opinion; instead, the majority opinion of the court was announced.[8]

No doubt one of the most important decisions ever made by any Supreme Court session was the case of *Dred Scott v. Marlborough.* Some historians have argued that the *Dred Scott* decision precipitated the Civil War because the Court decided that Scott, an escaped slave who had already lived free for seven years, was still the property of his former owner. The Court further held that the law prohibiting slavery in any new territory of the United States was unconstitutional. This ruling led Congress to pass the Thirteenth, Fourteenth, and Fifteenth Amendments to the Constitution, ending slavery in the United States.[9]

It was during the Franklin D. Roosevelt administration that the Supreme Court interpreted the Constitution to vastly increase the power of the federal government. Thereafter, the Warren court (1953–1969) became an advocate of civil rights when it overturned *Plessy v. Ferguson*, an 1869 decision favoring segregation. The court also held that the Constitution supports the right to privacy and that schools cannot engage in official prayer or mandatory Bible reading. Numerous other such decisions led Chief Justice Warren to proclaim, "We make the law."

Subsequently, the Warren Burger court ruled that abortion is a legal right (*Roe v. Wade*). That court also dealt with affirmative action, the death penalty, and other moral issues.

In *Roe v. Wade*, the Court held that most state laws prohibiting abortion violate the constitutional right to privacy and that therefore the mother may abort a pregnancy up to the point when the fetus becomes "viable." The decision has led to endless controversy as to when the fetus is viable, who should decide this, and whether religion has any place in this dispute.[10]

It was the *Bakke* case that led to a great deal of controversy concerning "affirmative action," a means by which members of minority groups are allowed preference in admission to higher education and employment even if their qualifications are less than those of applicants belonging to the Caucasoid race. Allan Bakke, a Caucasian, claimed that he was the victim of racial discrimination when, despite his high grades, he was refused admission to the University of California's medical school. The Supreme Court had ruled in that case that race or ethnicity may be one factor in making decisions as to admission to medical school but that race cannot be the only factor considered.[11]

The Supreme Court has no means of enforcing its rulings. Instead, the Court relies on the acquiescence of those affected by the opinions of the Court and the principle of legitimacy. This means that Americans have viewed the Supreme Court's decisions as legitimate even if they do not agree with those decisions. As a consequence, the Court's orders have been obeyed, with the exception of the refusal of President Andrew Jackson in *Worcester v. Georgia*.

In 2003, James Gibson, Gregory Caldeira, and Lester Spence published a study concerning attitudes toward the U.S. Supreme Court. Using a number of public opinion surveys to answer their question ("I am going to name some institutions in this country. As far as the people running these institutions are concerned, would you say you have a great deal of confidence, only some confidence, or hardly any confidence in them?"), the authors concluded that slightly less than a third of Americans express a great deal of confidence in the Supreme Court. This does not mean that a majority of Americans have no further loyalty to the Court. It does mean, however, that many Americans do not know or care to know the members of the Court. The institution per se is regarded as important not only by those who have a great deal of confidence in the Court but also by many who disagree with the important decisions of the Court.[12]

THE DISTRICT COURT JUDGES

Although the district courts did at one time hold numerous trials, this function of district courts is declining more and more not only because criminal trials are fewer and fewer but also because civil "filings" are down. According to Judge D. Brock Hornby of the Maine District Court, "In the twenty-first century, the federal district courts' primary role in civil cases have become law exposition, fact sorting, and case management—office tasks, not umpiring trials."

Even in criminal cases, says Hornby, trials and sentencing discretion by judges are gone and are not coming back. Instead, district judges are engaged in law elaboration and fact finding, supervising federal offenders after prison, and safeguarding the integrity of the criminal process.[13]

There are 13 circuits in the federal system. The chief justice is assigned to the District of Columbia circuit and one justice is assigned to the "federal circuit." The other justices are assigned to one or more of 11 circuits across the country. These courts hear civil as well as criminal cases and are subject to review by the U.S. Supreme Court. The reviews are provoked by the petition of any party not satisfied with the judgment of the highest court in a state. Such a review is called a "writ of certiorari," meaning "to be searched." The English language could be used, and a request for a review could be called just that. However, using Latin envelops the courts in a mystery created by an ancient and generally little-known language. The use of Latin serves to segregate the justices from the American populace and gives the illusion that Supreme Court justices are scholars. A similar approach is used by physicians and, of course, the clergy.

District court judges are politicians who have usually held other political offices. An example of such a career was that of Eugene Nickerson, who served as judge for the Eastern District of New York. Nickerson had been Nassau County executive from 1961 to 1964. Failing to win reelection, he joined a law firm bearing his name. Then, in 1977 President Jimmy Carter appointed him to the federal bench in Brooklyn.

Nickerson made numerous attempts at gaining public office before and after his term as county executive. He failed in an attempt to be elected county surrogate in 1959. He also lost in an effort to become U.S. senator in 1968 and lost the primary contest to become New York State governor in 1970. In 1980, Nickerson was nominated to become judge on the U.S. Court of Appeals for the Second Circuit of New York. The Senate refused to confirm Nickerson for this position, and so he remained a circuit judge.

Nickerson descended from Presidents John Adams and John Quincy Adams. His first American ancestor was William Nickerson, who bought Cape Cod from the Indians in 1637. A son of privilege, Nickerson attended St. Mark's School in Southborough, Massachusetts, and thereafter became a student at Harvard University. He later earned a law degree at Columbia University. The media labeled Nickerson a "patrician," a term applied to those who belong to the aristocratic class of Americans.

During his career as a judge, Nickerson presided over several important trials. One was the trial of John Gotti, reputed Mafia boss, and another the trial of Vincent Gigante, also a capo in organized crime. Nickerson struck down the Defense Department's policy concerning homosexuals, a policy called "Don't ask, don't tell," but his decision was overruled by the court of appeals. Nickerson also presided over the Abner Louima case. The Louima trial led to the conviction of two police officers for torturing Louima. Nickerson was later in charge of a number of other sensational New York trials.[14]

Another federal circuit court judge, Harold Barefoot Sanders, began a political career as a Texas state legislator in the 1950s. He had graduated from the University of Texas law school and then joined his father's law firm in 1950. He served three terms in the Texas House but lost in an effort to become a member of the U.S. House of Representatives in 1958. President John F. Kennedy appointed him federal attorney for Dallas in 1964. One year later, Sanders joined the Justice Department in Washington, D.C., and thereafter became legislative counsel at the White House in 1967. President Lyndon Johnson sought to appoint Sanders to the appeals court. This attempted appointment failed, since the Senate would not confirm him. He also failed in his effort to become a U.S. senator when John Tower defeated him in 1972.

Like Nickerson, Sanders was appointed to the federal bench by President Carter in 1979, remaining there until his retirement in 1995. As a judge, Sanders presided over Dallas school desegregation efforts. He associated himself with former speaker of the House Sam Rayburn; Lyndon Johnson, first a member of the House and the Senate and then president; Senator Ralph Yarborough; and Texas Governor John B. Connolly. Indeed, his entire career was devoted to politics, as are the careers of almost all circuit judges in the federal system.[15]

Charles Lamont Brieant was appointed to the federal bench by President Nixon in 1971. Prior to that appointment, he had been an Ossining, New York, town justice; a Westchester County, New York, assistant district attorney; the village attorney for Briar Cliff, New York; the Ossining town supervisor; and the Westchester County supervisor.

Brieant, a graduate of the Columbia University Law School and an Air Force veteran, made a number of rulings in cases of race and gender discrimination. He decided that Alcoholics Anonymous is akin to religion with reference to the separation of church and state. His most controversial ruling was his decision that Texaco, a giant oil company, did not have to post a $12 billion bond in a case brought by Pennzoil.

Judge Brieant also approved a $115 million discrimination suit by a number of blacks against Texaco after his court was given documents and tape recordings in which Texaco executives made racist remarks. In addition, he ruled that third-graders should not be subject to religious exercises in school. He wrote that children should not be taught superstition "at a young and impressive age." Brieant wrote more than 700 opinions in his 36 years on the federal bench.[16]

Federal district court judges preside over a variety of cases ranging from terrorism issues to organized-crime accusations and home foreclosures. For example, Judge Emmet G. Sullivan of the District Court of Columbia in Washington was appointed to that position by President Ronald Reagan in 1984. A graduate of Howard University, Sullivan has questioned accusations by the U.S. government that some of the detainees at Guantanamo Bay are terrorists. This stance is illustrated by Judge Sullivan's refusal to accept the government attorneys' accusation that Binyam Mohamed, an Ethiopian-born British subject, had planned a radioactive bomb attack on the United States. When the government dropped the charge that Mohamed had planned to assault the United States with a "dirty bomb," Judge Sullivan questioned whether the allegations against Binyam Mohamed were ever true. According to government prosecutors, Mohamed confessed to the "dirty bomb" charge. This accusation was countered by Mohamed's lawyer, Zachary Katznelson, who claimed that Mohamed was tortured into making a false confession.[17]

Mark L. Wolf is a federal district court judge in Boston. There, he presided over the trial of Vincent Ferrara, accused of being a Mafia capo and of ordering the murder of John Limoli after Limoli stole drugs from the Patriarca crime family. When Walter Jordan, an associate of Vincent Ferrara, testified that he had himself killed Limoli without Ferrara's permission, as recorded by a detective, the judge ordered the prosecutors to give a copy of the detective's notes to the defense. The prosecutors refused to do so and thereby violated the defendant's due process rights. This violation forced the judge to release Ferrara in 2005. The judge then demanded that the Justice Department sanction the prosecutor, Jeffrey Auherhahn, but without success.[18]

Missouri's federal district judge Jean C. Hamilton ruled in March 2008 that the Army Corps of Engineers was entitled to release hundreds of thousands of gallons of water from a dam in the Missouri River despite the catastrophic flooding experienced that week by the Missouri population. The Corps of Engineers was allowed to release the water because doing so would help the sturgeon population.[19]

A recent foreclosure case in Ohio illustrates the involvement of federal district court judges in yet another area of dispute. Judge Christopher A. Boyko of the Cleveland, Ohio, District Court dismissed 14 foreclosure cases in November 2007 on the grounds that the owners had not proved ownership. Whereas foreclosure cases were at one time easily won by property owners without proof of ownership, the avalanche of such cases in 2007 and later caused judges to demand proof of ownership before foreclosing on delinquent borrowers. For example, Judge Thomas M. Rose of Dayton's Ohio Southern District 6th Circuit Court demanded that lenders prove ownership of properties within 30 days if they wanted to seize homes for the homeowners' failure to make mortgage payments. The usual owners of mortgages are such banks as Citibank, which sought to foreclose on a $191,000 home on the grounds that the borrower had defaulted for over a year. In another case, involving HSBC Bank, the homeowner defaulted on a $144,000 mortgage for two years.

According to a study by a law professor, in the past, 40 percent of creditors seeking to foreclose on debtors did not demonstrate proof of ownership. Such proof is required by law, which had seldom been enforced before the present housing crisis.[20]

The foregoing examples demonstrate that federal district judges are called upon to rule on a great diversity of cases, including organized crime, terrorism, flood control, school desegregation, religion, and house foreclosures. Undoubtedly, many more issues come before federal district judges every day.

Perhaps the most recognized state court judge in America is Judge Lance Ito of California. Ito owes his prominence to the trial of O. J. Simpson for the murder of Simpson's wife, Nicole, and Ron Goldman, who happened to be at the home of Nicole. The 1995 trial of football star Simpson made Ito a household name, although the judge is not otherwise generally known.

As a Japanese American, whose parents met in an internment camp in Wyoming during Word War II, Ito understands Japanese American culture. Ito thus refused all lucrative offers to write a book about the Simpson trial. No doubt Ito could have profited immensely from such an enterprise, but in keeping with traditional Japanese expectations, he refused to write about the trial lest he bring dishonor to his family.

A graduate of UCLA and the University of California Law School at Berkeley, Lance Ito began his career at a private law firm in Los Angeles and from there became a deputy district attorney working in the organized-crime division and in the antiterrorist division. Later, he became special assistant to the chief deputy. Ito wrote a number of proposals changing criminal law, including a provision that made it a felony to carry a weapon into a courthouse. In 1987, Ito, a Democrat, was appointed to the Los Angeles Municipal Court by the Republican governor George Deukmejian. Two years later, he was appointed to the California Superior Court.[21]

At the other end of the country, in New York City, James Yates was elected to a 14-year term to the New York State Supreme Court of New York County in 1998. A seasoned politician, Yates had previously spent six years on the New York State Court of Claims, to which he had been appointed by Governor Mario Cuomo. Yates, a Democrat, is considered a liberal and was therefore appointed general counsel to New York Governor David Patterson in 2008. Yates declined the appointment and remained a judge.

A graduate of Yale University, Yates earned a JD from Rutgers University in 1973. He began his career with the New York Legal Aid Society. Thereafter, he became counsel to the New York State Assembly majority leader from 1987 to 1989 and followed this by serving in the same capacity to the assembly speaker from 1989 to 1993.

Yates also taught part-time at several New York City–area law schools, including New York University, the New York Law School, Queens College, Cardozo School of Law of Yeshiva University, and the Pace University School of Law. All these appointments were, of course, dependant on Yates's loyalty to the Democratic Party.

Yates has presided over numerous criminal trials, including the sensational trial of Peter Braunstein in 2007. Braunstein was convicted of assaulting a woman in her own apartment by tying her naked to a bed for 13 hours and "groping" her. Braunstein first drugged his victim with chloroform. He had made smoke bombs, which he used to gain entrance to the victim's apartment. Apparently "insane" in the legal meaning of that phrase, Braunstein had written numerous pathological treatises that exhibit his total inability to discern myth from reality. Nevertheless, he was sentenced to 18 years in prison.[22]

Judge William C. Christianson of Minnesota had a unique experience in the course of his career in that he served as the presiding judge at the trial of Hitler's cabinet from 1947 until the end of the trial in 1949. The trial included 21 defendants accused and later convicted of war crimes. Included were several storm trooper generals as well as Nazi war planners and espionage directors. Christianson based his judgment on international law as agreed to and signed by the German government before World War II. This meant, said Christianson, that the argument that one needed to obey a superior's orders was not a valid excuse for the crimes in question.

Christianson, a graduate of the University of Chicago School of Law,[23] began his political career when he managed the election of Governor

Edward Thye of Minnesota. In turn, Thye appointed Chistianson to the supreme court of Minnesota to serve an interim term of one year. When Christianson failed to be elected, he accepted appointment to the Nuremberg military tribunal. On Christianson's return to Minnesota, Governor Youngdahl appointed him judge in the first judicial district of the state.

Hiller B. Zobel is one of the most courageous judges ever to serve on the Massachusetts Superior Court. Because the Massachusetts constitution requires judges to retire at age 70, Zobel retired in 2002.

Zobel earned a BA from Harvard University and in 1959 graduated from there with a degree in law. He was appointed to the Massachusetts Superior Court in 1979 after having litigated admiralty cases for eight years. Thereafter, he taught law at the Boston College of Law and served as libel counsel at a local television station.

Judge Zobel is also the author of a number of books, including *The Legal Papers of John Adams, The Boston Massacre, Massachusetts Rule Practice*, and *Doctors and the Law*. In addition, he has written numerous articles for *American Heritage Magazine* and other journals.

In 1997, a Massachusetts jury convicted Louise Woodward, an English child care worker, of killing an eight-month-old boy by shaking him. The jury had voted to convict Woodward of murder, which would have carried a sentence of life in prison. Because such a conviction seemed utterly unfair to Zobel, he reduced her conviction to manslaughter and then sentenced her to the nine months she had already served in jail before her trial. The Massachusetts Supreme Judicial Court upheld the right of Judge Zobel to reduce Woodward's sentence, and so she returned to her home in England.

There is no doubt that Woodward caused the death of the infant. Nevertheless, her ignorance of the "shaken baby syndrome" cannot be compared to willful murder, as indicated by the jury verdict. Undoubtedly, Zobel was entirely right in reducing her sentence and letting her go home.

This case led to immense publicity in the United States and England, where the American criminal justice system was viewed as utterly foreign to common sense and decency.

Few judges are willing to stand up to public opinion or the wrath of the media and reduce the sentences of those unjustly treated by juries, prosecutors, or police. It is therefore to Judge Zobel's credit to be one of the few unwilling to preside over injustice.[24]

APPEAL

A court of appeals is the intermediate appellate court. It costs a great deal of money to appoint lawyers who specialize in appeals, and so appeals are not available to the poor unless lawyers can be found who will take an appeal case pro bono publico, that is, "for the good of the people."

If a party loses in a circuit court and believes a mistake was made, that party may file an appeal. The court of appeals in each state handles all appeals other than those that are within the province of the Supreme Court of the United States. The appeals would be issues involving constitutional questions, as well as death penalty cases. Although cases heard by a court of appeals may be further appealed to the Supreme Court, less than 10 percent of such cases are heard by the Supreme Court.

As already seen, the U.S. system of criminal justice is responsible for a long history of convicting innocent persons. This sorry record is partly the result of mistakes by police, prosecutors, and juries. It is mainly caused, however, by the deliberate deceit of law enforcement officers and prosecutors who violate the law. It is thus essential that judges protect the innocent from the machinations of "law enforcers" who benefit from the imprisonment and even the death of innocent citizens. Therefore, judges serving on a court of appeals are most instrumental in rectifying the many false charges and convictions occurring regularly in our criminal justice system. Courts of appeals are not the only agencies capable of freeing imprisoned innocent citizens. Circuit court judges can do so under some circumstances, and governors as well as the president of the United States can pardon those rightfully convicted as well as those deemed innocent.

On Wednesday, December 17, 2008, Judge Everett Young of the Texas Court of Criminal Appeals decided that Michael Roy Toney was wrongfully convicted of a 1985 bombing that killed three people on Thanksgiving Day in 1985. Judge Young was supported in his decision, not only by Toney's defenders, but even by the Tarrant County district attorney's office, who admitted that Toney's 1999 trial was unconstitutional because the then-district attorney withheld 14 documents that could have cast doubt on the testimony of two so-called eyewitnesses claiming Toney had killed three members of the Blount family.[25]

Judge Deborah Hedlund of the Hennepin County District Court in Minnesota has made significant contributions to that court during the two decades she has served there. A graduate of Kansas University, she earned a JD from the University of Minnesota School of Law and thereafter became a public defender in Hennepin County. In 1974, she entered the Minnetonka city attorney's office. Appointed Minnetonka city attorney in 1976, she stayed in that position until her appointment by Governor Quie of Minnesota to the Hennepin County Municipal Court in 1980.

Judge Hedlund has a family, including three children, of whom one is adopted. In 1978, *NBC Nightly News* broadcast a segment depicting Deborah Hedlund as an example of a woman who can be professionally successful and simultaneously raise a family.

It was Judge Hedlund who commuted Sherman Townsend's 20-year sentence for burglary to the 10 years he had already served. Hedlund did so because another man, David Anthony Jones, confessed that he had committed the burglary of which Townsend had been convicted. In fact, Jones had been the principal witness against Townsend. Prosecutors had promised Jones a reduced sentence for the burglary he himself had committed if he would implicate Townsend. Jones did so, and Townsend was thereby falsely convicted. After 10 years, lawyers working for the Innocence Project of Minnesota convinced Judge Hedlund that Townsend was innocent and succeeded in having him released.[26]

On September 11, 2007, Judge David Ashworth of the Court of Common Pleas of Lancaster County, Pennsylvania, dropped all charges against Charles T. Dubbs. He had spent 5 years in prison, having been sentenced to serve 12–40 years though he had committed no crime.

On graduating from Gettysburg College and the Widener University School of Law, Ashworth became a civil trial attorney for 20 years and one of the founding partners of Wagman, Ashworth, Kreider and Wright. Ashworth participated in numerous civic organizations and was elected to a number of boards. He speaks frequently to students in Lancaster schools about drugs and teaches in the People's Law School of the Lancaster Bar Association.

It fell to Judge Ashworth to free Charles Dubbs, who had been the victim of the deliberate effort of the Lancaster district attorney to hide his responsibility for the cruel injustice done to Dubbs. In May 2002, Dubbs was sentenced for sexually assaulting two women who both identified him as their attacker. Yet, Wilbur Cyrus Brown had confessed to both attacks and to 13 other rapes. Brown had raped both women on a jogging trail that Dubbs had never visited. In fact, Dubbs did not know the trail existed. Nevertheless, the district attorney labeled Brown's confession "a joke."[27]

Dennis G. Jacobs is the chief judge of the U.S. Court of Appeals for the Second District. He became chief judge in October 2006 and became responsible for releasing Derrick Bell from prison in 2007.

Jacobs began his professional career as an English teacher but decided to enter law school at age 26. Thereafter, he litigated 22 years for a private New York law firm. In 1992, he was nominated by President George H. W. Bush.[28]

Despite his reputation as a conservative, Judge Jacobs has, on repeated occasions, ruled against prosecutors, including the erroneous conviction of Derrick Bell, who was sent to prison for 12.5 to 25 years for shooting Brentono Moriah despite Moriah's inability to identify Bell as his assailant on July 28, 1996. The Second Circuit Court of Appeals under Judge Jacobs determined that Bell not only had had an utterly inadequate defense but that he had been falsely prosecuted. Bell served 11 years in prison before he was exonerated through the efforts of two pro bono lawyers working at a private firm.[29]

On October 10, 2007, the governor of North Carolina, Mike Easley, signed a "pardon of innocence" concerning Dwayne Dail, who had spent 18 years in prison.

Easley, a graduate of the University of North Carolina, earned a law degree from North Carolina Central University School of Law. After several years in private practice, he was elected district attorney in 1982 and became North Carolina attorney general 10 years later. In November 2000, he was elected governor of the state.

By freeing Dwayne Dail, Easley alleviated a gross injustice that can, of course, never be undone. In 1989, Dail was falsely convicted and imprisoned on the allegation that he raped a 12-year-old girl, Tomeshia Artis. Artis wrongly identified Dail as her assailant. While her motive for this falsehood is not known, it is evident that the police and the prosecutors ignored the evidence that William Jackson Neal Jr., and not Dail, had committed that crime. They nevertheless railroaded Dail into prison, where he remained until a DNA test on a nightgown proved his innocence. Indeed, the state has paid Dail $750,000 and allowed him to attend college at public expense. Nevertheless, Dail is severely damaged by the brutal treatment he received in prison for his being a "child rapist."[30]

When Connie Nardi was murdered in Portage County, Ohio, in 1988, prosecutors promised Troy Busta that he would escape the death penalty for committing this murder if he would testify against Randy Resh and Bob Gondor, who were also suspects in this rape-murder. Convicted by a jury that was not allowed to hear any exonerating evidence in their favor, Resh and Gondor were sentenced to life in prison.

In June 2002, Judge Charles J. Bannon ruled that both men had been convicted improperly and ordered their release. However, Bannon's order was overturned by two judges of the 11th District Court of Appeal at Warren, Ohio. Judge Cynthia Rice and Judge Mary DeGenaro declared the original verdict "reliable" on the grounds that the testimony of Troy Busta was true despite the evidence that he had been prosecuted on a lesser charge in exchange for his false testimony against the other two men.

Evidently, all three men had been in the same nightclub in which the victim was a dancer. Nardi's body was found outside that bar, where Busta had killed her. Resh and Gondor were not acquainted with Busta, nor were they in any manner involved in the murder. Nevertheless, Busta claimed he saw them kill Nardi.

Then, in December 2006, the Ohio Supreme Court decided that both Resh and Godnor were to be given a new trial on the grounds that Busta's testimony was unreliable. The Portage County prosecutor, Victor Vigliucci, complained that the Supreme Court had forced him to retry a 20-year-old case. He did not complain that two innocent men had been in prison for 18 years.

At a new trial held in April 2007, Resh was found not guilty. Gondor was not tried again, and both were released on the order of Justice Paul Pfeiffer. A graduate of Ohio State University, Pfeiffer earned a law degree from the College of Law at Ohio State University in 1963. Subsequently, he practiced law privately and then entered politics when he was elected to the Ohio House of Representatives in 1970. In 1976, he was elected to the Ohio Senate, where he remained until 1982, when he was defeated in an attempt to become a U.S. senator. In 1992, Pfeiffer was elected to Ohio's supreme court. Reelected several times, he will serve until 2011.

The brutal manner in which Resh and Gondor were persecuted by the Ohio criminal justice system depicts once more that for many prosecutors and police officers, career and personal advantages are far more important than the constitutional guarantees on which this democracy rests.[31]

Judge Twyla Mason Gray was elected a district judge in Oklahoma City in 1998. Since then, she has been reelected two times. Prior to becoming a district judge, she was a municipal judge in Oklahoma City for four years after serving as a corporate lawyer. Her political career began when she became the chief of staff for the mayor of Tulsa, Oklahoma, and later assistant to a congressman from Oklahoma's first congressional district.

Gray graduated from the University of Central Oklahoma and earned a law degree from the University of Tulsa. She is the recipient of numerous honors from a variety of civic organizations.

In May 2007, Judge Gray freed Curtis E. McCarty after he had been in prison for 22 years, 16 of which he spent on death row. McCarty was victimized twice as the police, the prosecutor, and a police chemist, Joyce Gilchrist, deliberately falsified evidence leading to two trials and two death sentences for this innocent man.

First, McCarty was convicted and sentenced to death for the murder of 18-year-old Pamela Willis, who was raped, strangled, and stabbed on December 10, 1982. In 1989 the Oklahoma Court of Appeals overturned that verdict on the grounds of police and prosecutorial misconduct. McCarty was retried that year and again sentenced to death. That sentence was thrown out and then reinstated in 1996. Then, in 2005 the court of appeals overturned the conviction again.

The prosecutor in the McCarty case, Robert H. Macy, sent 73 people to death row and bragged that executing innocent persons was justified because it allowed the state to keep the death penalty.[32]

The United States has no political prisoners, it is commonly believed, because in a free country political affiliation or opinion cannot be punished by the government. That belief is grounded in the Constitution of the United States, with particular reference to the First Amendment.

Evidently, the U.S. Constitution is unknown to a good number of prosecutors, including U.S. attorney Steven Biskupic, who prosecuted Georgia Thompson, a Wisconsin civil servant, on the preposterous charge of illegally steering a state contract to a travel agency whose principal owner made campaign contributions to Wisconsin Governor Jim Doyle. Thompson was convicted and sent to prison for 18 months beginning in May 2007.

In August 2007, the 7th District Court of Appeals reversed Thompson's conviction and ordered her immediate release, with Chief Judge Easterbrook calling her conviction and imprisonment "preposterous." There can be little doubt that Thompson was prosecuted in an effort to embarrass the Democrat governor, who was reelected despite these nefarious efforts by the Republican opposition.[33]

Frank Easterbrook graduated from Swarthmore College in 1970 and earned a law degree from the University of Chicago in 1973. Editor of the *Chicago Law Review*, he became a clerk to a judge of the U.S. 1st District Court of Appeals and thereafter joined the solicitor general's office. He became deputy solicitor general of the United States before becoming a professor of law at the University of Chicago. From there, he was appointed judge of the U.S. 7th District Court of Appeals. Judge Easterbrook has also been editor of the *Journal of Law and Economics* and has written a book and numerous scholarly articles.[34]

Joan Humphrey Lefkow is a U.S. judge for the Northern District of Illinois. She was nominated by President Clinton in 2000 and confirmed by the Senate that year. A native of Kansas, she graduated from Wheaton College and earned a JD from Northwestern University in 1971. Thereafter, she became a law clerk for Judge Thomas Fairchild and then became a U.S. magistrate until 1997, when she was appointed a U.S. bankruptcy judge.

Shortly after her appointment as U.S. district court judge, Lefkow presided over the enforcement of a trademark infringement case against the World Church of the Creator. In that connection, Lefkow ruled against a white supremacist, Matthew Hale. Hale thereupon solicited the murder of Judge Lefkow by contacting an undercover FBI agent. Subsequently, Hale was sentenced to 40 years in prison for soliciting the murder of Judge Lefkow.

Then, in February 2005, Judge Lekow found that her husband and mother had been murdered in her home. Evidently, a hate group was involved in the killings. This conclusion was confirmed when Bart Ross killed himself just before being apprehended for the killings. At the time of his suicide, he had not admitted to the murders.[35]

It was Judge Lefkow who freed Marion Pendleton, who had spent 12 years of a 20-year sentence in prison for a rape that another man had committed in 1992. Pendleton had lost two appeals in the Illinois Appellate Court and also lost two times in the Illinois Supreme Court.

Earlier, Pendleton had asked for a DNA test but was refused on the grounds that there was insufficient material available for such a test. Yet, in 2006, there suddenly emerged enough material to make the test. Judge Lefkow was willing to hear Pendleton's appeal, sponsored by the Innocence Project in Illinois.[36]

THE INNOCENCE PROJECT

For 25 years, ever since 1983, it has become more and more evident that innumerable Americans have been convicted, sentenced to long prison terms, and even death, although they were and are innocent of any crime.

The first to recognize that the American criminal justice system regularly convicted innocent people was the Rev. James McCloskey, who founded Centurian Ministries for the purpose of clearing the numerous prisoners who are absolutely innocent of the crimes for which they have been convicted. McCloskey's efforts led to the release of 14 innocent people from prison.

In 1992, two professors at the Cardozo School of Law, Barry Scheck and Peter Neufeld, founded the Innocence Project there. The Cardozo School of Law is part of Yeshiva University ("yeshiva" is Hebrew for "community"). This project relies on the use of DNA (deoxyribonucleic acid), a structure first discovered by Rosalind Franklin in the 1950s. Based on DNA tests, over 200 innocent Americans have been freed from prison because they were found to have been unjustly convicted. The project, first confined to New York City, has now spread to the entire nation and is also used in Europe to determine whether or not someone accused or convicted of a crime could have been the perpetrator.

Almost all those innocents convicted and imprisoned and later freed owe their freedom to the Innocence Project in their state. The recent success of this project nationwide demonstrates the imperfection of the U.S. criminal justice system and emphasizes the unreliability of eyewitnesses, the malfeasance of prosecutors, the willingness of juries to rush to judgment, and the failure of police work in identifying offenders instead of blaming the innocent. Further, DNA testing delivers a serious blow to trial by media, who have for years decided guilt based solely on their prejudices.

THE JUVENILE COURT

The first American juvenile court was established in Cook County, Illinois, in Chicago, in 1899. The reason for this development was the effort of the progressives in politics and journalism to alter the conditions under which children were tried and incarcerated.

In 1869, 30 years before the establishment of the juvenile court, Illinois housed 98 children under the age of 16 in 40 different jails. The jails were "filthy and full of vermin" and "moral plague spots" where children were "turned into greater criminals."[37] It was the belief of the Illinois legislature that a separate court for young people would alleviate the bad conditions by sending "delinquent" children to houses of refuge and other institutions that did not hold adults. Special judges were therefore appointed to deal with children, whose crimes were adjudicated as civil rather than criminal acts. It was the belief of the originators of the juvenile courts that the judge would deal with the child as a whole rather than with the particular offense that led to the child's appearance before the court. No lawyers were needed, since the adjudication was viewed as a civil action. Further, the determination of the court was seen, not as punishment, but as a means of dealing "in the best interests of the child."[38]

Because the names of youthful offenders may not be revealed in the media, specific examples of youth crimes cannot be portrayed here. The FBI's Uniform Crime Report attributes approximately 17 percent of all violent crimes to youths under 18. However, juvenile judges are assigned to deal not only with violent crimes but also with nonviolent crime, as well as with such "status offenses" as failing to attend school, drinking alcohol, engaging in sexual encounters, or failing to obey parental authority.

Delinquency is therefore defined as conduct that would be adjudicated a crime if committed by an adult. Juvenile court judges also deal with child neglect or offenses committed by adults against children.

One juvenile court judge is Brenda Harbin Forte of Alameda County, California, Juvenile Court. Judge Forte was admitted to the California Bar in 1979. She had graduated from the University of California at Berkeley and thereafter attended law school at the same university. After practicing law in a private firm for several years, Forte served as clerk at the 9th District Court of Appeals in California. She is the recipient of numerous awards and has been active in the judicial education program in California.

The cases that may be heard by a judge in the juvenile courts around the country can consist of such minor issues as school attendance or "incorrigible conduct" at home. Yet, there are cases that come before juvenile court judges that would undoubtedly be felonies if committed by adults. A few examples suffice to recognize this.

In 2004, two boys in Montclair, New Jersey, were charged with rape. Montclair has 39,000 citizens and is a wealthy suburb of greater New York City. To the upper-middle-class and upper-class citizens, the charge of rape is repugnant not just because of the crime itself but because such allegations, it is feared, sully the community's reputation.[39]

In Toledo, Ohio, a 14-year-old girl was arrested in school wearing a low-cut midriff top under an unbuttoned sweater. This apparel did not conform to the school dress code. When she refused to wear a bowling shirt given her by the school and also refused to wear a T-shirt brought by her mother, she was sent to a holding cell in the local courthouse until her mother came to get her after work. She was charged with a misdemeanor.[40]

Lee Malvo was sentenced to life in prison without chance of parole because at age 17, he murdered six unsuspecting citizens in Montgomery County, Maryland. Malvo, accompanied by an adult, John A. Muhammad, participated in attacking citizens at random in both Maryland and Virginia. Malvo was tried as an adult despite his age at the time the crimes were committed.[41]

In Long Beach, California, nine black teenagers were convicted of felony assault for beating three young white women with skateboards and other objects at Halloween in 2006. The teenagers were also convicted of a hate crime. The defense claimed that the perpetrators were the victims of racism and that "they didn't do anything."[42]

Although the juvenile court was at first conceived as an informal civil court in which no lawyers were needed or admitted, the Supreme Court has ruled that every American has a right to counsel; consequently, lawyers are now active in juvenile courts. In theory, the juvenile court is not a part of the criminal justice system. Nevertheless, an overview of the juvenile court system is included here not only because public opinion has eroded this view over the past century but also because the law has accorded children all the rights and protections demanded by the U.S. Constitution.

CONDUCT OF AMERICAN JUDGES

There are undoubtedly judges who do not need the power and adulation they demand from the public and the citizens who come before them. Generally, however, judges seem to believe that they are entitled not only to their salaries but also to those ancient European customs once associated with royalty. Judges demand that their fellow citizens stand up when they enter a room and one of their sycophants shouts "all rise." Judges must be addressed as "Your Honor" or called "The Honorable," a label also associated with other politicians. Judges reserve the right to jail anyone anytime for "contempt of court," an offense that usually signals a judge's displeasure with a citizen who is not sufficiently obsequious. Such ritual behaviors are remnant reminders of the British tyranny overthrown by the American Revolution and are most un-American. Judges have no right to forget that the United States is a democracy in which *all* men and women are equal and none should be obligated to rise before a fellow citizen.

The worst abuses by judges in the United States occur in small towns in every state. In September 2006, William Glaberson of the *New York Times* published three articles concerning such abuses. Glaberson wrote: "People have been sent to jail without a guilty plea or trial, or tossed from their homes without a proper proceeding, in violation of the law. Defendants have been refused lawyers or sentenced to weeks in jail because they cannot pay a fine. Frightened women have been denied protection from abuse."[43]

The judges who deal such injustices are seldom lawyers. There are 1,250 judges in New York alone. These judges have little education. Some are not even high school graduates. They include hairdressers, state troopers, and phone company technicians, among others. Some judges have subjected defendants to crude racial insults, others have imposed themselves sexually on female defendants, and yet others have jailed defendants illegally though they themselves are barely literate.[44]

SUMMARY

This chapter reviews the early history of the Supreme Court together with some of its most important decisions. The district courts are also described, as are backgrounds of some of the judges who function there, together with examples of the cases these judges hear. The courts of appeal are recognized as important rectifiers of injustices perpetrated by prosecutors or resulting from false eyewitness identification.

Although the juvenile court is not a criminal justice court, it does become involved in many serious criminal cases adjudicated by the same judges who hear complaints about truancy and joyriding.

Our next chapter deals with the treatment of offenders in the American criminal justice system.

NOTES

1. U.S. Constitution, Article 3, Section 1.

2. Judiciary Act of 1789, Chap. 20, Section 1.

3. Ronald L. F. Davis, *History of the Supreme Court*, 3, http://www.history ofsupremecourt.org/overview.htm.

4. "Judicial Gowns: Their Use by *Nisi Prius* (Unless before) Judges in Virginia," *Virginia Law Review* 10, no. 7 (May 1924): 565–66.

5. U.S. Constitution, Article 3, Section 2.

6. *Chisholm v. Georgia*, U.S. (2 Dall) 419 (1793).

7. Ibid.

8. *Marbury v. Madison*, 5 U.S. (1 Cranich) 137 (1803).

9. John Vishneski, "What the Court Decided in *Dred Scott v. Sandford*," *American Journal of Legal History* 32, no. 4 (1988): 373–90.

10. 410 U.S. 113 (1973).

11. 438 U.S. 265 (1978).

12. James L. Gibson, Gregory L. Caldeira, and Lester Spence, "Measuring Attitudes toward the United States Supreme Court," *Journal of Political Science* 47, no. 2 (April 2003): 355.

13. D. Brock Hornby, "The Business of the U.S. District Courts," *The Green Bag* 10, no. 4 (Summer 2007): 453–68.

14. *New York Times*, "Eugene Nickerson, Ex-Nassau Politician and Judge in Louima Trial," January 3, 2002, A20.

15. Douglas Martin, "Barefoot Sanders Dies," *New York Times*, September 24, 2008, B5.

16. Dennis Hevesi, "Charles L. Brieant, Longtime Federal Judge," *New York Times*, July 27, 2008, A24.

17. William Glaberson, "Questioning 'Dirty Bomb' Plot, Judge Orders U.S. to Yield Papers on Detainee," *New York Times*, October 31, 2008, A17.

18. Adam Liptak, "Federal Judge Files Complaint against Prosecutor in Boston," *New York Times*, July 3, 2007, A11.

19. Malcolm Gay, "U.S. Judge Upholds Water Release in Flood Area," *New York Times*, March 26, 2008, A17.

20. Gretchen Morgenson, "Judge Demands Documentation in Foreclosures," *New York Times*, November 17, 2007, C8.

21. Don Ray, "Hon. Lance A. Ito," *Daily Journal*, n.d., http://www.donray.com./LanceIto.htm.

22. Anemona Hartocolis, "This Season's Must-See Criminal Trial," *New York Times*, May 13, 2007, New York Region, 3.

23. Bruce Benidt, "Ex-state Justice, Nuremberg Judge Christianson Dies," *Star Tribune*, May 28, 1985, n.p.

24. Carey Goldberg, "Massachusetts High Court Backs Freeing Au Pair in Baby's Death," *New York Times*, June 17, 1998, A1.

25. Alex Branch, "Conviction Cleared in Death Row Case," *Star Telegram*, December 17, 2008, n.p.

26. David Hanners, "St. Paul Man Freed after 10 Years," *Twin Cities Pioneer Press*, October 2, 2007, n.p.

27. Pete Shellem, "Guest Shot: How Justice Gets Done in Spite of the Justice System," *Harrisburg Patiot News*, September 14, 2007, n.p.

28. Joseph Goldstein, "Meet the 2nd Circuit Court's New Judge," *New York Sun*, October 16, 2006, n.p.

29. Mark Hamblett, "2nd Circuit Upsets Conviction," *New York Law Journal*, September 6, 2007, n.p.

30. Lynne Bonner, "Payouts to the Wrongly Jailed Get a Big Boost," *News and Observer*, July 19, 2008.

31. Ed Meyer, "Resh Not Guilty," *Akron Beacon Journal*, April 18, 2007.

32. Cheryl Camp, "Convicted Murderer Is Freed in Wake of Tainted Evidence," *New York Times*, May 22, 2007, 16.

33. Stephanie Francis Ward, "When Honesty Is Not Best Politics," *ABA Journal*, August 2007: 18.

34. "Frank Easterbrook," University of Chicago Law School, http://www.law.uchicago.edu./faculty/easterbrook.

35. *New York Times*, "2 Bodies Found at Residence of U.S. Judge," March 1, 2005, natonal section.

36. Maurice Possley, "Always Knew I Was Innocent," *Chicago Tribune*, November 24, 2006, n.p.

37. A. M. Platt, *The Child Savers* (Chicago: University of Chicago Press, 1977), 119.

38. Bradford Kinney Peirce, *A Half Century with Juvenile Delinquents* (Montclaire, NJ: Patterson and Smith, 1969), 41.

39. Jeffrey Gettleman, "Montclair and Its Model School Try to Cope with a Rape Charge," *New York Times*, October 18, 2004, 1.

40. Sara Rimer, "Unruly Students Facing Arrest, Not Detention," *New York Times*, January 4, 2004, 1.

41. *New York Times*, "Young Sniper Is Sentenced to Six Life Terms," November 9, 2006, A28.

42. Lisa Munoz, "Black Teenagers Convicted of Beating of 3 White Women," *NewYork Times*, January 27, 2007, A14.

43. William Glaberson, "In Tiny Courts of N.Y., Abuses of Law and Power," *New York Times*, September 25, 2006, New York Region.

44. Ibid.

Chapter 8

THE PRISON-INDUSTRIAL COMPLEX

PRISONS AS A NECESSARY EVIL

L osing one's freedom is an awful condition even in a minimum security prison. Nevertheless, American society has not found any other means of protecting normal citizens from the violence perpetrated by citizens who murder, rape, assault, and rob others. It is evident, therefore, that prisons and jails are needed for the protection of all who seek to lead a peaceful existence. It is true, of course, that imprisonment does not protect against individuals who behave violently and are not incarcerated. In fact, criminologists recognize that 85 percent of those who have been convicted of a violent crime come from a violent home, so the most fruitful way of preventing violence would be to teach our citizens not to do violence to their families, and particularly to prevent children from witnessing violence or becoming the victims of violence. As long as education against violence does not succeed, we have no alternative but to imprison those who harm others and endanger innocent people among us.

Therefore, it is of the greatest importance that prisons be used only as a last resort against those who threaten our lives and well-being. Unfortunately, the people in charge of our criminal justice system cannot always be trusted to prosecute, sentence, or imprison only dangerous offenders. For too long, the prisons of the United States have been misused by some people in power to imprison sick people who are addicted to illegal substances, for example, or to incarcerate people who are innocent of any crime or those who are too poor to be defended by a competent attorney. It is not the purpose here to seek the abolition of the criminal justice system or to claim that all who commit violence against their fellows should go free. Instead, it is the intent here to show how the prison-industrial complex can be improved and the criminal justice system made more just.

THE RATE OF INCARCERATION

In 1998, Eric Schlosser, writing in *The Atlantic Monthly*, defined the prison-industrial complex as ''a set of bureaucratic, political and

economic interests that encourage increased spending on imprisonment, regardless of the actual need."[1]

The aforementioned "interests" have succeeded in bringing about
the incarceration of over 2 million Americans in jails and prisons
throughout the United States. In 2007, local jails held 780,581 prisoners,
and state and federal prisons held over 1.5 million prisoners. This
means there were about 750 prisoners in American institutions for
every 100,000 residents. This figure indeed reflects the highest rate of
imprisonment recorded for any country in the Western world. For
example, in the United Kingdom (i.e., England, Scotland, Northern
Ireland, and Wales), the imprisonment rate per 100,000 population is
340. In France, the imprisonment rate is 93; and in Germany, 98. Likewise, other European countries have imprisonment rates ranging from
352 per 100,000 population in Latvia to 37 in Iceland.[2]

The argument that the United States has far more crime than other
countries cannot account for this immense rate of imprisonment
because the U.S. violent crime rate has declined steadily for a number
of years. For example, in 1977, the American homicide rate was 7.7 per
100,000 population. In 1980, that rate had risen to 10.2 and continued
to exceed 9 per 100,000 through 1994. From then until 2007, the homicide rate declined each year, reaching a low of 5.5 in 2004 and increasing slightly to 5.9 in 2007. Similar rates of decline were recorded for
forcible rape, which decreased by 2.5 percent between 2006 and 2007;
and robbery, which decreased by 1.2 percent between 2006 and 2007
and showed a 5.5 percent decline since 2003. Aggravated assault
decreased by 1 percent between 2006 and 2007 but had decreased by
21.5 percent since 1998. Evidently, violent crime in the United States
declined mainly because the birthrate had decreased; as a result, the
proportion of young men who commit the most violent offenses was
smaller in 2007 than in earlier years.[3]

In 1910, the U.S. birthrate per 1,000 population was 30.1. This
declined to 23.7 in 1960 and further declined to 14.0 by 2005. The rate
remained there for three years thereafter.[4]

It is debatable, of course, whether nonviolent offenders should be
incarcerated. In the United States, this debate has been decidedly won
by those law enforcers who seek to imprison as many citizens as possible by criminalizing all kinds of conduct that is by no means criminal
elsewhere in the world and by increasing the length of sentences
handed individuals convicted of various crimes. It should be remembered that American prisons hold innumerable innocent people as well
as drug addicts and other ill people who fill up our jails and prisons,
all to the benefit of the prison-industrial complex and to the detriment
of tax-paying citizens.

CONSTRUCTING PRISONS

New construction of prisons is not related to a reduction in crime. It is instead related to improving the income and finances of the people who benefit from victimizing the poor, the illiterate, the ill, and the helpless. Included in the prison population are a considerable number of innocent people, a large number of individuals addicted to drugs other than alcohol, nonviolent white-collar offenders, and individuals whose conduct has been deliberately criminalized to increase the prison population.[5]

In the early 1990s, California taxpayers spent $400 million to build two towers in downtown Los Angeles. Both towers are used as jails. It takes over 800 employees to move more than 6,000 prisoners through these facilities every day. The prisoners are booked, fingerprinted, sorted, and locked into cells already crowded with other prisoners, who have been there longer. Since 1980, California has built 21 new prisons, which are the ultimate destination of most of the people locked in the local jails. This growth in the prison industry has led to a sevenfold increase in the California prison population. Prison construction costs during the years since 1980 have forced taxpayers to spend $5.3 billion. In addition, it costs the state $4.8 million a year to maintain these prisons. This is only one example from one state of the huge investment in prisons that American politicians have promoted at taxpayers' expense.[6]

The phenomenal growth in prison populations is not limited to California. Instead, we find that while the U.S. population has grown by 20 percent in the past 20 years, the prison population has doubled. Another example of the growth of prisons may be found in Oklahoma. There, five criminal justice bills passed by the legislature in 2007 cost taxpayers over $46 million. In addition, another bill costing $42 million more was passed by legislators who wanted to be reelected on the grounds that they are "tough on crime," a phrase without substance other than its effect on the electorate. As prison construction increased, the state gained 900 new inmates in one year alone. As a consequence, the Oklahoma Department of Corrections is seeking another $40 million in a supplemental appropriation.[7]

Yet another example of the considerable cost of prison construction may be found in Dallas County, Texas. There, the Dallas County Detention Center was built in 2007 at a cost of $61.7 million. That facility is a 330,000-square-foot, four-level, medium security prison holding more than 2,300 inmates. Evidently, a prison of such size needs a steady stream of prisoners to ensure that the cells are always full and politicians can claim they are protecting the public. The fact is that as such prisons are built, more and more bodies are needed to fill them. That goal is achieved by seizing on those who cannot pay for lawyers, who are innocent, or who are victims of drug abuse. The Constitution of the United States is also a victim of the incarceration craze, as the erstwhile guarantee that everyone is innocent unless proved guilty by a jury of one's peers appears forgotten or ignored, especially by the media.[8]

In Arkansas, the Department of Corrections, using prison labor, is spending $40 million to construct a 339,442-square-foot concrete addition to an existing prison; and in Louisiana, $16.4 million was spent to build a new jail in Livingston County. In Mississippi, the Adams County Prison is being expanded at a cost of $105 million, thereby employing 450 workers who would otherwise be unemployed as the economy suffers a nationwide downward trend.

Such spending on prisons, which can be found nationwide, began in 1963, when Senator Barry Goldwater of Arizona sought to improve his chances of becoming president of the United States by using the fear of crime to attract voters. Subsequently, Richard Nixon used the same tactic during his successful 1968 campaign. Then, in January 1973, the then-governor of New York, Nelson Rockefeller, demanded in his State of the State address that every illegal drug dealer be imprisoned for life without parole.[9]

In New York, the construction of prisons on a large scale began during the administration of Mario Cuomo, who was elected governor of New York in 1982. At that time, the prison population of New York had increased considerably because of the Rockefeller drug laws. Seeking reelection, Cuomo needed public approval and chose the worn-out "tough on crime" slogan to achieve this. In view of the defeat of a $500 million bond issue to build more prisons, Cuomo used the state's Urban Development Corporation to build prisons instead of housing for the poor. Cuomo spent $7 billion building prisons in upstate New York, above Watertown in the rural Adirondack district. There had been considerable unemployment in that area of New York, so the construction of 27 new prisons in "the north country" employed many people in construction work and later as prison guards. Since Cuomo was also opposed to the death penalty, he sought to ward off criticism that he was "soft on crime" by increasing the prison population in his state.[10]

The cost of incarceration in 2008 was indeed phenomenal. On the average, it costs about $29,000 a year to house one prisoner in a double-bunk-bed cell in a minimum security prison. The cost rises to $61,000 for a double-bunk bed in a medium security prison and becomes $110,512 a year to house one person in a maximum security prison. It is understood, of course, that costs vary from state to state and from prison to prison. Nevertheless, these expenditures are the outcome of politics in that legislators, whether county, state, or federal, want to be reelected by shouting the "tough on crime" slogan, no matter what it costs the taxpayer. Few voters think about these costs. Those who vote, and they are always a small minority of those eligible to vote, make their decision on the basis of the emotion of the moment. The majority of eligible citizens do not vote in state and local elections and therefore have no influence on the spending habits of incumbents.

In October 2007, Senator Jim Webb of Virginia held a Joint Economic Committee hearing entitled "Mass Incarceration in the United States: At What Cost?" That hearing revealed that the United States spent $49 billion on prisons in 2006 compared to $17 billion in 1987. Whereas the world average rate of imprisonment is 166 per 100,000, the U.S. average imprisonment rate (750) even exceeds that of Russia, which imprisons 628 residents per 100,000. The U.S. imprisonment rate is so high despite the constant decrease in the American crime rate since 1990. Evidently, the increase in incarceration is not the result of increases in the crime rate but results from changes in penal policy. Two such changes have brought about the mass imprisonment of Americans. One of the changes has been the criminalization of conduct heretofore not recognized as criminal. The other change is motivated by profit, which the incarceration of over 2 million citizens provides for numerous politicians and greedy business establishments.

Among those who profit from the misery of the semi-slaves locked into our prisons are construction companies and the politicians who receive financial support from them at the next election. Then there is the telephone company, the suppliers of goods and services, private prison corporations, and numerous residents of small towns whose employment depends on the prison industry. Often, the town's citizens are members of the powerful prison guards' unions, whose votes are needed by politicians at their next reelection effort. All those interests militate against the reduction of U.S. prison population even as the money spent prevents the funding of such vital needs as the education of children and young adults, the support of the homeless, and the feeding of the poor.

THE WAR ON DRUGS

Alcohol is a drug. Therefore, the prohibition of the use of alcohol in the United States, which went into effect in 1920 and ended in 1933, constituted a war on drugs. It is common knowledge, of course, that Prohibition failed because Americans wanted to use alcohol and did so despite the law. In fact, laws that are contrary to the mores of American society cannot succeed because they do not gain support from the public. Law is but one form of custom. Other customs, or social laws, are folkways, defined as such conduct as shaking hands on greeting someone or eating ham and eggs for breakfast. Mores involve social conduct supported by popular opinion but not enforced by legal means; keeping oneself clean, using polite language, respecting one's elders, or attending religious exercises are all mores. Laws are statutes that either order that something be done—paying taxes, for example—or prohibit such an action as stealing or using drugs.

When Prohibition was repealed by the Twenty-first Amendment in 1933, numerous law enforcement agents and prison operators were threatened with losing their jobs and their careers. Therefore, it became vitally important to the people who benefited from the imprisonment of alcohol suppliers and users to continue by other means some form of prohibition, though not of alcohol. Those other means were the introduction of laws prohibiting the use of drugs other than alcohol.

It had become evident by 1930 that alcohol would shortly be reintroduced as a legal substance because its suppression had visibly failed by then. As a consequence, there began in 1930 a campaign against the use of marijuana. This drug, also known as cannabis, became the target of people who viewed it as especially dangerous because of its association with Mexicans (the term "marijuana" is Mexican for "Mary Jane"). That this bigotry is a principal reason for the campaign against marijuana is best illustrated by taking a look at the leading annual causes of death in the United States. The data reveal that in the years 2000, 2001, 2002, 2003, and 2004, more people died from tobacco-related diseases than any other category of death-inducing conditions. Tobacco killed about 435,000 Americans in each of those years, yet tobacco has not been prohibited. Alcohol-related deaths amounted to about 85,000 each year, and prescription drugs killed 32,000 people legally each year. Yet, by contrast, all illicit drug uses were responsible together for 17,000 deaths in each of the years from 2000 through 2004.[11]

It was also found by researchers that marijuana alone has never caused even one death, although marijuana in combination with other drugs, notably alcohol, has killed some users.[12]

The foregoing findings demonstrate that the laws prohibiting some drugs other than alcohol were not derived from scientific analysis regarding the danger of their use but are the products of political decisions based on the interests of those who have a financial stake in having these laws enforced.

Harry J. Anslinger, the son of Swiss immigrants, became the first commissioner of the Federal Bureau of Narcotics in 1930. It was Anslinger and William Randolph Hearst, the newspaper magnate, who incited American politicians against marijana and other drugs and brought about the continuation of prohibition practices after the repeal of Prohibition in 1933. Anslinger recognized that his career depended on the suppression of the use of alcohol and that he needed to promote the war on drugs by targeting other substances to maintain his income and his power. In this war, he was helped by the Hearst chain of newspapers, which were, before the advent of television, widely read. A highly sensational antimarijuana campaign by all the Hearst-owned newspapers began in 1930.[13]

In 1914, Congress had passed the Harrison Act, which demanded that physicians who prescribed marijuana and other drugs be licensed to do so. It did not prohibit the use of these drugs. However, law enforcers interpreted the Harrison Act in such a fashion as to give them authority to imprison physicians who prescribed marijuana and other drugs. So, the members of the medical profession relinquished their right to do so and left drug distribution to organized crime instead. In short, it can be justifiably said that law enforcement is more responsible for the widespread importation of illegal drugs from South America and Asia than is any other factor in its dissemination and use.[14]

In the 1950s and continuing into the 1960s, the Harrison law was amended by Congress to increase the penalties for possession of illicit drugs even as many states also increased such penalties. Federal prisoners were deprived of parole, so anyone convicted in a federal court had to serve the entire sentence, up to 20 years or more. Such sentencing compares poorly with murder convictions, which usually lead to a sentence of 11 years in prison but normally allow the convicted killer to leave prison after 8 years because of eligibility for parole in state institutions.[15]

The ever-harsher laws did nothing to reduce the number of drug users in the country. They did, however, increase the number of prisoners. That situation was particularly true of the federal prisons, which increased their prison population from 145,416 in 2000 to 199,618 at the end of 2007. During these same years, the states increased their prison population from some 1.2 million to almost 1.4 million. At the end of 2007 American jails held 780,581 prisoners, so that over 2.3 million Americans were locked up at that time. The latter figure equals the entire population of Houston, Texas, or the population of Nevada. During the seven years 2000 to 2007, the U.S. population increased by 6.4 percent while the incarceration rate increased 15 percent.[16]

Such figures demonstrate that imprisonment in the United States is related not only to the commission of crimes but also to the monetary and psychic income derived from the policies of prison employees and the numerous businesses that earn large sums at the expense of those who remain in jails and prisons without posing any threat to anyone. Included in the prison population are the 600,000 citizens and residents of the United States whose sole crime is the possession of illegal drugs. Those convicts are people who are ill because of their addictions, who need help; indeed, they are not only the victims of their addiction but are victimized a second time by the so-called system of criminal justice.

The war on drugs affects women a good deal more than men. In fact, researchers have shown that the war on drugs is a war on women. The Bureau of Justice Statistics (BJS) has shown that in 2004 there were 28,487 federal prisoners charged with drug offenses. Only about 12.4 percent of these prisoners were female. The BJS also reported that in 2004 one-half of state prisoners had been using alcohol or other drugs. About 6 in 10 female prisoners described themselves as drug users during the month before their arrest. In 1986, only 1 female prisoner in 8 was jailed for drug possession. The Bureau of Prisons reported, in 2006 and 2007, that 80 percent of female prisoners are incarcerated for drug-related offenses. One-third of the increase in male imprisonment since 1986 has been drug related. One-half of the increase in female imprisonment has also been drug related.[17]

It is an axiom of sociological insight that the vast majority of men and women who serve as the raw material for the prison-industrial complex are those individuals whom no one wants and who have no place in conventional society. This axiom is even more true for women than for men. Women who end up in prison are generally the product of battering by significant others, be they husbands or boyfriends; substance abuse from alcohol to cocaine; economic disadvantage; and unsupported parenting. The failure to help women subject to such difficulties has led to incarceration as the standard technique for dealing with all those handicaps.[18]

The facts concerning women in prison may be gleaned from BJS publications. Accordingly, at the end of 2007, the number of women in prison, 114,420, represented an increase since 1980 at double the rate of increase for men. In December 2007, there were almost 1.5 million men in prison and more were in jail. The number of women in prison increased eightfold since 1980, although there was no increase in women's criminality in those years.

Thirty percent of women in prison are of African descent, and 16 percent are Latinas of both races. Women are much more likely to be imprisoned for a drug offense than are men (29 percent to 19 percent) or a property offense (30 percent to 20 percent) and less likely to be incarcerated for a violent offense than are men (35 percent to 53 percent). The women generally committed violent offenses against men who had assaulted them. Three-quarters of women imprisoned for any offense had used drugs shortly before their arrest. Two-thirds of women in prison were mothers of minor children, and 37 percent of women in prison had an income of less than $600 a month. One-fourth of women in prison had a history of mental illness. Many women in prison tested positive for HIV—18 percent in New York and 41 percent in the District of Columbia. More than half of women in prison had been sexually or physically abused.[19]

In view of the lesser risk women pose to the public than do men, it is incongruous to apply male characteristics to women offenders. Because women are a small minority among prisoners, their needs have generally been invisible in the same sense as minorities are almost always invisible, even in history books.

The differences between men and women are not limited to sex. In fact, it is the social interpretation of sex differences, called "gender," that determines the treatment of women everywhere, including in prison. The evidence is that the belief that women should be treated equally with men has led to an increase in female imprisonment greater than ever in U.S. history. It has also led to more brutality inflicted on women prisoners, even as the war on drugs has given sadists an opportunity to vent their hatred of humanity on helpless prisoners.

The prime example of sadistic cruelty inflicted on even minor offenders in our jails and prisons is the treatment of prisoners in Maricopa County, Arizona. There, Sheriff Joe Apaio has reduced food to two meals a day. The food is so disgusting that green bologna is standard fare. The meals cost only 40 cents a day and literally resemble the food given concentration camp prisoners during the Nazi era. The jailed prisoners are housed in outdoor tents in heat exceeding 120 degrees and sleep on cots without pillows. In addition, all prisoners must wear pink underwear. Apaio also operates chain gangs, including female chain gangs.[20]

Apaio's practices, which serve only to satisfy the sadism of an out-of-control sheriff, unnecessarily increase the number of American prisoners and do so at taxpayers' expense. Moreover, the imprisonment of people ill from the use of drugs in no way increases the safety of the public, as almost all ex-prisoners who return to the world outside prisons resume their drug habits.

PRISON GUARDS

The growth of America's prisons is evidently not related to an increase in criminal behavior in this country. Instead, it is related to the attraction the prison industry holds for those who see their financial advantage in the prison system and who also enjoy the power that domination over others permits them.

Prison guards, unionized and politically influential, are a major force in the growth of the American prison industry. Prison guard unions have grown immensely since 1980, when the membership was no more than abut 2,000 guards. Since then, the prison guard union in California alone has reached 25,000. American prison guards earn an average salary of $36,000 a year, which is 34 percent below the median American income of $48,000 in 2007. According to the Bureau of Labor Statistics, there were about 500,000 "correctional officers" working in the United States in 2007. Of those, 18,000 were federal employees; the others worked for state and county governments. Because of the constantly rising rates of incarceration, the Bureau of Labor Statistics estimates a growth for this occupation of 16 percent between 2007 and 2014. Of course, the downturn in the American economy as of 2009 may make such growth impossible, for economics has frequently determined results quite different from those expected.[21]

In view of the large membership in the prison guards unions, the unions have considerable clout at election time. Because the relatives and friends of guards are also voters, state legislators can seldom risk antagonizing the prison guard unions if they seek reelection. Such election concerns are particularly true in California, where prison guard unions have been a major force in the growth of the prison industry. The California Correctional Peace Officers Association funnels money to politicians to ensure a "lock 'em up" policy in the state. The growth in political clout is best illustrated by the growth of the prison guard union, which collects about $15 million in union dues each year, leading to contributions to gubernatorial candidates of at least $1.5 million. The union also finances a so-called Crime Victims Political Action Committee, which in turn supplies political candidates in California with money toward their campaigns. Prison guard unions also demand laws that lead to mandatory life sentences as well as longer sentences for all offenders. While California is one example of the influence of prison guard unions, these tactics are used in every state. Lawmakers who want to keep their jobs know that it is dangerous to oppose union demands. Therefore, prison guard unions are yet one more factor contributing to the huge incarceration rate experienced in the United States.

INCARCERATING THE INNOCENT

An accurate number of innocent people spending time in American jails and prisons is not available. Nevertheless, one can calculate the approximate number of innocent Americans in prison. Considering that the Bureau of Justice Statistics reports that over 2.2 million people, or more specifically, 2,236,871 convicts, are in our jails and prisons, it is evident that if only 0.5 percent of the prisoners are innocent, then 11,184 innocent people would be so victimized. If 1 percent of all prisoners are innocent, then the criminal justice system will have victimized 22,237 citizens; and if 2 percent of prisoners are innocent, then our (in)justice system is destroying the lives of 44,474 people. Given the large number of exonerations resulting from DNA testing, it is highly likely that at least 10 percent of incarcerated individuals are innocent, as estimated by the Rev. James McCloskey, the founder of Centurion Ministries, an organization devoted to freeing the innocent from American prisons. Therefore, there are about 224,000 innocent people in American prisons as of 2009.

Nevertheless, the administrators of our system of criminal justice resist all efforts to right wrongful incarcerations. The reason for this is the failure of the U.S. Department of Justice to make any effort to discover the presence of innocent people in American jails and prisons and the concomitant effort by police, prosecutors, judges, and prison officials to hide from the public the conviction and imprisonment of innocent people.

Of the seven most common causes of wrongful convictions in the United States, eyewitness misidentification ranks first. Eyewitness accounts are such an unreliable method of identifying an offender that as an examination of exonerations in the United States and Canada revealed, 76 percent of wrongful convictions were based on so-called eyewitness testimony. The Northwest University Law Center also found that in 70 cases in which 84 men and two women had been sentenced to death based on eyewitness testimony, all were later legally exonerated. In another examination of 74 DNA cases of wrongful convictions, eyewitness mistakes provided 81 percent of the errors.[22]

In addition to eyewitness identification, unreliable "science" and forensic science fraud, false confessions, prosecutorial misconduct, informants or "snitches," and poor lawyers lead to numerous false convictions.

Forensic science, which was widely used before DNA testing became available, can be manipulated by scientists who seek to please the police departments employing them. One of the worst examples of the fraud committed by forensic scientists involved Joyce Gilchrist, who for years testified at trials in the courts of Oklahoma City, claiming that she had made scientific tests that proved the guilt of those accused of murder, rape, and other crimes of violence. Between 1980 and 2001, Gilchrist had testified in thousands of cases, including 23 in which defendants were sentenced to death. Eleven of those sent to death row were executed on the basis of Gilchrist's scientific evidence. In 2001, she was dismissed from her job after the FBI found that she had deliberately withheld evidence from the defense, claimed to have achieved scientific results that no other scientist had ever achieved, and failed to perform tests that might have cleared the accused.

Gilchrist's fraud was discovered after DNA testing proved that she had sent Jeffrey Pierce to prison for 65 years for a rape that Pierce had nothing to do with. Then, it was found that Robert Lee Miller was innocent of a murder attributed to him by Gilchrist's science while the same Gilchrist had cleared the real killer. Gilchrist had been suspected of fraud for years, but the attorneys who accused her were ignored by the judges and the prosecutors and even the forensic scientists to whom the complaints were made. It has been estimated that many prisoners who confessed to crimes they did not commit did so in order to lessen sentences they would otherwise have received by reason of Gilchrist's manipulations.[23]

In West Virginia, Fred Zane, a police forensic specialist, falsified DNA tests that he had never carried out. His false report led to the conviction of Glen Dale Woodall, who was convicted of two abduction rapes although he had nothing to do with the crimes. His lawyers succeeded in having the DNA test done over again by another laboratory; the test results showed that Woodall could not have committed these rapes. This led to the investigation of Zane's work, with the result that in 133 cases Zane had either never carried out any lab work or reported inconclusive results as certain results.[24]

In January 2001, a lawsuit against the city of Chicago included a report revealing that a supervisor at the Illinois State Police crime lab had given false testimony in nine cases, including trials that resulted in wrongful rape convictions of three Chicago men. The supervisor of the crime lab, Pamela Fish, deliberately withheld evidence that would have served to establish the innocence of John Willis, falsely accused of numerous rapes. Willis was sentenced to 100 years in prison and labeled "the beauty shop rapist" by the media, always in a hurry to convict innocent people. When DNA tests proved seven years later that not Willis but another man had committed the rapes, Willis was paid $2.6 million in compensation and Fish was fired. Consequent examination of the Illinois crime lab work revealed widespread fraud promoted by that laboratory. The scientists who worked there regarded themselves as members of the prosecution and were eager to please the police and the district attorneys who employed them. Such bias is found in almost all states, since crime labs are usually not independent of the prosecutors. In fact, 90 percent of crime labs in the United States are affiliated with law enforcement agencies and therefore report whatever prosecutors want to hear. Governor Ryan suspended the death penalty in Illinois after it was revealed that 13 of the 24 men on death row were innocent, as proved by DNA test results.[25]

Dr. Ralph Erdmann worked as a medical examiner in more than 40 rural counties in Texas from the early 1980s until September 1992, when he pleaded "no contest" to seven felony counts of falsifying autopsies in three Texas counties. He was sentenced to 10 years' probation and had to return $17,000 he received for examinations never performed. Erdmann repeatedly falsified toxicology reports to please prosecutors who sanctioned his deceit so they could win their cases, resulting in imprisonment and the death penalty for innocent people. Erdmann also testified falsely to release criminals who were friends of district attorneys.[26]

In 1993, Willie Simpson was charged with the murder of Phillip Mancini, a Vineland, New Jersey, high school teacher. Dr. Larry Mapow, the medical examiner in Cumberland County, New Jersey, concluded that Mancini had been killed by several blows to the head with a blunt instrument. When the Mancini family asked another pathologist to conduct another autopsy, the pathologist, Dr. Claus Speth, discovered that Mancini had died from two bullets and not from blows to the head. In another New Jersey case, Willie Simpson was charged with the murder of Robert Webb. The medical examiner claimed that Simpson had killed Webb with a gunshot to the head. Yet, Dr. Michael Baden, the foremost medical examiner in the country, concluded that Webb was killed by a brick and not a gunshot. Baden concluded that "there is not a shred of evidence that Webb was killed by means of a gun." It then turned out that another man, not Simpson, had killed Webb.[27]

Perhaps one of the most atrocious miscarriages of justice was inflicted on Barry Beach, a resident of Poplar, Montana. Beach was sentenced to 100 years in prison when a jury convicted him in 1984 of killing 17-year-old Kimberly Nees in 1979. That conviction was obtained by a prosecutor in the attorney general's office, Marc Racicot, who was guilty of "prosecutorial misconduct," a phrase meaning that he deliberately railroaded Beach into prison. Racicot later became governor of Montana.

The evidence is that Beach had nothing to do with the murder of Nees but that she was killed by a group of girls who had together murdered Nees and left their footprints and fingerprints all over the car in which they transported the dead body to a nearby river. In fact, the girls who murdered Nees confessed having done so to a number of Poplar residents. Still, the police and prosecutors did not want to hear that. Instead, Beach was tortured into confessing to the crime. Only 17 at that time, he wanted to escape his tormentors and did so by falsely confessing to whatever the police told him. Seeking to protect their own reputations and careers, the prosecutor, police, parole board, and other politicians implicated in this monstrous injustice have consistently refused to free Beach or investigate the real killers, who still live in Poplar, secure in the knowledge that politicians will protect them from the consequences of the murder they committed.[28]

Unreliable eyewitnesses, fraudulent science, malicious prosecutors, and poor lawyers are thus mainly responsible for numerous false imprisonments in the United States. Added to the preceding list, however, are victims' rights spectators, more recently allowed in the court room. The spectators generally display buttons, T-shirts, and other paraphernalia intended to influence the jury to convict those accused of a crime. Such demonstrations erode the right of any defendant to a fair and impartial trial as guaranteed by the Sixth Amendment, since jurors are, of course, influenced by the demonstrations by relatives and friends of the victim. While a victim's rights should be recognized, it is obvious that courts need to ban spectators' demonstrations, which as such contravene the fundamental right of any defendant to a fair and impartial jury.

As of June 2008, 217 people of those wrongfully convicted have been exonerated by means of DNA tests. For every person freed through DNA evidence and by other means, there are thousands who are innocent of any crime but are nevertheless in prison, even on death row, or who have been wrongfully executed by the state and its agents. It was for those reasons that New Jersey abolished the death penalty in December 2007.[29]

Well before Barry Scheck and Peter Neufeld founded the Innocence Project in 2000 at the Benjamin Cardozo Yeshiva University School of Law came an earlier effort to free innocent people from prison and death row. That effort began in 1978, when the Rev. Jim McCloskey devoted his life to rescuing innocent people from the horrors of the American criminal justice system. Since 1983, when McCloskey first succeeded in freeing an innocent man from prison, his organization, called the Centurion Project, has freed 43 inmates. Because McCloskey began his work before DNA testing became available, he and his associates use other means to free the innocent. The Centurion group studies old documents concerning cases of people they believe to be innocent. They also interview witnesses and talk to people the police never dealt with because the police feared that those people would contradict their theories. McCloskey says that it takes five years to investigate a case and another five years to free the innocent. The reason for the decade-long effort is that it takes so long to find evidence in favor of the innocently convicted because prosecutors and judges will do anything to avoid being proved wrong. The cost of investigating such cases ranges from $150,000 to $300,000, which must be borne by the Centurion Project, since the wrongfully imprisoned have no money.[30]

In sum, we find that 600,000 American prisoners are incarcerated unnecessarily because they are ill through drug addiction. In addition, there are 224,000 innocent prisoners in our penal facilities. So, taxpayers could easily be relieved of nearly half the cost of imprisonment were it not for the graft of politicians, the cruelty of prosecutors, and the greed of building contractors and those who run private prisons at taxpayer expense.

THE PRIVATE PRISON BUSINESS

A private prison is one managed by a nongovernment agency on behalf of the state. It is also defined as "a place of confinement managed by a private company under contract to the government."[31] Thus, the private prison business is derived from public law and resembles the leasing of prison labor, which was practiced widely in the United States in the early nineteenth century. With the ending of those practices, it became the norm that states ran all the prisons except those of the federal government. The practice continued until the 1970s, when private prison companies first organized.[32]

Two large companies dominate the private prison business in the United States. Corrections Corporation of America (CCA) and Wackenhut Corrections Corporation profit the most from the imprisonment of Americans. In fact, CCA forms the sixth-largest correctional system in the United States, exceeded only by California, Texas, Florida, New York, and the Federal Bureau of Prisons.[33]

After the 1970s, both companies expanded quickly. By 1989, they were managing 44 prisons and jails holding 15,000 prisoners. By 1996, 118 prisons were privately owned; these prisons held 78,000 prisoners in 25 states. In November 1999, 162 private prisons and jails held 125,000 prisoners, and now over 360,000 prisoners are held by private prison companies, which lobby state legislators to pass more and more "get tough" laws so as to hold prisoners longer and therby increase the companies' profits. For example, CCA stock rose from $8 a share in 1992 to about $30 a share at the beginning of the twenty-first century, and investors in the Wackenhut prison business have enjoyed an 18 percent increase in profits since 1995—all this, while the crime rate has declined precipitously. Of course, former state and federal prison executives retire early and are then appointed to lucrative jobs in the private prison business even as the corporations make considerable contributions to the election of politicians who are influential in passing laws that criminalize more and more common behavior and send more and more of the poor to prison.[34]

CHILDREN IN PRISON

Although the juvenile court was first established in Cook County, Illinois (Chicago), in 1900, there are today thousands of children 13 years of age and younger who are imprisoned in state adult prisons for life. Thus, young children are virtually condemned to death in prison by the 19 states that follow such practices.[35] Among those states are Alabama, Arizona, Arkansas, California, Colorado, Delaware, Florida, Illinois, Iowa, Michigan, Mississippi, Missouri, Nebraska, North Carolina, Pennsylvania, South Dakota, Tennessee, Washington, and Wisconsin.[36]

Connecticut leads the nation in the number of children condemned to die in prison. Nationwide, there were 2,266 children in adult prisons in 2007, of whom 2,225 were serving life sentences without the possibility of parole. Prisons are physically unsafe even for adults. For children, prisons are even more dangerous. The evidence is that children in adult prisons are twice as likely as adults to be beaten by staff. Children are also much more often attacked with a weapon than is true of adults. Children in prison are often subject to male rape and other prison violence. Such children have no opportunity to go to school, so they are precluded from gaining employment beyond minimum-wage jobs should they ever be released. Such youths, even if ever released, will have spent a good deal of time with adult career criminals. Furthermore, children in adult prisons are given the same diet as the adults incarcerated there and are therefore deprived of milk, fruit, and other dietary supplements available to children in children's institutions.[37]

In Florida, for example, children as young as 9 are imprisoned in adult prisons, although the majority of such imprisoned children are between the ages of 14 and 17. The Florida legislature has passed laws allowing the massive prosecution of children in adult courts. More than 7,000 children are so prosecuted in Florida each year. The laws are called "tough love" laws, although the word "hate" might be more appropriate.[38]

One argument for sending children to adult prisons is the view that the juvenile court system has failed. The fact is that the evils of locking children in prison with adults led to the invention of the juvenile court in the first place when Chicago became the seat of the Cook County, Illinois, Juvenile Court. That court was a unique American development brought about when Lucy Flowers, Jane Addams, and Julia Lathrop pushed state lawmakers to create a separate system of justice for children. By 1925, 46 states had created separate juvenile courts.[39]

Theoretically, the juvenile court is engaged in determining the needs of the child rather than seeking to determine guilt and punishment as called for in adult courts. The original idea in creating the juvenile court was to provide guidance and rehabilitation for the child as well as protection of society from predators. It was understood, when the juvenile courts were first organized, that the brutal consequences of treating children as adult prisoners would only increase adult criminality because almost all who were then in prison would be released at some time. Adult prison experiences led child prisoners to be more vulnerable on release than they had been before imprisonment, particularly because they met adult criminals who would befriend them when released alone into a hostile world.[40]

Florida has incarcerated so many children as adults that the state is an excellent example of the effects of sending children to adult prisons. *The New York Times* carried an article in 2000 concerning the experience of Jessica Robinson.

> When Jessica Robinson was 13, she took part in a crime that Judge Barbara Levinson called "horrible," "vile," and one of the most "deeply saddening" cases she had ever heard in her courtroom. On July 18, 1997, animated by a vague plan to go to Disney World with their spoils, Jessica and two older teenagers robbed their grandparents in their Miami home. . . .
>
> Though Jessica had not actually wielded the knife or herded the victims onto the porch, she was charged with assault and armed kidnapping as well as armed robbery and sentenced to nine years in an adult prison.[41]

Likewise:

> Tiffany Landoo who . . . had never committed a crime, was convicted of felony murder [for] being with a man and another teenager who murdered a Palm Beach businessman. Lindoo, then 14, went to a motel with her new boyfriend, Lewis Crocker, 17, and another couple, Shannon Wofford, 16, and Mike Yates, 22. Palm Beach County businessman Ed Strother, then 45, met the girls outside the motel and made plans to take them out later that night.

When he returned and entered their room, Yates and Crocker beat him to death with a bat and the butt of a gun.[42]

Instead of running out and reporting the murder to the police, Lindoo went with the others to the dead man's house and helped rob it. She got 14 years for second-degree murder.

There are hundreds of cases like those of Jessica Robinson and Tiffany Lindoo, who participated in crimes committed by adults or adolescents older than they were and who, by association, were themselves then charged as adults. These children are obviously the product of neglect and the dupes of older criminals who lead them into situations they never understood or planned or anticipated. In fact, such children are twice victimized: first by the adult criminals who associate with them and then by the so-called criminal justice system, which by imprisoning them hurts them further, for they will be released from adult prisons with so much damage that their recidivism is practically assured. In fact, a detailed study of the recidivism rate of children sent to adult prisons as compared with children held in juvenile facilities shows decisively that those held in adult prisons commit more crimes later and are more likely to commit felonies than those held in juvenile facilities.[43]

Children in adult prisons are eight times more likely to commit suicide than is true of children in juvenile reformatories. In Ohio, 30 percent of children in adult prisons have attempted suicide, particularly because children in adult prisons are easily sent to "segregation"—also called "the box"—on the grounds of being disciplinary problems.[44]

It needs to be remembered that those children adjudicated by an adult court have lifelong felony convictions on their records. Unlike children adjudicated in a juvenile court, whose record is sealed, convicted children are also deprived of an education available in children's institutions but absent in adult prisons. Such young adults, released in their early twenties without job opportunities, money, or home, are thus literally programmed to be the next generation of adults in prisons, mental institutions, or hospitals. They become the 6 percent of Americans who participate in lifelong dependency on public institutions and services and then have children who follow in their footsteps as generation after generation continues in that pattern.

Most of the children who have been sentenced to die in prison at 13 or 14 come from violent and disorganized homes. They have usually been physically and sexually abused by parents who may be prostitutes, drug addicts, alcoholics, or drug dealers. Generally, such children have grown up in extremely poor and violent areas where health and safety were absent from everyday life. In fact, the U.S. Department of Health and Human Services reports that, in 2007, approximately 900,000 children in 50 states were victims of abuse and neglect. The report breaks down the condition of such children into 60 percent who are the victims of neglect, 15 percent who are physically abused, and 10 percent who are sexually abused; the rest are emotionally abused. The report further recognizes that 80 percent of the perpetrators of child abuse are parents; 7 percent, other relatives; and 13 percent, such nonrelatives as foster parents and employees of institutions.[45]

It is evident that children are not adults and that a return to the nineteenth-century treatment of children can only make the United States less safe, increase the rate of mental illness, increase unemployment and homelessness, and promote every social ill that prisons cannot cure.

SUMMARY

Although prisons may be a necessary evil, prisons should not be misused by those entrusted with the administration of the American criminal justice system. Nevertheless, the evidence is that the United States has an excessive rate of imprisonment, not because of an excessive amount of crime, but because numerous individuals and agencies profit from the unnecessary incarceration rate at the expense of the taxpayer. Huge amounts of money have been spent on unneeded prison construction in order to imprison ill drug users, innocent men, women, and children. This state of affairs is mainly the result of the greed of businesses that profit from the prison industry as well as of the activities of prison guards' unions, corrupt police, and prosecutors whose election to office is more important to them than the incarceration of the innocent and of children.

NOTES

1. Eric Schlosser, "The Prison Industrial Complex," *Atlantic Monthly*, December 1998, 51–77.

2. U.S Department of Justice, Bureau of Justice Statistics, *Prison Statistics* (Washington, DC: GPO, 2008).

3. U.S Department of Justice, FBI, *Uniform Crime Reports* (Washington, DC: GPO, 2007).

4. U.S. Public Health Service, *Vital Statistics of the United States* and *Statistical Abstract of the United States, 1900–2007* (Washington, DC: GPO, 2008).

5. *Philadelphia Inquirer*, editorial, "Prison Reform Always Misses the Point," February 5, 2007, B02.

6. Vince Beiser, "How We Got to Two Million: How Did the Land of the Free Become the World's Leading Jailer?" *Mother Jones,* July 10, 2001, 1.

7. Barbara Hoberock, "New Bills Require Fresh Look at the System," *Tulsa World,* July 22, 2007, A20.

8. Staff, "Dallas County Detention Center South Tower Cost: $61.7," *Texas Construction* 15, no. 6 (June 2007): 47.

9. Ian Fisher, "Stiff Sentences and Crowded Prisons," *New York Times,* January 30, 1995, Metropolitan Desk.

10. David Remnick, "One Sure Thing," *New Yorker,* November 21, 1994, 49.

11. Ali H. Mokdad, James S. Mrks, Donna F. Stroup, and Julie L. Gerberding, "Actual Causes of Death in the United States," *Journal of the American Medical Association* 291, no. 4 (March 10, 2004): 1238–41.

12. U.S. Department of Justice, Drug Enforcement Administration, "In the Matter of Marijuana Rescheduling Petition," Docket 86–22 (September 6, 1988): 57.

13. James A. Inciardi, *The War on Drugs: Heroin, Cocaine, Crime and Public Policy* (Palo Alto, CA: Mayfield, 1986), 231.

14. "Mental Secquaelae of the Harrison Law," *New York Medical Journal* 102 (March 15, 1915): 1014.

15. Gilman C. Udell, *Opium and Narcotics Laws* (Washington, DC: GPO, 1968), ii–iv.

16. U.S. Department of Justice, Bureau of Justice Statistics, "Prisoners in 2007," by Heather C. West and William J. Sabol, *Bureau of Justice Statistics Bulletin,* December 2008, 1.

17. Barbara Bloom and Meda Chesney-Lind, "Women in Prison: Vengeful Equity," in *It's a Crime: Women and Criminal Justice,* ed. Roslyn Moraskin, 2nd ed. (Upper Saddle River, NJ: Prentice Hall, 2000), 183.

18. Barbara Owen, *In the Mix: Struggle and Survival in Women's Prison* (Albany, NY: SUNY Press, 1998).

19. U.S. Department of Justice, Bureau of Justice Statistics, *Prison Statistics* (Washington, DC: GPO, December 31, 2007): 1.

20. Sue Anne Pressley, "Sheriff's Specialty: Making Jail Miserable," *Washington Post,* August 25, 1997, A1.

21. U.S. Department of Labor, Bureau of Labor Statistics, *Occupational Outlook Handbook, 2008–2009* (Washington, DC: GPO, 2009), n.p.

22. Samule R. Gross, "Lost Lives: Miscarriage of Justice in Capital Cases," *Law and Contemporary Problems* 61 (Autumn 1999): 125.

23. Belinda Luscombe, Wendy Cole, Maggie Sieger, and Amanda Bower, "When the Evidence Lies," *Time Canada* 57, no. 20 (May 21, 2001): 26–28.

24. Alicia Montgomery, "Angels of Justice," *Salon,* March 17, 2000, 1.

25. Steve Mills, Flynn McRoberts, and Maurice Possley, "When Labs Falter, Defendants Pay," *Chicago Tribune,* October 20, 2004, 1.

26. Roberto Surro, "Ripples of a Pathologist's Misconduct in Graves and Courts of West Texas," *New York Times,* November 22, 1992, 22.

27. Jon Nordheimer, In New Jersey, Slip-ups Show Autopsy Deficiencies," *New York Times,* October 20, 1993, A1.

28. Danile J. Gengler, "The Story of Barry Beach's Innocence," *Helena (Montana) Independence Record,* January 23, 2008, 1.

29. Elizabeth Sierra, "The Newest Spectator Sport: Why Extending Victim's Rights to the Spectators' Gallery Erodes the Presumption of Innocence," *Duke Law Journal* 58, no. 2 (November 2008): 275.

30. Sarah Golin, "McCloskey Labors to Exonerate Innocent Prisoners," *New Jersey Star-Ledger*, October 2, 2008, 1.

31. Charles Logan, "Well Kept: Company Quality of Confinement in Private and Public Prisons," *Journal of Criminal Law and Criminology* 83, no. 3 (1992): 577.

32. D. C. McDonald, "Private Penal Institutions," In *Crime and Justice: An Annual Review of Research*, ed. Michael Tonty, vol. 16 (Chicago: University of Chicago Press, 1992), 370.

33. Prison Reform Trust, *Prison Privatization Report International* (London: Prison Reform Trust, 2007).

34. Ken Silverstein, "US: America's Private Gulag," *CorpWatch*, June 1, 2000, 1.

35. Mara Dodge, "A Mood of Defeat and Dejection Prevails: One Hundred Years of Reform at the Cook County Juvenile Court," *Children's Legal Rights Journal* 19 (1999): 34.

36. Brian Stevenson, "Cruel and Unusual: Sentencing 13 and 14 Year Old Children to Die in Prison," Equal Justice Initiative, Montgomery, AL, 2008, available at http://eji.org/eji/files/20071017cruelandunusual.pdf.

37. Martin Forst, Jeffrey Fagan, and T. Scott Vivona, "Youths in Prisons and Training Schools: Perceptions and Consequences of the Treatment-Custody Dichotomy," *Juvenile and Family Court Journal* 39 (1989): 1.

38. Lisa Rodriguez, "Juvenile Legislation: Where's the 'Love' in 'Tough Love'?" *Florida Bar Public Interest Journal*, July 2006, 11.

39. Vincent Schiraldi and Steven Drizin, "100 Years of the Children's Court," *Corrections Today*, December 1999, 24.

40. Rod Smith, "Toward a More Utilitarian Juvenile Court System," *Florida Journal of Law and Public Policy* 237 (1999): 245.

41. Margaret Talbot, "The Maximum Security Adolescent," *New York Times Magazine*, September 10, 2000, 46.

42. Meg Laughlin, "Years in Prison for Adults Keep a Child Frozen in Time," *Miami Herald*, October 1, 2000, 31.

43. Donna M. Bishop, "Juvenile Justice under Attack: An Analysis of the Causes and Impact of Recent Reforms," *Florida Journal of Law and Public Policy* 129 (1998): 145–46.

44. Talbot, "The Maximum Security Adolescent," 46.

45. U.S. Department of Health and Human Services, Administration on Children, Youth and Families, "Child Maltreatment" (Washington, DC: GPO, 2007).

Chapter 9

PROBATION AND PAROLE

THE HISTORY OF PROBATION

Probation began in the United States when, in 1841, a Boston shoemaker, John Augustus, posted bail for a man convicted of drunken conduct. Augustus had worked with alcoholics in the past and therefore convinced the Boston police court that he could rehabilitate the alcoholic involved. Augustus asked the judge, who was about to sentence the drunk to jail, to let him, Augustus, supervise the drunk for three weeks. The three weeks were sufficient to convince the judge that the drunk would remain sober, and thus the judge sentenced the man to only a fine. This episode led to the concept of probation, which has existed in the United States ever since.

Although law enforcers opposed the efforts of Augustus, the courts in Boston gradually accepted the view that not all offenders needed to be incarcerated and therefore let Augustus bail out over 1,800 persons. Augustus continued in his efforts until he died in 1859. He made himself liable for $231,234, which was an enormous sum in his day. Augustus helped his probationers to find employment and a place to live and gave them support in their effort to rid themselves of their alcoholism. It should be noted that Augustus carefully selected those candidates for his attention who were salvageable and appeared not to be violent or untrustworthy.[1]

Because Augustus lived in Massachusetts, his efforts led to the establishment of the first American probation department in that state. In 1878, the Massachusetts legislature passed the first statute authorizing the appointment of the first American paid probation officer. At first, the mayor of Boston appointed the probation officer. Then the law was changed in 1891, and the courts appointed the probation officers. The second state to appoint probation officers was Vermont in 1898.[2] Thereafter, probation became national in that more and more states adopted provisions allowing probation. On March 4, 1925, President Calvin Coolidge signed the National Probation Act. That law, passed by Congress earlier, allowed every state to appoint one probation officer to a position paying $2,600 a year. Two years later, in 1927, Georgia, Illinois, New York, Pennsylvania, and West Virginia appointed probation officers.[3]

Thereafter, probation on the federal and state level became universal, so that at the end of 2007, 5.1 million Americans were supervised in the community. Of those, more than 80 percent, or almost 4.3 million, were on probation; the others were on parole. This meant that at the end of 2007, 1 in every 45 American adults was being supervised. One-half of probationers had been convicted of committing a misdemeanor—that is, an offense punishable by imprisonment for one year or less in a county institution. The others had been convicted of a felony, which is an offense punishable by incarceration for more than a year in a state or federal prison. Of those individuals on probation, 27 percent had been convicted of a drug offense. Women constituted 23 percent of probationers in 2007. Furthermore, 55 percent of probationers in 2007 were white, 29 percent black, and 13 percent Hispanic, either white or black. The average length of probation in the United States is 27 months, and the cost of the supervision is $9.61 per day.[4]

PROBATION OFFICERS

Caseloads for probation officers should average 29 probationers. So low a caseload is seldom achieved, however. Because caseloads are generally far larger, the cost of probation compared with the average cost of jail is a good deal less, for probation amounts to $9.61 per day, whereas prison averages $63.51 per day. Earnings of probation officers vary from $28,000 to $71,000 per year. The middle salaries, that is, the amount paid to about one-half of all probation officers, range from $34,000 to $56,000 a year. State governments, which employ the majority of probation officers, paid an average annual salary of $46,000.[5]

Probation officers, also called community corrections officers, usually need a bachelor's degree in criminal justice, sociology, psychology, social work, or related social sciences. Some employers require a master's degree in social work, whereas others regard a master's degree as at least one cause for promotion to a supervisory position.[6]

Usually, employers require newly appointed probation officers to undergo a training program sponsored by the state or federal government and leading to a certification test and a permanent position after one year's experience. In 2006, there were approximately 94,000 probation officers working in federal and state jobs and supervising between 6 million and 7 million adults.[7]

New York City's probation department is one example of the work probation officers do. There, 58 percent of probation officers are women, many having been recruited from social work, both public and private. The armed probation officers of the Field Services Unit are charged with rounding up probation violators, a job at one time the assignment of the police department. Because the New York police are overworked, it has become the task of the probation department to seek out violators, although the probation department in New York City is also overworked, given that the average caseload of probation officers tops 200, a number far above the average for the nation as a whole.

The New York City Field Services Unit probation officers work in groups of four. They seek out violators and arrest them. Doing that can be a dangerous assignment, as many probation violators are armed and violent and often subject to the use of crack cocaine.[8]

The work of probation officers is most important to the adjudication of those arrested. That is so because probation officers conduct personal investigations designed to determine whether a defendant can be trusted to live in the community and accept supervision. The fact is that judges have no more information concerning an accused or convicted citizen than that which probation officers provide. The judge may read the pre-sentencing report submitted by the probationer, though that would be most unusual. Generally, judges rely on the probation officer's report and recommendation as to imprisonment or release on the probationer's own recognizance.

Probation officers conduct pre-sentence investigations and report their findings to a judge. When the judge imposes certain conditions to be obeyed by the probationer, the probation officer can decide which violations to report to the court. Thus, probation officers have a great deal of discretion concerning which conditions to enforce. When a convict goes to prison, the probation officers also send their pre-sentence reports to the prison.

Judges thus generally rely on the probation officer's pre-sentencing report. Such reports usually contain information about the seriousness of the crime, the defendant's circumstances, a summary of sentencing options, and a recommendation for or against imprisonment.[9]

Probation is frequently interpreted by the media as a way of "coddling criminals." The media's failure to understand probation leads to a poor image of probation. So, the public hardly supports probation despite the evidence that if well supported, probation works and saves the taxpayer a great deal of money. If probation officers had manageable caseloads, probation would lead to successful reintegration of ex-offenders into the community. Because probation is unpopular, it is therefore poorly funded, and so, many a probation officer has a caseload of 100 or more. Large caseloads guarantee that many probationers are not sufficiently supervised, leading to the accusation that probation does not work and that probation officers are "soft on crime."[10]

The negative image of probation is fostered by the media, who are quick to report on probation failures but seldom mention probation successes. If a probationer commits another crime, particularly a spectacular offense like murder or rape, numerous reporters create the impression that probation is always a failure. The same media hardly ever report that a probationer earned a high school diploma or succeeded in business.

For example, the *Detroit News* published an exposé in 2003, "Felons on Probation Often Go Unwatched." The report dealt only with those individuals who failed probation and committed another crime but said nothing about the excessive caseload probation officers face, nor did it investigate the numerous low-risk probationers who had succeeded in their effort at rehabilitation.[11]

In 2007, the American Probation and Parole Association issued a report that revealed that 77 percent of probation officers nationwide considered their caseloads too large. At that time, the average caseload was 106 probationers. The survey indicated that probation officers considered a caseload of 77 manageable. The discrepancy means that according to the officers themselves, the workload of probation officers is about 37 percent higher than can be managed successfully. The evidence is that caseloads for probation officers have doubled since 1980, so community corrections agencies are expected to supervise more offenders with fewer resources. The failure to support probation leads, in turn, to public perceptions fueled by the media that "nothing works" and that probation is a failure.[12]

One reason for the increase in probation caseloads is the use of probation as a means of alleviating prison overcrowding. Whereas probation was at one time reserved only for such low-level offenders as drunks or petty thieves, it now includes major felons who can be most dangerous to the community. Therefore, "probation roles increasingly mirror the prison population so that more than half of probationers today are convicted felons."[13]

Because probation officers are overworked and underpaid, they are conditioned to lose sight of some of their probationers, leading to sensational stories in the media concerning probationers who have committed terrible crimes while on probation. One method used by the media to exploit the weaknesses of probation is to popularize failure without ever mentioning the successes of the probation department.

Probationers

One example of how violent probationers slip through the cracks because probation officers have excessively large caseloads is the case of Daniel Tavares Jr., who had spent 16 years of an 18- to 20-year sentence in the Massachusetts prison system for killing his mother in 1991. Tavares had earned "automatic good time" and was released in 2007. Before his release, Tavares threatened to kill correctional officers and Governor Mitt Romney. Tavares was therefore rearrested on release because he assaulted a corrections officer. Nevertheless, he was given probation by Judge Kathe Tuttman and released on condition he would work, live with his sister in Massachusetts, and visit his probation officer three times a week. In November 2007, Tavares was arrested on charges of having murdered Brian and Beverly Mauck in Washington State after arguing over a $50 debt.[14]

A more infamous case of a similar nature concerns Willie Horton, who was convicted of a brutal murder in 1974 but released for an unguarded weekend furlough on June 6, 1987. He never came back. On April 20, 1987, Horton entered the house of Clifford Barnes in Oxon Hill, Maryland. He pointed a gun at Barnes and pistol whipped him and then cut him several times. When Barnes's fiancée returned that evening, Horton gagged her and raped her twice. Horton then stole Barnes's car. Later captured by police, Horton was imprisoned for life in Maryland.[15]

Joseph P. Smith abducted 11-year-old Carlie Brucia in February 2004 and killed her in Sarasota, Florida. Smith, who was on probation, had a long history of using violence, including hitting a woman in the face with a motorcycle helmet. He was also a drug offender who had failed to pay a fine imposed by a court and punched a man in the face, breaking his nose and tearing his left retina. Despite these and other violent offenses, Smith was released on probation by Judge Harry Rapkin, who relied on a Department of Corrections report that did not request prison for Smith. Investigation after the Carlie Brucia murder showed that the probation officers involved with Smith were so overworked that they made a few clerical errors, among them a failure to check a box on a form, which then allowed Smith to go free.[16]

A subsequent study by the staff of the *St. Petersburg Times* revealed that over 70,000 probationers in Florida had been accused of violating the terms of their probation and that of these, 426 had committed serious forms of violence but were nevertheless granted probation. The acts of violence included murder, manslaughter, rape, robbery, home invasions, sexual battery, false imprisonment, shooting a rocket into a dwelling, and numerous forms of child abuse.[17]

Another unnecessary burden on probation officers is the introduction of probation conditions by judges, legislators, and the media, none of whom know much about probationers and who prescribe one-size-fits-all conditions for probationers. By increasing the conditions of probation, many of which are unreasonable and unnecessary, the chances of a probationer violating his or her probation also increase. The conditions, imposed by those who have never worked in probation and are playing to the media with the intent of labeling themselves "tough on crime," cause probationers to be returned to prisons already overcrowded with white-collar offenders and users of controlled substances. It is rare that judges or legislators ask the opinions of probation professionals concerning the effectiveness of probation conditions, since the true purpose of imposing all kinds of conditions is the reelection of politicians and not the safety of the public.[18]

The advantages of probation are evident. The costs are lower than the cost of imprisonment, there are increased opportunities for rehabilitation, and the risk of criminal socialization is a good deal less. Furthermore, probation reduces the overcrowding problem in American prisons. It is therefore important that probation be given favorable coverage by the media and that its benefits be better explained to the public and the professions.[19]

Looking now at the annual probation survey of the Bureau of Justice Statistics, one finds that in 2007, the total correctional population of the United States included over 7.3 million persons, of whom just over 5 million were under "community supervision" and over 2 million were in prison. That means that in 2007, 3.2 percent of the adult population of the United States was on correctional supervision, of whom 69.8 percent were under community supervision and 2.2 percent of all adults in America were so supervised.[20]

In 2007, men were 72 percent of probationers. The female share of 28 percent represents an increase of 2 percentage points since 1995.

WHO GETS PROBATION

Probation is applied a great deal in cases of a first offense or because the prisons are already overcrowded. It is also used because many defendants are most likely to remain in the community where they were convicted, because the offense for which they were convicted does not rise to the level of a felony, or because the defendants are politically connected or have the means of hiring an expensive attorney.

For example, a former National Hockey League player, Rick Tocchet, was arrested in New Jersey in 2007 for running an illegal sports gambling ring. Although that offense could have resulted in five years in a state prison, he was ordered to serve two years' probation on the grounds that as a first-time offender who pleaded guilty to a fourth-degree crime, he was eligible for the lesser punishment.

Because of his fame as a hockey player, Tocchet became the target of media speculation, including rumors of ties to organized crime. While first-time offenders are generally given probation, it is also evident that sports figures, even with prior convictions, are often given probation because the public wants its team to win. Should a judge deprive a team of the chance of winning because a star player has been sent to jail, the judge risks losing reelection by the star's fans.

Judges often combine probation with a suspended sentence. That is a "split sentence" and refers to the conditions under which probation is granted. It is assumed that if the probationer violates the agreed-on conditions, the probationer goes to jail. The conditions are generally recommended by the probation officer, who thereby becomes the unseen and unofficial judge. Probation revocation is subject to "due process" as interpreted by the Supreme Court in *Morrissey v. Brewer*.[21]

Probation may be seen as punishment. Those critics who are opposed to punishment claim that punishment does not promote public safety. The media and public opinion support punishment, as do most criminal justice employees. Victims of crime are particularly adamant in wishing to see perpetrators punished. Therefore, probation officers need to find a means of achieving rehabilitation even as probation is also punitive. Probationers include violent offenders, domestic or "significant others" offenders, sex offenders, white-collar property offenders, drunk drivers, and drug offenders, among others. It is, therefore, exceedingly difficult for probation officers to deal with so diverse a caseload.

VIOLENT OFFENDERS ON PROBATION

Darrell Lee Frazier is an example of a violent offender who lost probation because he could not control his anger. Charged with rape and battery, he was nevertheless put on probation, which he promptly violated. His probation was revoked because he failed to stop after an accident and also sold a controlled substance.[22]

In Massachusetts, the number of violent criminals on probation has increased considerably since the 1990s. The range of offenses of violent offenders includes attempted murder, rape, assault, and the use of deadly force. As a result, the number of violent offenders under "intensive" supervision has increased as well. Such violent offenders are monitored by the probation department of Massachusetts at all times. The reason for the increase in violent offenders on probation is related to an increase in female violence, parental violence at youth sports events, school violence, and a general increase in the use of violence in daily life, including road rage and the willingness to kill those with whom we disagree. Most important is the willingness of women to report domestic violence to the police. Reporting domestic abuse was uncommon before 1980 and was then regarded as unimportant. Now, the police are likely to arrest someone accused of domestic violence.[23]

In Brooklyn, New York, city probation officers are using electronic bracelets to monitor domestic violence offenders on probation. Such a violation can include going within 500 feet of a victim's home. The probation department also installs electronic signal devices in the homes of domestic abuse victims. Previous to this arrangement, judges would issue orders of protection. The orders were largely ignored. Now the offender must wear a bracelet that sets off a loud signal device, attached to the victim's telephone, if the offender approaches within 500 feet. In addition, a monitoring company calls 911 and dispatches the police.[24]

One example of domestic violence perpetrated by a probationer was the conduct of Jim Brown, the former football player. Brown, a member of the Hall of Fame, was in 2002 declared "the greatest ever football player" by The Sporting News. He had played nine years with the Cleveland Browns as a running back, but that did not prevent him from wrecking his wife's car with a shovel. He had a history of attacks on women when he was convicted and sentenced to three years' probation in 1999 at the age of 63.[25]

In 2003, the Buffalo News reported that a local councilman had pleaded guilty to several misdemeanors in a number of domestic violence incidents, for which he was sentenced to three years' probation and required to undergo counseling. Richard Zarbo had violated an order of protection that resulted from an earlier domestic incident, which subsequently led to fighting the police, who seized numerous weapons from his home, including 31 pistols, rifles, and shotguns. Zarbo was also ordered to undergo counseling courses ranging from anger management to family relations.[26]

Likewise, Tom Sizemore, a movie actor, violated his probation on a domestic violence charge involving his ex-wife, Heidi Fleiss. Sizemore failed a drug test when it was discovered that he had attached a false penis to his underwear. The apparatus contained clean urine that was not his. Sizemore, having starred in a television show and a movie called Black Hawk Down, sought to gain sympathy from a judge by claiming to be destitute and living in a garage.[27]

During the decade ending in 2009, sex offenders have come to be regarded as the most dangerous of all predators. While there are undoubtedly sex offenders who subject children to their needs and have even been known to kill their victims, it is reasonable to hold that some sex offenders can be placed on probation. Of course, some sex offenders do violate probation, and their violations increase the hysteria already surrounding such offenses.

SEX OFFENDERS ON PROBATION

Stalking can be a sex offense. Therefore, Jack Jordan was sentenced to three years' probation in Manhattan, New York, for stalking actress Uma Thurman. Jordan was ordered to undergo psychiatric treatment. The treatment order resulted from a court-ordered psychiatric evaluation that discovered that Jordan suffers from a psychiatric disorder. Jordan had been convicted by a New York City jury because he repeatedly arrived at the front door of Thurman's house both by day and at night. He called her on the phone and left messages at her doorstep, including drawings of a bizarre nature and a drawing of a headless woman.[28]

Patrick Naughton was sentenced to five years' probation and fined $20,000 because he flew to California with the alleged intent of seducing a 13-year-old girl who turned out to be an FBI agent. Naughton had met the girl online. The FBI agent told him she was a blonde, weighed 110 pounds, and was 5 feet tall. Naughton had entered an online chat room, where he met the sex-police agent. Evidently, the FBI employs agents whose interests lead them to conduct such forms of entrapment. Since Naughton had been a Disney executive, the media enjoyed the spectacle entirely induced by the law enforcement community.[29]

Fredy E. Bonilla was arrested in March 2005 for abusing a 12-year-old girl. In May 2005, Bonilla, then 25 years old, was deported to his native El Salvador with the understanding that he would not reenter the United States. At that time, he was also placed on probation. Nevertheless, Bonilla returned to New York, where he was again arrested for a probation violation in 2006. Reentry after deportation for committing a crime is a felony punishable by no less than one year and one day in a federal institution.[30]

New York City has instituted a Special Targeted Offenders Program. Among other efforts to prevent well-known sex offenders from attacking anyone, probationers are required by the program to report to their probation officer four times a month, including at least one home visit.

Probation officers will also impose curfews on convicted sex offenders, who are also required to comply with the New York State Sex Offender Registration Act. According to that law, sex offenders must register their addresses with the police. To uphold the law, the New York City police department has organized a Sex Offender Monitoring Unit. There are about 500,000 registered sex offenders in the United States.[31]

In Westchester County, New York, fear of sex offenders has reached such a level that sex offenders have been required to attend a four-hour educational program on Halloween night. In New Jersey, sex offenders are prohibited from answering their door on Halloween if trick-or-treaters come knocking on their door. Such prohibitions are also in effect in Texas. In Virginia, sex offenders must report to their probation officer between 4:30 P.M. and 8:00 P.M. on Halloween night. Since most children who have been victimized are the victims of relatives or friends of the family, not of strangers, these measures appear to be mostly grandstanding by politicians without ensuring the safety of children.[32]

It is to be hoped that teenage boys and girls have an interest in the opposite sex. Nevertheless, such normal interests are viewed by the sex police as "molestation," as demonstrated by the imprisonment of a 17-year-old Minnesota boy, Joseph Leroy Driscoll. Driscoll was sentenced in November 2008 on three felony counts of second-degree criminal sexual conduct. At age 17, Driscoll was given an adult sentence of 39 months in prison and a 10-year conditional release period should he fail to comply with his probation requirements until his 21st birthday. His crime was "molesting" three girls. Evidently, conduct dictated by nature and viewed as common and normal for centuries has become the target of hysterical adults who seek to return to the Puritan traditions of the seventeenth century.[33]

WHITE-COLLAR OFFENDERS ON PROBATION

In September 2008, movie actor Ryan O'Neal and his son by actress Farrah Fawcett, Redmond, were arrested and booked by the Los Angeles police on suspicion of narcotics possession. Narcotics were found in their home when the police searched their bedrooms. Redmond was on probation in 2008 because he had pleaded guilty to a drug possession charge a year earlier. At that time, he was sentenced to three years' probation and a $1,500 fine. Ryan was also on probation on charges of assault with a deadly weapon after firing a gun at another son, Griffin O'Neal.[34]

Marion Barry, former mayor of Washington, D.C., was given probation after he failed to file federal and District tax returns. He pleaded guilty on two counts of tax evasion in 2006 because he had not filed tax returns for six years. Nevertheless, he again did not file tax returns in 2007. Barry had been convicted in November 2005 of testing positive for marijuana and cocaine during his probation on the tax charges. Despite the test result, the judge would not jail Barry on probation violation charges as requested by the district attorney.[35]

Widespread publicity accompanied the trial of Martha Stewart, a TV show host, on charges of lying about a stock trade that saved her $45,000. Stewart was convicted and sentenced to probation. It is fairly certain that the prosecution was mainly motivated to gain a conviction because Stewart is wealthy, had a great number of followers derived from her TV show, and is a woman. Prosecutors frequently go after people who have achieved success because they are often the targets of popular resentment. There are only a few women who are successful in the media business, and that makes them a target. Stewart had been known to be rude to those who worked for her. Furthermore, the very idea of a woman "lording it over" men angers many a prosecutor who needs to get even with such female success. Prosecutors are anxious to stigmatize celebrities also because it is easier to inflame a jury with tales of arrogance and bossy behavior. It is likely that every juror eligible to serve at the Stewart trial had already read about her tyranny over her employees.[36]

As more and more business executives and other white-collar offenders are convicted in American courts, the decision to sentence a defendant to probation rather than jail or prison can be influenced by showing the judge that the defendant has a record of community involvement, has done good deeds in the past, and has references from prominent citizens. All this is arranged for a fee of $300 an hour by the National Center of Institutions and Alternatives (NCIA). The NCIA prepares a presentencing report for the judge showing the defendant's "better side." Such a report lists the defendant's contributions to charity, notes his or her history of volunteering for work among the poor, and also states the defendant's willingness to make restitution. For example, a physician convicted of tax evasion volunteered to contribute his medical skills on an American Indian reservation, which led the judge to grant him probation instead of sending him to a federal prison. The NCIA tries to persuade charities to accept white-collar criminals as volunteers, which is not always easy because many such organizations fear that the presence of a convict will damage their image and affect contributions to their cause.[37]

JUVENILE PROBATION

At the end of 2008, the Office of Juvenile Justice and Delinquency Prevention of the U.S. government published statistics concerning juvenile crime in 2005. The report indicates that in that year, the juvenile court delinquency caseloads were four times higher than they had been in 1960. In 1960, the courts across the nation handled about 400,000 delinquents. In 2005, that number had risen to 1.9 million; and in that year, an estimated 556,500 young people, or 48 percent of juveniles who received any kind of sanction, were put on probation.[38]

The statistics include New York City, which has the Court Employment Project, a program designed to counsel and tutor young offenders who have been given probation instead of prison. The purpose of that project is to give defendants six months of help. This is done with the agreement of the court. The defendants are mostly those who have committed robbery, burglary, and similar crimes and who may well benefit from probation and save the taxpayer a great deal of money. Included in the probation experience are such work projects as converting an unheated tenement into modern housing. The workers, all of whom are on probation, receive minimum wages. The young probationers have, in the main, left high school or achieved an equivalency diploma, which has little value outside the positive psychological value it may possess for some of the probationers.[39]

In Philadelphia, the Family Court's Juvenile Probation Department supervises about 6,000 juveniles on probation at any one time. The probation department works together with the Philadelphia police department with a view of sharing information concerning violent behavior with particular reference to gang activities. The goal of that program is to identify groups of youths involved in violence and to increase probation supervision to prevent it.[40]

In Washington, D.C., juvenile probation officers enforce curfews imposed on 1,700 probationers who have been ordered to stay home between 3:30 P.M. and 9:00 P.M., the hours when street violence peaks. In addition, other officers drive around between 7 P.M. and midnight daily. They have the names of young offenders who need to be monitored in order to reduce violence in the district. The officers knock on doors, climb stairs in tenements, and walk through housing projects to make sure juveniles are not on the streets. Some of those individuals being monitored await sentencing; others are waiting for admission to detention facilities.[41]

In Los Angeles, the county operates juvenile probation camps, a practice mirrored in other California counties. There are 28 counties in California operating 67 probation camps. Five of the camps are for girls. This means that there are, on average, 3,880 boys and 480 girls in these camps, at a cost of $900 million a year. Not all probationers are located in the camps. There are also probationers who live in the community, costing the taxpayer about $1,712 per juvenile offender. The probation camps resemble juvenile prisons but are not called that for symbolic interactionist reasons. California also operates boot camps and other facilities as wilderness camps, which have not reduced the recidivism rate of juvenile delinquents but are operated nevertheless because politicians find that these camps demonstrate to the public that the politicians are "tough on crime," a sure means of gaining reelection.[42]

In February 2007, four girls were sentenced to probation by Judge Gibson Lee of the Long Beach, California, juvenile court. A gang of black girls had been convicted of a hate crime because they had attacked and beaten a white woman on a residential street. The girls beat three white women so badly that they suffered multiple facial lacerations and concussions. All the assailants were sentenced to probation with 60 days' house arrest and 250 hours of community service.[43]

In Bucks County, Pennsylvania, a fifth-grade boy, Joseph Ramos, was placed on probation, charged with burglary of the home of a friend. There, he and another boy had stolen $340 in cash, a video game, and other items. Because juvenile courts do not find a child guilty, such an admission was not required. The child did, however, have to write a letter of apology to the victim of the burglary and pay $370 in restitution, which became the obligation of his parents. In such cases, probationers can have the record of their misdemeanors expunged if they finish probation successfully.[44]

CORRUPTION IN THE PROBATION AND PAROLE COMMUNITY

In February 2009, Sandra Brulo, a high-ranking probation official in Luzerne County, Pennsylvania, was charged with obstruction of justice by federal prosecutors. The charge stemmed from the alteration of records in the probation department. This conduct was related to Brulo's culpability in the kickback scheme by two judges, Mark A. Ciavarella Jr. and Michael T. Conahan, who both pleaded guilty to taking payoffs of more than $2.6 million paid them by two privately run detention centers. Both judges had sent numerous youths to these private prisons even when their offenses would ordinarily result only in probation. Both judges had ordered the closing of a county-owned and state-run detention center on grounds of its alleged poor condition. Doing that allowed the two to send children to the privately owned detention center. Brulo evidently manipulated the paperwork to make the activities look legal and justified.[45]

Sexual exploitation by members of the criminal justice community is by no means uncommon. Such conduct was engaged in by probation officer Keith Cochran, who resigned his job in St. Petersburg, Florida, after he was accused of making sexual advances to a female probationer. Cochran, who had worked for the probation department for 16 years, had been accused of similar conduct on several previous occasions. In this instance, Cochran allowed the female probationer to drink alcohol, use drugs, and ignore her house arrest. As a consequence, Cochran was prosecuted not only for his illegal relationship but also for destroying documents to protect the woman from prosecution. Four women independently recounted similar events concerning Cochran and added that they had complained to the probation department, which refused to believe such complaints.[46]

Likewise, probation officer Nicole Waite, 36 years old in 2004, admitted to having sex with a 17-year-old client in return for a good conduct review if he agreed. She admitted to having sex with the youth on three occasions, including in her office. Despite the admission, the judge dismissed all charges on the grounds that the prosecution did not prove its case.[47]

Misconduct by probation officers is not always active. It may also be passive in the sense that probation officers fail to enforce the rules required by law. In San Diego, 23 probation officers were dismissed on grounds that they failed to make mandatory checks of inmates at Juvenile Hall. Instead, they entered into log books that they had made regular checks on inmates every 15 minutes.[48]

Twelve Hamilton County, Ohio (Cincinnati), probation officers were disciplined in 2000 for failing to conduct court-ordered drug tests. The failure was discovered by an audit conducted for the judges who had requested the tests. Such tests are important to judges, who rely on them to decide whether or not someone should go to jail or remain free on probation.[49]

PAROLE

Although there is a great deal of similarity between probation and parole, there are two major differences. Probation refers to those who have not been incarcerated, so that probation may be considered serving a sentence outside the walls of a prison. Parole refers to early release from prison on conditions imposed by a parole board. The second difference is that an administrative board grants parole, whereas probation is granted by a judge.

The word "parole" is French and means "speech" or "promise" in the sense that a military prisoner is released on his word of honor not to continue fighting the enemy who has captured him.

Parole was first introduced into the criminal justice system in 1840 when a British naval officer, Captain Alexander Maconochie, was put in charge of the English penal colony on Norfolk Island in the South Pacific. Maconochie introduced incentives for good behavior by providing a mark system that allowed inmates to earn points toward early release. This system led to the indeterminate sentence through which freedom could be gained through hard work and good behavior. Adopted by Zebulon Brockway, the first superintendent of the Elmira Reformatory in New York, the system spread from there to other American states and continues to this day, though in altered form.[50]

In 2006, there were 52 parole supervising agencies in the United States. That number included all states, the District of Columbia, and the California Youth Authority, which is distinct from the California Parole Board. In 2006, the adult parole population in the United States numbered 660,959. Five agencies supervised half that number because they are located in the heavily populated states of California, Texas, Illinois, New York, and Pennsylvania. There, 65,000 full-time and 2,900 part-time workers were employed by the numerous parole boards. Caseloads for parole officers alone amounted to approximately 38 persons. Drug offenders and sex offenders were the majority of those individuals paroled in 2007.[51]

In 1984, Congress abolished parole for federal prisoners as part of the Sentencing Reform Act. Since then, federal prisons have become immensely overcrowded as more and more prisoners are incarcerated to serve long sentences without hope of early release. The abolition of parole came about after Marvin Frankel, a federal judge for the Southern District of New York, complained that because judges could impose any sentence they wanted, similar offenders received widely disparate sentences in federal courts. The Sentencing Reform Act created guidelines for judges to follow in sentencing and abolished parole.[52]

Since then, the House of Representatives has passed legislation to reinstate parole in federal prisons. That bill died at the end of the 110th Congress and was re-introduced on March 12, 2009. If it passes again, it will have to be submitted to the Senate. Therefore, as of March 9, 2009, there is still no federal parole in the United States. As a result of the extant policy, there are U.S. prisoners who serve life sentences without a chance of getting paroled. There are, of course, many states that do grant parole, sometimes with frightening results. In 22 states, so-called lifers have no way out. In 14 other states, less than 10 percent of life prisoners gain release, so that the number of life prisoners increased to over 132,000 as of 2005.[53]

PAROLEES AND PAROLE VIOLATORS

Fear of parolees is widespread, particularly because the media give parole violators wide publicity. An example of a parole violator was Kalik Church, who was killed by police in 2005 as he fired a gun at the police who tried to arrest him for a parole violation. Church shot a police officer who came after him because of a traffic altercation. The parolee ran from the scene of the fight but then shot an officer in the groin. Thereafter, another officer shot Church in the head, killing him. Church had been in and out of prison several times during his brief life and is an example of an entire group of Americans who spend almost all their time in that "revolving door."[54]

Lionel Tate is the youngest American in years to be sentenced to life in prison. Yet, after 52 days behind bars, he was paroled in October 2004. He was convicted in 1999 of beating to death a 6-year-old child, Tiffany Eunick. At the time of the murder, Tate was 12 years old. The victim, who weighed only 48 pounds, suffered more than 35 injuries, including a fractured skull. Tate violated his parole in November 2004 by associating with a teen who had been arrested several times. Tate had been told not to deal with such friends and to avoid all contacts that could lead to more trouble.[55]

There are numerous parolees who commit additional crimes once paroled. Rashid B. Hall of Philadelphia was stopped by police in Wilkes-Barre, Pennsylvania. He gave the police a false name and also called 911, claiming a domestic dispute involving a gun was occurring at a fake address. In fact, Hall was wanted on a parole violation and made the fake 911 call to avoid arrest.[56]

Adam L. Pallas violated his parole by dealing drugs in Bryan, Texas. Pallas had been paroled after serving time in a Texas prison for drug dealing. Yet, he continued to deal drugs while on parole. Caught with numerous plastic bags in his car, all of which contained methamphetamine, he was charged with manufacturing and delivering a controlled substance. Conviction carries a possible prison sentence of 5 to 99 years. Pallas also carried a weapon, which is also a felony, carrying a possible prison sentence of 20 years.[57]

Corey Cox was already in jail for a parole violation related to a 2005 robbery when he admitted to the fatal shooting of Robert Kowalewski in July 2004. Cox made his admission after he was taken into custody for violating his parole. He had shot Kowalewski in the abdomen and now faced a life sentence. Cox's earlier conviction on a robbery charge led to only a brief prison term because New York prisons are so overcrowded that parole is used as a means to reduce the pressure.[58]

A most unusual parole was granted Sara Jane Olson, a name adopted by Olson after she pleaded guilty of taking part in a bank robbery in Carmichael, California, during which a bank customer was shot and killed. Olson also planted bombs under police cruisers, which did not detonate, and stole wallets in order to make fake identifications. She did all this as a member of the Symbionese Liberation Army, a group of terrorists operating in California in the late 1970s.

Sara Jane Olson was born Kathleen Soliah. She disappeared in 1976, when she moved to Minneapolis and married Dr. Fred Peterson, with whom she had three children. She became a soccer mom and participated in numerous community activities, including many leftist causes. It was not until 1999 that the FBI arrested her. She was sentenced to 14 years in prison and paroled on March 17, 2008, on the grounds of good behavior, only to be rearrested four days later because as a result of administrative error, she had been released one year too soon. She was once again released on March 17, 2009.[59]

Parole of illegal aliens has become routine in California and other southwestern states, with the result that numerous former convicts return to the United States after being deported to their native lands. An example is Jose Hernandez, apprehended for parole violations in connection with the possession of an assault weapon, participation in a street gang, and violation of immigration law. Hernandez carried an UZI submachine gun and a high-capacity magazine in his car.[60]

SUMMARY

Probation began in the United States when a Boston shoemaker, John Augustus, vouched for the good behavior of several drunks whom he took home and rehabilitated. Thereafter, probation spread all over the United States. It has been abolished for federal prisoners. While a number of conditions are usually attached to a probation decision, some of these conditions are unreasonable. Probation may be extended to various kinds of offenders, ranging from violent offenders to white-collar criminals and juvenile offenders.

Parole may be extended to prisoners in all states but has been abolished by the federal government. Because of frequent parole violations, parole violation is well known in all the states.

NOTES

1. John Augustus, *First Probation Officer* (New York: National Probation Association, 1939), 26.

2. Robert Panzarella, "Theory and Practice of Probation on Bail in the Report of John Augustus," *Federal Probation* 66, no. 3 (December 2002): 38.

3. Richard A. Chapell, "Look Back at Federal Probation: Recollections of the Early Years," *Federal Probation* 24, no. 4 (December 1975): 26–30.

4. U.S. Department of Justice, Bureau of Justice Statistics, "Probation and Parole Statistics" (Washington, DC: GPO, December 14, 2008), 1.

5. U.S. Department of Labor, Bureau of Labor Statistics, "Probation Officers and Correctional Treatment Specialists," *Occupational Outlook Handbook, 2008–2009*, http://www.bls.gov/oco/ocos265.htm.

6. U.S. Department of Justice, Bureau of Justice Statistics, *Prior Abuse Reported by Inmates and Probationers*, by Caroline Wolf Harlow (Washington, DC: GPO, 1999).

7. U.S. Department of Justice, Bureau of Justice Statistics, "Probation and Parole in the United States," by Leonard Glaze and Thomas Boneczar (Washington, DC: GPO, 2007).

8. Celestine Bohlen, "Armed Dangerous Life of a Probation Officer," *New York Times*, December 30, 1988, B3.

9. U.S. Department of Justice, Bureau of Justice Statistics, *Sentencing in the Federal Courts*, by D. C. McDonald and K. E. Carlson (Washington, DC: GPO, 1993).

10. Andrew R. Klein, *Alternative Sentencing, Intermediate Sanctions and Probation* (Cincinnati: Anderson, 1997), 72.

11. Michael Claxton, N. Sinclair, and Robert Hanson, "Felons on Probation Often Go Unwatched," *Detroit News*, December 10, 2002, 2.

12. Matthew T. Michelle, *Probation and Parole's Growing Caseloads and Workloads Allocation: Strategies for Managerial Decision Making* (Lexington, KY, 2007), 45.

13. F. Taxman, D. Young, and J. Byrne, "Transforming Offender Reentry into Public Safety: Lessons from OHP's Recent Partnership Initiative," *Justice Research and Policy* 5, no. 2 (2003): 101–28.

14. Debra J. Saunders, "Willie Horton, 2008," *San Francisco Chronicle*, November 27, 2007, B7.

15. Robert J. Biddinotto, "Getting Away with Murder," *Reader's Digest*, July 1988.

16. Curtis Krueger, Richard Rafke, and Dong-Phuong Nguyen, "The Problem with Probation," *St. Petersburg Times*, June 13, 2004, 6.

17. Ibid., 6.

18. Karl Lucken, "The Dynamics of Penal Reform," *Crime, Law and Social Change* 26 (1997): 367.

19. Patrick Langan, "Between Prison and Probation: Intermediate Sanctions," *Science* 264 (1994): 791.

20. U.S. Department of Justice, Bureau of Justice Statistics, "Probation and Parole in the United States, 2007 Statistical Tables," by Lauren E. Glaze and Thomas P. Bonczar (Washington, DC: GPO, 2008), Table 1.

21. *Morrissey v. Brewer*, 408 U.S. 471, 477 (1972).

22. Betsey Martin, "Violent Criminal Loses Probation," *Atkansas Matters.com* (December 23, 2007): 1.

23. "Violent Criminals on Probation in Bay State Increase by 200 Percent," The Massachusetts Court System, Office of the Commissioner of Probation, January 26, 2002.

24. David M. Herszenhorn, "Alarm Helps to Fight Domestic Violence," *New York Times*, July 27 1999, B3.

25. *New York Times*, "Brown Draws Probation," October 6, 1999, D8.

26. T. J. Pignataro, "Zarbo Gets Three Years' Probation in Domestic Violence Case," *Buffalo News*, June 18, 2003, B3.

27. *New York Post*, "Black Hawk Star Jailed," February 12, 2005, 10.

28. John Elgon, "Uma Thurman's Stalker Sentenced to Three Years' Probation and Treatment," *New York Times*, June 3, 2008, New York Region 1.

29. Randy Dotinga, "Ex-Disney Executive Gets Probation in Sex Case," Associated Press, Los Angeles, August 10, 2000, 1.

30. Julia C. Mead, "Police Arrest Sex Offender: Can Be Deported to El Salvador," *New York Times*, May 2, 2006, NewYork Region 1.

31. William K. Rashbaum, "A Closer Eye on the Worst Sex Offenders," *New York Times*, February 25, 2009, B.

32. Anahad O'Connor, "Sex Offenders See New Limits for Halloween," *New York Times*, October 26, 2005, N1.

33. Gretchen Schlosser, "Teen, Already in Sex Offender Treatment Faces New Sex Charges," *Willmar (Minnesota) West Central Tribune*, February 26, 2009, 1.

34. Andrew Blankstein, "Ryan O'Neal, Son Redmond Booked on Suspicion of Drug Possession," *Los Angeles Times*, September 17, 2008, 1.

35. Carol B. Leoninng and Yolanda Woodlee, "Barry Escapes Jail Time on Probation Violation," *Washington Post*, March 13, 2007, B01.

36. Jonathan B. Glater, "Stewart Celebrity Created Magnet for Scrutiny," *New York Times*, May 7, 2004, N1.

37. Barbara Lyne, "Giving the Bad Guys a Shot at Redemption," *New York Times*, March 28, 1993, 108.

38. Charles Puzzanchera and Melissa Sickmund, "Probation as a Court Disposition," *Juvenile Court Statistics, 2005* (Washington, DC: Office of Juvenile Justice and Delinquency Prevention, 2008), 1.

39. Kathleen Teltsch, "Alternative to Prison in New York: Six Months of Counseling and Therapy," *New York Times*, February 1, 1988, 49.

40. Barbara Boyer, "New Program Targets Gangs, Violence in South Philadelphia," *Philadelphia Inquirer*, January 17, 2008, B5.

41. Keith L. Alexander, "Did the Crime? Watch the Time," *Washington Post*, November 8, 2007, DZ01.

42. Marcus Niets, "Probation Camps and Ranches" (Sacramento: California Research Bureau, November 2008), 117.

43. Joe Mosingo, "4 Girls Get Probation in Hate Crime Trial," *Los Angeles Times*, February 6, 2007, 1.

44. Larry King, "Bucks Boy, 11, Get Probation over Burglary," *Philadelphia Inquirer*, April 4, 2007, AO1.

45. Ian Urbina, "Judge Guilty in Kickback Is Accused of Fixing Suit," *New York Times*, February 21, 2009, A10.

46. Cary Davis, "Officer's Undoing Began Long Ago," *St. Petersburg Times*, June 15, 2003, 1.

47. *New York Times*, "Probation Officer Is Cleared by Judge," March 5, 2004, B4 L.

48. Luis Monteagudo, "23 Probation Officers' Firings Upheld," *San Diego Union Tribune*, July 18, 2002, 1.

49. Dan Horn, "Probation Officers to Be Disciplined," *Cincinnati Enquirer*, November 30, 2000, 1.

50. John V. Barry, "Captain Alexander Maconochie," *Victorian Historical Magazine* 27 (June 1975): 5.

51. U.S. Department of Justice, Bureau of Justice Statistics, "Characteristics of State Supervising Agencies, 2006," by Thomas P. Bonczar (Washington, DC: GPO, 2007), 1–12.

52. Richard D. Hartley, "Sentencing Reform and the War on Drugs," *Journal of Contemporary Criminal Justice* 24, no. 4 (November 2008): 437.

53. Adam Liptak, "Serving Life with No Chance of Redemption," *New York Times*, October 5, 2005, A1.

54. Fernanda Santos, "Trenton Man Killed by Police Was Wanted on Parole Violation," *New York Times*, November 14, 2005, B4.

55. Daman P. Gregory, "Lionel Tate Gets Third Chance at Freedom," *Caribbean Today* 15 (November 2004): C4.

56. Bob Kalinowski, "Driver Accused of Making False 911 Call to Avoid Arrest," *Wilkes-Barre Citizens Voice*, March 4, 2009.

57. *Bryan Eagle*, "Man Had Drugs: Club," March 7, 2009, 1.

58. Matt Gryta, "Inmate Indicted in 2004 Slaying," *Buffalo News*, March 7, 2009, 1.

59. Don Thompson, "Controversy Follows Ex-radicals Parole," *Internatonal Business Times*, March 28, 2008, 1.

60. Beatriz E. Valenzuela, "Illegal Alien Arrested for Carrying an UZI," *Victoria Daily Press*, February 14, 2009, 1.

Chapter 10

THE DEATH PENALTY: *NON OMNIS MORIAR*

CONVICTING THE INNOCENT

The phrase "death penalty" implies that those who are killed by the representatives of the government are penalized for the crime of murder. This implication is based on the decision of the U.S. Supreme Court, which ruled in 2008 that the death penalty is unconstitutional as punishment for the rape of a child or an adult. That decision overturned the death penalty rape laws of Louisiana, Georgia, Oklahoma, Montana, South Carolina, and Texas. The Court ruled out the death penalty for any crime, other than treason or espionage, in which the victim's life was not taken. The case under consideration involved Patrick Kennedy, who had been convicted of brutally raping his eight-year-old stepdaughter.[1] As a consequence of the ruling, Kennedy was removed from death row.

The *Kennedy* decision was preceded by *Coker v. Georgia* in 1977, when the Supreme Court ruled that the death penalty could not apply to the rape of an adult woman because the sentence was deemed disproportionate to the crime. The *Coker* decision resulted in the removal from death row of 20 inmates awaiting execution for rape.[2]

The *Kennedy* and *Coker* decisions make murder, but not all murders, the only crime to which the death penalty may apply. According to the Supreme Court's decision in *Ford v. Wainwright* (1986), it is also unconstitutional to execute a person who is insane.[3] In addition, in 1988 the Supreme Court ruled in the case of *Thompson v. Oklahoma* that according to the Constitution, youths younger than 16 could not be executed.[4]

In June 2002, the Supreme Court also ruled that the legal killing of mentally retarded defendants is also unconstitutional on the grounds that killing the retarded violates the Constitution. According to the Court, a "national consensus" no longer supports the killing of retarded persons. The Court ruled on the case of a Virginia man with an IQ of 59. The Court viewed such an execution as a violation of the provision prohibiting "cruel and unusual punishment" by the Eighth Amendment to the Constitution.[5]

It is noteworthy that those who are paid to kill for the state use the subterfuge "execute," meaning "to carry out" or "perform," instead of the word "kill." Evidently, those who do so seek to lessen the disgust their activity provokes in others by covering up the fact that an executioner is a paid killer.

That the convicts killed by the state must all be guilty of murder is, of course, an assumption that can be questioned based on evidence produced by DNA testing, available after the discovery of the composition of deoxyribonucleic acid, or DNA, by Erwin Chargaff and its double-helix structure by Rosalind Franklin in the 1950s. While it is possible that the police, prosecutors, judges, and juries could have made honest mistakes in identifying and convicting people who committed crimes before DNA matching became available in the 1980s, that excuse has become hardly feasible since then.

Consequently, numerous death row inmates have been found innocent by the application of DNA matching; meanwhile, innumerable other innocents have been killed or remain incarcerated because no DNA evidence is available to exonerate them. As of 2008, 130 death row inmates were exonerated. There have, however, been more than 7,000 death sentences since the Supreme Court reinstated the death penalty in 1976. It has been estimated that the number of false convictions for death row inmates is somewhere between 2.5 and 5 percent, involving at least 175 people. This means that 175 innocent people have been sent to death row with the lame excuse that this number is a small percentage of those convicts actually guilty of murder. The truth is that even the conviction of one innocent person is a heinous crime.

There can be little doubt that over the many years since the founding of the American Republic in 1789, innumerable innocent people have been killed by the state for alleged murder and other crimes with which they had nothing to do. When on August 23, 1987, the then-governor of Massachusetts Michael Dukakis declared Sacco and Vanzetti Memorial Day, he highlighted perhaps the best-known convictions of two innocent men, a pair whose executions were for murders attributed to them solely because they were unwanted immigrants. Their executions were indeed legal murders.[6]

The states involved in legal murders are the 36 states that continue to support the death penalty, as does the federal government. Fourteen states and the District of Columbia do not participate in such killings.

One example of an innocent man sent to death row and later exonerated and released is Dave Roby Keaton, the first death row inmate released in 1979 after spending eight years in prison. Keaton had nothing to do with the murder of a deputy sheriff, Thomas Reeve, in 1971. Nevertheless, the police, using threats and lies, coerced a confession from Keaton after three days of relentless interrogation. In addition, the polygraph operator who extracted the confession from Keaton had a history of obtaining false confessions from suspects who were frightened and had no lawyer. Keaton is black. An all-white jury convicted him, and Keaton was sentenced to death. Newspaper publicity and the conviction of three other men for the murder of the deputy led to a review of Keaton's case and his eventual release.[7]

A more recent case of prosecutorial misconduct victimized Michael Blair, who was falsely accused in 1993 of abducting and killing 7-year-old Ashley Estell from a playground in Plano, Texas. The evidence against Blair consisted of a few hairs and a small fiber. Prosecutors argued that the hairs on Ashley's body were Blair's and that hair found in his car belonged to Ashley. They also claimed that a fiber found on her body came from Blair's car. A jury took only 27 minutes to convict Blair of murder and 90 minutes of deliberation to recommend the death penalty, promptly imposed by the judge.

Blair's attorneys appealed, and Blair's execution was delayed. Then, in 2007, DNA testing of the hair samples was performed by order of the court over the objections of the Texas attorney general. That test revealed that the hairs used to convict Blair did not belong to him or to the victim. As usual, the forensic hair comparisons used by the district attorney proved wrong.[8]

In October 1967, James Joseph Richardson, a poor black fruit picker, was arrested and later convicted in Fort Myers, Florida, and sentenced to death for killing his seven children by poison. Richardson was framed by the sheriff and the prosecutors, who refused to investigate Betsy Reese, the children's babysitter, who admitted the murders. Instead, the sheriff asked a deputy to beat prisoners in the holding jail where Richardson was incarcerated before trial so that they would testify Richardson had admitted the crimes.

Twenty-one years after Richardson's conviction, Janet Reno, then-chief prosecutor in Miami, reviewed the conviction and concluded that prosecutors deliberately failed to disclose evidence that would have cleared Richardson. Richardson was released in 1989.

In 2009, Richardson applied for compensation for unjust imprisonment under a new law that awards the wrongfully convicted. Yet, even then, the state's attorney opposed such compensation on some technicality in the law because payment of compensation to Richardson would definitely have compromised the state attorney's office as guilty of malicious prosecution.[9]

The federal government has a law providing compensation for the wrongfully incarcerated. The Innocence Protection Act passed by Congress and signed into law by President George W. Bush in 2004 provides for the payment of $50,000 per year for those innocents incarcerated. In the case of death row inmates, the compensation by the federal government is $100,000 per year of incarceration.[10]

In addition, 16 states provide compensation for inmates innocent of the crimes attributed to them. Those states are Alabama, which provides for a minimum of $50,000 for each year of false imprisonment; California, which compensates at $100 per day; the District of Columbia, which has no cap on the amount of possible compensation; Illinois, which pays the imprisoned innocent up to $35,000 per year of imprisonment; Iowa, which compensates the falsely imprisoned at the rate of $50 per day and lost wages up to $25,000 per year; Maine, which pays $300,000 maximum compensation; Maryland, which has no cap on possible compensation; New Hampshire, which pays a maximum compensation of $20,000; New Jersey, which pays twice the amount a falsely imprisoned person earned before incarceration plus attorney's fees; New York, which has no limit on possible compensation; North Carolina, which pays a limit of $500,000; Ohio, which pays $40,000 per year of imprisonment plus lost wages and attorney's fees; Tennessee, which instructs its court of claims to hear cases of false imprisonment and decide each case on its merits; Texas, which pays $25,000 for each year of false imprisonment plus one year of counseling for a total possible payment of $500,000; West Virginia, where the court determines the amount of compensation to be paid to the falsely imprisoned; and Wisconsin, where the maximum is $25,000 total or $5,000 per year unless the state claims board seeks more compensation by applying to the legislature for more money.[11]

It should be noted that among the states that compensate the falsely imprisoned, the District of Columbia, Iowa, Maine, New Jersey, New York, West Virginia, and Wisconsin do not have a death penalty.

ARGUMENTS FOR AND AGAINST THE DEATH PENALTY

There is no more forceful argument against the death penalty than the list of the 130 innocents released from death row between 1973 and 2008. The conviction of the innocent should suffice to abolish the barbarism of state execution from civilized society. There are, however, a number of arguments for the death penalty as well as against it that are as old as Julius Caesar, who in 63 BC argued that the death penalty should be replaced by life in prison. Caesar was dealing with a Roman citizen, Cataline, who had been found guilty of treason, having sought to overthrow the Roman Republic by force and violence. Whereas the orator and writer Cicero favored the death penalty, Caesar opposed it on the grounds that it demeaned the state.[12]

THE ARGUMENT OF POPULARITY

Arguments concerning the death penalty begin by citing its popularity. The most recent Gallup poll does indeed indicate that the American public favors the death penalty for murder by 64 percent to 30 percent, with 6 percent having no opinion. The statistics lead some critics to claim that since the majority rules in a democracy, the death penalty is legitimized by the numbers. The problem with that argument is, of course, that the majority does not rule in the United States. The presidential election of 2008 gave the winner, Barak Obama, almost 69.5 million votes and John McCain over 59.9 million votes. Since the population of the United States exceeds 300 million, it is evident that the president was elected by a minority of citizens. The winner did not receive a majority because anyone under age 18 could not vote, and a large number of others did not vote though eligible to do so. In addition, the Constitution provides that electoral votes, not the popular vote, shall decide elections of the U.S. president. Therefore, the majority does not rule.

The First Amendment to the U.S. Constitution also guarantees freedom of religion. Thus, minority religions can practice their religion, though the vast majority of Americans are Christians. It is in this area, religion, that the issue of the death penalty becomes an important challenge to religious believers, most of whom are opposed to the death penalty but are forced to pay taxes for the killing of their fellow citizens despite their religious beliefs.[13]

If religious freedom is to be meaningful, then it is defeated by all-powerful judges who send men and women, including innocent people, to their deaths. This is also true of prosecutors and juries who participate in judicial killings and is even more egregious on the part of the paid killers, the executioners, who carry out these atrocities.

Religious organizations are almost unanimous in condemning the death penalty. In 1972, the American Jewish Committee, speaking for all but the most fundamentalist Jews, adopted this resolution: "WHEREAS capital punishment degrades and brutalizes the society which practices it . . . WHEREAS . . . we agree that the death penalty is cruel, unjust and incompatible with the dignity and self respect of man, NOW THEREFORE BE IT RESOLVED that the American Jewish Committee is recorded as favoring the abolition of the death penalty."[14]

The American Jewish Committee has made this commitment on the grounds that the Jewish scriptures also reject the death penalty in Ezekiel 18:23: "Have I any pleasure at all that the wicked should die saith the Lord God but not that he should return from his ways and live?" Assuming that all Jews, whatever their denomination, view the Old

Testament, specifically the Torah, as the essence of their beliefs, it can reasonably be assumed that Judaism rejects the death penalty on theological grounds despite the numerous references to it in the Five Books of Moses. Rabbinic opinion has held that a Sanhedrin—meaning "to sit together or assemble"—that executes even one person in 70 years is destructive. Consequently, modern Israel has abolished the death penalty.

In 1957, the Church of the Brethren also rejected the death penalty. Likewise the Episcopal bishops, at a meeting in 1979, passed a resolution that stated: "RESOLVED, the House of Bishops concurring that this 66th General Convention of the Episcopal Church reaffirms its opposition to capital punishment."

The Lutheran Church of America passed a similar resolution in 1972, as did the Presbyterians, the Mennonites, the Reformed Church in America, and the United Church of Christ. The United Methodist Church "declares its opposition to the retention and use of capital punishment in any form or carried out by any means." That is the text of a resolution passed by the Methodists in 1980.[15]

The American bishops of the Roman Catholic Church have campaigned against the death penalty since 1978. This campaign was forcefully resumed in 2005 when the bishops once more organized a new campaign headed by Cardinal Theodore E. McCarrick of Washington, D.C. McCarrick bases his opposition not only on the view that the death penalty is morally flawed but also on the evidence that numerous innocent persons have been condemned to death. Furthermore, the Catholic Church has consistently opposed abortion, euthanasia, and stem cell research and therefore needs to link this demand for the sacredness of human life with the condemnation of the death penalty.[16]

If the First Amendment to the U.S. Constitution is to be meaningful, then the use of taxpayers' money to kill on behalf of the state violates that amendment even if the majority of Americans favor the death penalty. Because the majority cannot overrule the First Amendment, the majority does not rule in all those situations in which the Constitution guarantees minority rights. Freedom of religion is one of these.

THE ARGUMENT OF DETERRENCE

It is commonly believed that the death penalty prevents murder. Yet, even proponents of the death penalty admit that there is no proof that the notion is true. In fact, every effort to find such proof has come to naught.

It is instructive to compare the murder rates in states with the death penalty to those without it. The comparison plainly indicates that the death penalty does not deter murder because murder is much more dependant on the birthrate than on the death penalty. Because most killings are conducted by young men between the ages of 18 and 24, with a visible increase in offending rates for youngsters between the ages of 14 and 17, it is the number of children born in a particular generation that determines the rate of murder when that generation reaches the teens and twenties.

The Bureau of Justice Statistics reveals that the homicide rate in the United States fell to its lowest level in 2003.[17] Birth rates also fell dramatically after 1970. Prior to that year, American birthrates per 1,000 in the population were in the 20s. Thus, in 1950, the birthrate per 1,000 in the population was 24.1. It was 23.7 in 1960 and then fell to 18.4 in 1970. By 1980, it had declined to 16.9; and by 2000, it stood at 14.4. Evidently, the decline in the birthrate, including an increase in abortions, led to a decline in the murder rate.[18]

Consider, now, states with the death penalty adjoining states without the death penalty. Such a consideration must exclude New Jersey and New Mexico, which abolished the death penalty only recently. Following here are the murder rates of adjoining states as of 2007.

In New England, Connecticut, with the death penalty, registered a murder rate of 3.0 per 100,000 in 2007. Maine, also in New England, had only 1.6 murders per 100,000 residents, although Maine has no death penalty. Likewise, New York, without the death penalty, had a murder rate per 100,000 of 4.2 in 2007; whereas adjoining Pennsylvania, with the death penalty, had a murder rate of 5.7 that year.

In the Midwest, Ohio, with the death penalty, registered a murder rate of 4.5 in 2007; but Minnesota, without the death penalty, had only 2.2 murders per 100,000 that year. North Dakota, without the death penalty, accumulated a murder rate of 1.9; and South Dakota, with the death penalty, had a murder rate of 2.1 in 2007. Iowa adjoins Nebraska. Iowa, without the death penalty, had a murder rate of 1.2 per 100,000 in 2007; whereas Nebraska, with the death penalty, exhibited a murder rate of 3.8.

The foregoing statistics indicate that the death penalty is no deterrent to murder. Nevertheless, it is also true that some states with the death penalty have lower murder rates than states without it. For example, Massachusetts, without the death penalty, had a murder rate of 2.9 per 100,000 in 2007; but New Hampshire, directly adjoining Massachusetts, had a lower murder rate of 1.1 per 100,000 in 2007. New Hampshire has the death penalty. Wisconsin has no death penalty, with a murder rate in 2007 of 3.3. Washington, with a murder rate of 2.7, has the death penalty. The average murder rate for all states with the death penalty in 2007 was 5.5 and without the death penalty 3.3. The difference has a great dealt to do with the region of the country and differences in regional culture, but not with the death penalty.

Numerous other examples indicate that murder is not related to the death penalty. Its presence does not increase murder, nor does its absence increase murder. The highest murder rates in the United States for many years have been in Louisiana, with 14.7 per 100,000 in 2007, as well as such other southern states as Maryland, Alabama, New Mexico, South Carolina, and Georgia. In fact, the South has had a higher murder rate than any other region of the country for many years. For example, in 2001, the South had an average murder rate per 100,000 of 6.7, followed by the West at 5.5, the Midwest at 5.3, and the Northeast at 4.2. In subsequent years, the same distribution continued, so that in 2007 the South had a murder rate of 7.0, the West 5.3, the Midwest 4.9, and the Northeast 4.1.[19]

The Bureau of Justice Statistics reports that the homicide offender rate and the victim rate of blacks are and have been six times greater than that of whites. The ratio is particularly true in those states with the largest black populations, which are Alabama, at 26 percent black; Florida, with a black population of 15.1 percent; Georgia, which is 28.7 percent black; Louisiana, which is 32.5 percent black; Mississippi, at 37.2 percent black; South Carolina, whose citizens are 28.1 percent black; and Texas, with 11 percent. All these states suffer a homicide rate greater than the 5.5 per 100,000 nationwide rate.[20]

The argument of deterrence is flawed not only because DNA testing has shown that innocent people can become victims of the death penalty policy but also because racial bias can contribute to the killing of innocents by the state. The bias is so well known that 38 states have appointed commissions to investigate the relationship between race and the death penalty. Death rows are populated by blacks far in excess of their proportion to the population. This situation may well be true because blacks commit more murders than do whites. Yet, even if that is the case, the perception of discrimination is not alleviated by the facts. Beyond that, it is likely that blacks are more often sent to death row than is true of whites with similar murder convictions. In addition, it is a matter of record that blacks guilty of murdering whites are definitely more likely to be sentenced to death than is true of whites who have killed members of any race. Moreover, racial prejudice is the most important predictor of white attitudes toward the death penalty. Racial bias is well understood in the African American community, where the death penalty is regarded as a racially motivated form of punishment. Evidently, as long as the death penalty may be attributed to bigotry, it cannot be a deterrent as well.[21]

Then there are those people who believe that controlling guns would be a deterrent to murder. There has been considerable debate concerning gun control and homicide. Numerous studies have been inconclusive concerning the effect of guns on the American killing rate. The fact is that the United States had a murder rate of 11 per 100,000 in the 1970s, whereas in 2009 it is 5.5, even as the number of guns in the hands of the American public has remained the same. It should be noted that the number of gun deaths in the United States is indeed higher than in countries where few citizens own guns. The number of gun deaths does not, however, reflect the number of intentional gun murders because most victims of shootings are killed by guns deemed "not loaded" or fired "accidentally."

THE ARGUMENT OF COST

Several recent surveys have demonstrated that it is cheaper to hold a prisoner for life than to kill him or her. For that reason, the death penalty may finally be abandoned in the United States, since it appears to be 10 times more expensive to kill a prisoner than to keep him alive. Few American voters understand this reality because it is commonly assumed that someone sent to death is quickly killed and therefore costs the taxpayer no more. The opposite is the case.

Normally, it takes at least 10 years, and in the case of California 20 years, from conviction to execution. The time from conviction to execution is one reason that New Jersey abandoned the death penalty in 2007, since it cost the state $4.2 million for each death sentence. That is also why, as of 2009, eight additional states are considering abandoning the death penalty. These states are Colorado, Kansas, Maryland, Nebraska, New Hampshire, New Mexico, Montana, and Washington.

Death penalty cases are so expensive because they require the state to hire extra lawyers to deal with the numerous appeals by the prisoners. Death row prisoners are often represented by pro bono publico lawyers from major New York or Los Angeles law firms who oppose the death penalty and therefore represent the prisoners without compensation. In the numerous cases in which the accused has no money to hire a lawyer, the state must furnish counsel. These appeals specialists are expensive and few, and so their availability delays appeals for years. Then there are security costs as well as costs of providing DNA tests and other evidence. Because death row inmates are housed in segregated sections of prisons, it costs more to house them, with guards having to deliver everything from meals to soap—all things the other prisoners do themselves.

Considering that housing one person in a maximum security prison for a year costs an average of $110,512, it is evident that imprisonment at that level for 40 years would cost the state no more than to kill the prisoner. Furthermore, there is no reason to assume that someone convicted of murder needs to be held in maximum security. In fact, a medium security incarceration costs the state an average of only $61,000, so it becomes far cheaper to incarcerate than to kill.[22]

THE ARGUMENT OF RETRIBUTION

The argument of retribution does not rely on statistics, nor do retributionists claim that the death penalty is a deterrent. Those who believe in retribution argue only from a philosophical point of view in that they hold that a community that does not kill the killer becomes itself guilty of murder. This was the argument of the truly liberal German philosopher Immanuel Kant (1724–1804), who thought that if a community were to leave an island so as to dissolve the community, then the last act the community's members must perform would be the execution of the last murderer remaining in prison, since otherwise each individual who made up the community would be guilty of the murder the convict had committed. "If they fail to do so," wrote Kant, "they may be regarded as accomplices in this public violation of legal justice."[23]

There are some individuals who argue that if the state does not kill the murderer, then the friends and relatives of the killer will do so, leading to a blood feud. There is, however, no evidence that such feuds have developed in states without the death penalty. Those people who believe in retribution believe that killing the murderer "pays for" the murder. To them, the risk of killing an innocent person is less important than maintaining the death penalty on the grounds that we drive cars despite the accidental deaths derived from traffic accidents and that we play dangerous games like football and that we ride in airplanes despite the occasional crash of a plane, costing numerous lives.

SOME DEATH PENALTY FACTS

In 2008, there were 37 inmates killed by nine states. Of those executed, 18 were killed in Texas, 4 in Virginia, 3 in Georgia, 3 in South Carolina, 2 each in Florida, Mississippi, Ohio, and Oklahoma, and 1 in Kentucky. Of the total, 20 were white men and 17 were black men. Note that no women were executed. Lethal injection was used to effect 36 of these killings, and 1 was by electrocution.

At the beginning of 2009, there were 3,253 persons on death row in the United States. Of these, 56 were women. Of all prisoners on death row, 1 in 12 had a prior homicide conviction, and 2 in 3 had a prior felony conviction. At the time of conviction, the youngest inmate under sentence of death was 19 and the oldest was 92. The average age of prisoners under sentence of death in 2009 was 29. The 738 killers executed between 1998 and 2007 had murdered 1,531 victims in those nine years.[24]

THE TEXAS KILLING MACHINE

In no state of the union is the killing of those convicted of murder as common as in Texas. Executed have been those convicted of killing 1,415 Texas citizens in 2007 alone—in 2007, there were 16,929 persons murdered in the entire United States—as well as those persons innocent of any crime but convicted just the same. The Texas killing machine, as it is called, thus consists of the numerous Texas murderers as well as the state-employed killers, the executioners. Because more Americans are killed by the state-paid killers in Texas than any other state, the Texas killing machine is the best example of such killings in the country.

Huntsville, Texas, is known for its death house—its death row— because it is without doubt the location of the most prolific dealer in death anywhere in the United States. Mass killings are of considerable profit to the citizens of Huntsville. In fact, the mayor of Huntsville has declared that the death penalty is good for business. That is indeed the case, since motels that house the family and friends of the person about to be killed as well as the family and friends of the murder victims rent rooms to attend the execution of the condemned. The arrival of the media also brings profits to the motels as well as restaurants in Huntsville. Then there are those visitors who protest the execution and others who support it. Then comes a huge army of those who profit from "The City of Death" by drawing paychecks from tax dollars used for the execution. The paid killers, that is, the people who earn state salaries for their heinous occupation, include not only the administrators and guards of the death row prisons but also the prison chaplains, the doctors who pronounce the victim dead, the undertakers and grave diggers, the bureaucrats who fill out forms and record the ugly deeds, and the police used in crowd control.

In addition, bar owners, liquor distributors, drug dealers, both legal and illegal, lottery ticket sellers, and a host of other business enterprises profit from the killings. Furthermore, the pharmaceutical industry profits from the drugs used to kill the prisoners, as do the coffin makers, food distributors, and gasoline sellers.[25]

Over the years, numerous opponents of the death penalty have come to Huntsville to protest the killings. The groups have included church members, students, lawyers, and even visitors whose relatives were the victims of murder. In particular, the medical profession has opposed the presence of physicians at the killings. The American Medical Association has barred physicians from participating in the killing of prisoners on the grounds that the profession is devoted to healing, not killing. The injunction is particularly important in California because that state requires a physician to be present at executions, a requirement that runs counter to the principles of medical ethics on which the medical profession rests.[26]

The City of Death, Huntsville, Texas, the location of 6 of the 115 Texas prisons, is so immersed in the killing culture that it sponsors a prison driving tour, which among its sites of interest includes the prison cemetery. Indeed, the city is so proud of its achievements that it is the location of the Texas Prison Museum, which houses a collection of death instruments and other horror paraphernalia. The museum exhibits the history of the Texas penal system, which today houses 150,000 prisoners at a cost of $2.5 billion, or $16,666.67 per prisoner annually. The museum's prized possession is an electric chair named "Old Sparky," in which 361 prisoners died between 1924 and 1964. It is displayed in a replica "death chamber." In addition, the museum displays the tubing and straps from a lethal injection bed. There is also a gift shop that sells death row caps. Numerous other displays all enhance this macabre monument to Huntsville, Texas, culture, the culture of death.[27]

The museum is run by former warden James Willett of "The Walls" prison, where he presided over the killing of 89 prisoners from 1998 until his retirement in 2001 from 30 years in the Texas corrections department. In 2000 alone, 40 prisoners were killed in The Walls under Willett's watch. In a recent interview, Willett now questions whether killing "a perfectly healthy human being is right." Of course, no one can be forced to work in a death house. Therefore, such an ex post facto comment is hardly an excuse for participating in legal murder. It is, of course, also true that the death penalty would end at once if no one killed another human being and murder was no more.

Among those prisoners executed by Willett was Charlie Brooks, the first man in the United States to be killed by lethal injection. There is no doubt that Brooks was guilty of a truly cold-blooded murder. According to the *Fort Worth Star-Telegram* as well as the Texas Court of Appeals and the U.S. Supreme Court, Brooks and his friend Woodie

Loudres and a prostitute who lived with Loudres decided to go Christmas shopping on December 14, 1976. Using drugs and alcohol, the three drove a car handed as payment to the prostitute for favors given a used car salesman. When the car vapor-locked, the three left the car at a service station and walked to a used car lot where they persuaded another salesman, 26-year-old David Gegory, to let them test drive a vehicle. Gregory accompanied the three as they drove to Loudres's motel. Having arrived there, the three asked Gregory to enter the motel room, where he was bound, gagged, and shot in the head by Brooks or Loudres. Each of the defendants in the subsequent murder trial blamed the other. Loudres was sentenced to 40 years, and Brooks was executed. There are critics who argue that Loudres was the real killer. Nevertheless, both men promoted the death of an innocent man. Had they not done so, then Brooks would still be alive, and so it must be repeated that the best way we can abolish the death penalty would be the cessation of murder.[28]

Karla Faye Tucker was killed by injection in the Huntsville death house on February 3, 1998. Her life and death received extensive news coverage and resulted in the production of a play and several songs concerning her fate. Since she was the only woman killed by any state in many years, she received much more attention than did men who committed similar crimes.

Tucker was convicted of killing two people, a man and a woman, by hacking them to death with a pickax. One of her victims was Jerry Lynn Dean, who had been bludgeoned to death so that his head had unhinged from his neck. A pickax had also been used to puncture his chest and his back. His companion, Deborah Ruth Thornton, had also been murdered by a pickax embedded in her chest. Together with her boyfriend, Daniel Ryan Garrett, Tucker had entered Dean's apartment at night and murdered him and Thornton as they were sleeping so as to steal his truck and some motorcycle parts.

Tucker was high on drugs at the time, as she had been since first using drugs at age 9 and shooting heroin at age 10. At 11 she began having sex. She was constantly ejected from school for fistfights. Her divorced mother taught her how to roll a joint and how to make money as a call girl.

As a teenager, Tucker became "Ms. Tough Guy." She fought incessantly, as she became part of a motorcycle gang of men riding Harley-Davidsons and wearing provocative T-shirts. She visited gun shows and saw violent movies with her super-macho boyfriend, Dan Garrett, who promised to turn Karla into a hit woman. The end to that lifestyle came after she was arrested, convicted, and executed for the gruesome murders of Dean and Thornton. Once on death row, she found Jesus. Tucker's newfound religious zeal led to a great deal of sympathy for Tucker from people who believed that Tucker had become a changed person and could be rehabilitated through religion. The murders committed by Tucker once more lead observers to the conclusion that the best way to end the death penalty is the cessation of murder.

The Texas Execution Information Center reported in March 2009 that 35 men were killed in the Huntsville slaughterhouse in 1999 alone and that 40 more men were killed there in 2000. In subsequent years, that is, 2001 through March 11, 2009, the Texas killing center in Huntsville ended the lives of another 177 men. There is little doubt that the rate of slaughter will continue unless the people of Texas make it more profitable to end the slaughter than to continue it.

The executed in Texas are victims of the Texas killing machine. Those people who kill would seldom have an opportunity to end the lives of others were it not for those guilty of murder or those innocents railroaded into the death chamber.

Luis Salazar was killed at the Huntsville, Texas, killing facility on March 11, 2009. He was convicted of stabbing to death his next-door neighbor. In October 1997, Salazar had crawled through a window and attempted to rape a woman in the presence of her child. Because she resisted, he killed her. He spent 11 years on death row.[29]

Robert Hudson was killed at the Huntsville killing facility on November 20, 2008. He was convicted of killing Edith Kendrick because she had become involved with another man after having been Hudson's girlfriend for some time. Suspecting that Kendrick had invited a man into her apartment, Hudson kicked in the door and found Michael Speerman inside with Kendrick. Hudson then attacked Speerman with a knife. Seeing this, Kendrick tried to interfere, leading Hudson to stab her to death, leaving her with seven wounds in a pool of blood. He then stole $275 from Kendrick's purse, which the police found in his pocket. Hudson had three previous felony convictions, including burglary, forgery, and murder. Each time he was paroled but then continued his criminal activities.[30]

James Jackson was killed at the Huntington death house on February 7, 2007. Jackson had killed his wife and two stepdaughters. Jackson confronted one of his stepdaughters, Ericka, on April 8, 1997, and asked her how she felt about her mother's threat to divorce him. When Ericka expressed ambivalence about this, Jackson strangled her with his hands. Ericka was 18 years old when she died. Thirty minutes later, 19-year-old Sonny arrived home. Jackson asked her the same question and then strangled Sonny although she attempted to hug him. Shortly thereafter, his wife, Sharon, called and asked for a ride from work. Jackson picked her up and strangled her when they got home.

Before he left the apartment where he had murdered all three victims, Jackson left a note to the effect that he killed them because he had no job and could not support them. "I gave them back to God," wrote Jackson. He returned to the apartment as the police were present. He confessed to all three murders and told the police that he pawned his wife's sewing machine so he could buy drugs. Jackson had a previous felony conviction for shooting his children's grandfather. He had served 4.5 years of a 10-year prison sentence and was still on parole when he murdered his three victims.[31]

William Wyatt was killed at the Huntsville killing center on August 3, 2006. He was convicted of sexual assault and murder of a 3-year-old boy for whom he babysat while his live-in girlfriend was at work. Wyatt called 911 that evening and asked that an ambulance come to his home. There, the ambulance personnel found the little boy dead. According to Wyatt, the child had drowned in a bathtub. However, the physician at the hospital where 3-year-old Damien was pronounced dead discovered that the child had bruises all over his body and that his rectum had been invaded. The doctor determined that the child had died of homicidal violence. Wyatt explained after his arrest that he saw something on television that induced him to have sex. He also admitted to whipping the boy with a belt and placing a plastic bag over his head because he screamed. At his trial, Wyatt's girlfriend, Renee Porter, testified that Wyatt had molested the boy on previous occasions and that he had raped her.[32]

On September 14, 2005, Frances Elaine Newton was killed by lethal injection in the Huntsville killing center because she had killed her husband and her two children. Evidently, Frances Newton was having marital and financial problems. She and her husband dated others. She also took out $50,000 life insurance policies on her 23-year-old husband and her 21-month-old daughter. Her son already had a life insurance policy. She was 21 years old at that time.

On April 7, 1987, sheriff's deputies were dispatched to an apartment where they found Newton and her cousin, as well as the bodies of Adrian Newton, the husband, and the children, Alton and Farrah. All three had been shot in the head and were dead. Frances Newton admitted to having shot her victims with a .25 caliber semiautomatic pistol.

At her trial, Newton sought to blame a drug dealer for the murders. According to her testimony, the drug dealer was owed money from her husband, who used a good number of drugs. Several tests of the murder weapon revealed that it was indeed Frances Newton who had used it in these multiple murders. Therefore, her numerous appeals were all denied, and she was executed by state employees.[33]

DaRoyce Lamont Moseley was killed by lethal injection in Huntsville, Texas, on the August 28, 2007. Moseley, together with two other men, burst into a bar in Kilgore, Texas, just before midnight on July 21, 1994. There were four customers in the bar and a waitress, Sandra Cash. Shouting, "Give me the money, you white bitch," Moseley shot all four customers, who died. The waitress survived a shot that paralyzed her from the waist down. She called 911 as the killers fled.

A neighbor of Moseley's told the police the next day that he had heard Moseley discuss the possible robbery of the bar with his friends and that Moseley had a gun. On the evening of the murders, Moseley discussed the killings with Marcus Kaboo, a friend, and freely admitted that he had fired the shots. His benefit from these killings was only $77, since he had to divide the $308 found in the restaurant cash box with his companions in the robbery-murders.

TECHNIQUES OF NEUTRALIZATION

It is surely impossible for an American living in the twenty-first century not to know that killing men and women is revolting to almost anyone living in a civilized society. This sentiment is well known to the people who murder their fellow human beings outside the law as well as to those people whose killings are legally sanctioned because they are paid to kill on behalf of the state.

Therefore, it is necessary for those who murder or participate in state-sanctioned killing of others to find some excuse, some reason, to make it possible for them to condone killing their fellow human beings and live with that knowledge. Accepting one's role as a murderer or killer or as a deviant of any kind requires "techniques of neutralization."[34]

The first technique of neutralization is *denial of responsibility*. Such denial allows those who have killed others to claim that someone else is responsible for the killing and that the killer is, in fact, the victim. Such a means of living with the knowledge that one has destroyed the life of another human is quite evident among the paid killers, the executioners and administrators, who kill for the state as well as those who have private motives to murder. In an interview with a number of employees of the Huntsville, Texas, so-called Huntsville Unit, whose members execute a number of prisoners every week, this technique becomes quite evident. Kenneth Dean, a major of the Huntsville Unit, told National Public Radio's *All Things Considered*, on October 20, 2000, that he had participated in 120 killings. Dean describes how tying a victim to a death gurney "is down to a fine art." He said that he believed in his work, in "what I do," and that "I take my mind off it when I go fishing." Dean's principal reaction to all the killings he has committed on behalf of the state is that the state, not he himself, is responsible for the killings. That view, of course, conveniently overlooks the fact that no one is forced to do this horrible work and that those who kill are killers, whether working for the state or not. Murderers use similar techniques. They frequently deny responsibility by claiming that drugs, including alcohol, made them do it—made them kill—or that "I blacked out" or "didn't know what I was doing."

Another technique of neutralization is to *point out the culpability of the victim*, to say that the victim of the killing deserves it. A captain in a death squad working at the Huntsville killing center, Terry Green, excused his conduct as a professional killer by harping on the crime committed by the victim and telling his audience that he is only doing "what the people want done." Blaming the victim is also a notion used by murderers. Those who kill others often claim that they became enraged because their victim "got involved with another man," or "stole my money," or "threatened to kill me," or the like.

Professional killers working for the state like to claim that outsiders have no right to judge them, since they are only doing their job. Yet, not one has to do that job. Evidently, killing has its rewards over and beyond the money earned. Some people simply like to kill others, and death house guards are the best example of individuals who appear to have no conscience. This technique of neutralization involves *condemning the condemner*. Both murderers and state-employed killers claim that those who condemn their actions are hypocrites who are themselves criminals. Prison guards engaged in killing like to recite the crimes of their victims, and murderers will refer to misdeeds by the police or probation officers or "them."

Appeal to higher loyalties is yet another technique of neutralization. That approach was used extensively by Nazi officials during the Nuremberg trials. At every level, the accused claimed they had no choice but to follow orders from commanders above them. Likewise, state-paid killers appeal to their loyalty to the state or their wish to protect the public by killing the murderers.

The most important technique of neutralization is *approval of one's reference group*. The reference group is one with whom the perpetrator identifies and whose expectations the killer or murderer seeks to fulfill. Those who murder for organized crime, for example, will support their horrible conduct by being bolstered by the approval of the organization to which they belong. The need for the approval of one's reference group motivates not only those who kill but also ordinary people, who commonly seek their group's approval in everyday life. Thus, this neutralization technique is used by almost anyone, but in particular those who believe they have deviated from the expectations of their reference group or their expectations of themselves.

Loyalty to a higher purpose is yet another technique of neutralization used to engage in hundreds of death house killings. The "higher purpose" is, of course, the revenge motive, which supports legal killing. Just as organized-crime killers claim to support their organization by killing those who stand in the way of their business interests, death house guards claim to "protect the public" by killing their fellow men.

In sum, it is evident from reading the comments of the killers that some of them fit the profile of sociopaths—that is, of someone who has no conscience and is incapable of sympathizing with other human beings. That sort of deviance is known to psychiatrists and has never been adequately explained, though it is often associated with a lack of parental love starting at a very young age. It is also associated with neglect and brutal beatings or deprivation of young children before the age of five.

Martha Stout, a psychologist, in her book *The Sociopath Next Door*, indicates that about 4 percent of Americans have no conscience. Stout writes, "Imagine . . . not having a conscience, none at all, no feelings of guilt or remorse no matter what you do, no limiting sense of concern for the well being of strangers, friends or even family members."[35]

Of course, not all murders may be attributed to lack of conscience. In fact, Gerhard Falk found that sudden anger is the most frequent reason for murder, followed by victim precipitation and jealousy. Such motives do not apply to state-employed killers, whose methodical and unemotional killing is preplanned and therefore much more likely the province of sociopaths.[36]

THE RECENT HISTORY AND THE FUTURE OF THE DEATH PENALTY

In 1972, the U.S. Supreme Court struck down the death penalty temporarily but reinstated it in 1976. Between 1982 and 1999, there were 250 to 350 persons annually sentenced to death. In 1999, however, the figure declined to 100 persons executed; but since then, executions have continued to decline even in states that still maintain the death penalty. The decline was particularly the case when in 2000 the governor of Illinois imposed a moratorium on the death penalty because 13 inmates on death row had been cleared of murder charges by DNA testing, compared to 12 who had already been put to death.[37]

In view of DNA testing, more and more states have become willing to repeal death penalty laws. It is predictable, therefore, that the number of states whose laws allow the death penalty will dwindle in the face of scientific evidence. Elimination of the death penalty has certainly become the policy of New Jersey and of New Mexico, which is the 15th state to abolish the death penalty in recent years.

Internationally, abolition of the death penalty began in the nineteenth century, when Costa Rica, Venezuela, and San Marino ceased to enforce state-sanctioned murder. Since 2000, five more countries abolished the death penalty; however, China, the United States, Serbia, Montenegro, and Saudi Arabia have continued to support it.

The European Union (EU) has abolished the death penalty and made it a condition of membership that countries wishing to join must also abolish the death penalty. This pertains to Turkey, which abolished the death penalty in 2002 during peacetime, but not during war, in an effort to join the EU.[38]

In the United States, the death penalty is gradually losing public support. This change in the attitude of the American public is at least partially related to the imprisonment and execution of numerous innocent citizens whose innocence has been established by DNA evidence. It is also related to the reluctance of some juries to recommend the death penalty on moral grounds. Most important, the rate of violent crime in the United States has declined considerably in recent years as a decline in the birthrate preceded that decline.

SUMMARY

The conviction of innocent people by our criminal justice system is as old as the system itself. However, DNA testing has uncovered numerous such convictions, including convictions leading to the death penalty. In consequence, the federal government and a number of states have enacted laws compensating those people unjustly incarcerated.

There are a number of arguments for and against the death penalty, most of which date at least as far back as the first century BC. These are the argument of popularity, deterrence, cost, and retribution.

Because more convicts are killed in Texas than in any other state, the so-called Texas killing machine is featured as the best example of the administration of the death penalty in the United States. The large volume of executions causes those who kill the convicted as well as those who commit murder to use various techniques of neutralization in order to live with the knowledge that they have killed their fellow human beings.

NOTES

1. Linda Greenhouse, "Supreme Court: No Death Penalty for Child Rape," *San Francisco Chronicle*, June 26, 2008, A3.

2. *Coker v. Georgia*, 433 U.S. 584 (1977).

3. *Ford v. Wainwright*, 477 U.S. 399 (1986).

4. *Thompson v. Oklahoma*, 487 U.S. 815 (1988).

5. Linda Greenhouse, "Citing National Consensus, Justices Bar Death Penalty for Retarded Defendants," *New York Times*, June 21, 2002, 1.

6. Brian MacArthur, *The Penguin Book of Twentieth Century Speeches* (New York: Viking Penguin, 2000), 100–103.

7. Sydney P. Freedberg, "The Stigma Is Always There," *St. Petersburg Times*, July 4, 1999.

8. Tiara M. Ellis, "Appeals Court Overturns Michael Blair's Conviction in Ashley Estell Case," *Dallas Morning News*, June 25, 2008, 1.

9. Anthony Cormier, "Wrongfully Convicted Man's Murder Case Raises Questions," *Herald Tribune*, March 8, 2009, A1.

10. U.S. Public Law 108–405.

11. *The Innocence Protection Act of 2004*, Death Penalty Information Center, http://www.Deathpenalty.org.

12. Vincent M. Scarmuzza and Paul L. Kendrick, *The Ancient World* (New York: Henry Holt, 1988), 509.

13. First Amendment to the U.S. Constitution. "Congress Shall Make No Law Respecting an Establishment of Religion, Or Prohibiting the Free Exercise Thereof."

14. Religious organizing against the death penalty, "A Call to All People of Faith," (Philadelphia, n.d.).

15. National Inter-religious Task Force on Criminal Justice, *Capital Punishment: What the Religious Community Says* (New York, n.d.).

16. *Washington Post*, "Catholic Bishops Plan Drive against Death Penalty," May 21, 2005, AO4.

17. U.S. Department of Justice, Bureau of Justice Statistics, "Contents of Homicide Trends in the United States" (Washington, DC: GPO, n.d.).

18. U.S. Public Health Service, *Statistical Abstract of the United States* (Washington, DC: GPO, 2008), Table 77.

19. Death Penalty Information Center, *Nationwide Murder Rates, 1996–2007* (Washington, DC, 2008).

20. U.S. Census, *The American Community* (Washington, DC: GPO, 2004), 8.

21. Thomas J. Keil and Gennaro E. Vito, "Race and the Death Penalty in Kentucky Murder Trials," *American Journal of Criminal Justice* 20, no. 1 (1995): 17–36.

22. Deborah Hastings, "States Struggle with Cost of Execution," *Ventura County Star*, March 7, 2009.

23. Immanuel Kant, *The Metaphysical Elements of Justice* (New York: Bobbs Merrill, 1963), 102.

24. U.S. Department of Justice, Bureau of Justice Statistics, "Capital Punishement Statistics," *Summary Findings* (Washington, DC: GPO, March 26, 2009), 1.

25. George H. Russell, *The City of Death* (Huntsville, TX: Universal Ethical Church, n.d.).

26. Rich Daly, "Participation in Death Penalty: Where Should Line Be Drawn," *Psychiatric News* 41, no. 9 (May 5, 2006): 9.

27. Roadside America, *Texas Prison Museum* (Huntsville, TX, n.d.).

28. Rob Ray Sanders, "The First to Die by Injection," *Fort Worth Star-Telegram*, December 3, 2007, 1.

29. *New York Times*, "Texas Killer Is Executed," March 12, 2009, A17.

30. David Carson, "Robert Hudson," Texas Execution Information Center, November 24, 2008.

31. David Carson, "James Jackson," Texas Execution Information Center, February 8, 2007.

32. David Carson, "William Wyatt," Texas Execution Information Center, August 4, 2006.

33. David Carson, "Frances Newton," Texas Execution Information Center, September 15, 2005.

34. Gresham Sykes and David Matza, "Techniques of Neutralization," *American Sociological Review* 22 (1957): 664–70.

35. Martha Stout, Introduction to *The Sociopath Next Door* (New York: Broadway, 2006).

36. Gerhard Falk, *Murder: An Analysis of Its Forms, Conditions and Causes* (Jefferson, NC: McFarland, 1990), 48.

37. Patrick Cooney, "Death Penalty," *News Batch*, June 2008.

38. Ibid.

EPILOGUE

The first duty of government is to protect its country's citizens from foreign and domestic enemies. To do that, a criminal justice system is needed in all societies, large or small. The Constitution of the United States provides such a system, though it may seem antiquated because the document reflects life as it was in the eighteenth century.

It has, therefore, become necessary to interpret the U.S. Constitution in the light of present circumstances, a task assigned to the Supreme Court of the United States.

Of course, most Americans have no dealings with the criminal justice system outside of contacts with the police, and so public support for the American system of criminal justice depends mainly on the manner in which police organizations and their members are evaluated by citizens. Support for the criminal justice system depends largely on the manner in which the police are perceived by the citizens and that, in turn, is largely produced by the media. In fact, the media, and particularly television, portray police activities and the courts all the time and also show both real and fictional prison scenes—for example, TV programs like *Hill Street Blues, Crime Scene Investigation, Criminal Minds,* and *Law and Order: Criminal Intent.* The public is heavily influenced by such television portrayals of the U.S. criminal justice system. Yet, much of what is seen on television is exaggerated for the sake of its entertainment value. Some of what is shown is, in fact, wrong. It is thus one of the purposes of this book to deal in reality and countermand the fiction concerning the criminal justice system so frequently promoted by the entertainment industry.

Public relations are of the utmost importance to the police and the American public. It is therefore in the interest of police departments and their members to improve their image, in particular in the black community. There, police officers are frequently seen as the enemy. A cycle of violence between the police and black gun owners is a constant issue in the inner cities of the United States. Police, fearing that armed men will shoot them for minimal reasons, often react in advance of violence by using what appears to be excessive force. The arguments between police and citizens, particularly in the inner-city ghettoes, make it appear that the police are the enemies of the black community and that blacks must defend themselves at all times against provocative or aggressive police behavior in black areas of American cities. The solution to the misperceptions and the violence lies in promoting peaceful and instructive relationships between police and citizens, whatever their ethnicity. Here, mutual social affairs, role playing, and foot patrols can be of great help because these measures introduce individual police officers to community members. Friendly relationships reduce tensions and become a barrier against hearsay and angry responses to outsiders. People who know each other have far less reason to be suspicious of each other than do strangers. Familiarity is also why police foot patrols are superior to driving around in a squad car. In some cities, police have rented store fronts, where they can be visited by citizens at any time. Such store fronts also allow police to respond almost at once to violence or other problems in the community.

Police officers see themselves as a beleaguered minority who can trust only other police officers but not the public they reputedly protect. The resulting tensions and antagonisms between the police and the citizens they serve need to be alleviated. Tensions can be eased through role playing of explosive scenarios, by studying sociology and social psychology, for example, or by learning at least something about the constitutional rights of American citizens. Yet, more important than any other method of relaxing tensions between police and the minority community is an effort at building interpersonal relationships based on mutual respect and acquaintanceship between those who "serve and protect" and those who are to be protected.

Because the criminal justice system depends on prosecutors to represent the citizens in court, some prosecutors have a long history of going to any length to convict the accused. The introduction of evidence based on DNA testing has proved that a considerable number of past prosecutions led to the conviction of the innocent. It is justified to assume that a number of those convicted in the past were indeed innocent but were convicted because of eyewitness accounts. The evidence indicates that many eyewitnesses were actually wrong; they did not see what they believed they saw. Thus, prosecutors should not use eyewitness accounts as a reason to prosecute. In addition, it should be prohibited to use so-called jailhouse snitches to testify against a defendant to the effect that the defendant confessed guilt. Offering the prospect of gaining one's freedom in exchange for false testimony is so corrupting that no prosecutor should be given the opportunity to gain a conviction by such means.

Because prosecutors are elected, it is, of course, in their own best interest to gain as many convictions as needed to make a favorable impression on voters. The temptation to convict innocent citizens is therefore inherent in the short-term election cycle. To offset the temptation, the law should demand that a prosecutor who deliberately promotes the conviction of an innocent person shall be promptly relieved of his or her position. Likewise, police, judges, and others involved in railroading an innocent person should be subject to prosecution. Although there are provisions in most states for dealing with "malicious prosecutions," the laws are hardly enforced because those engaged in the criminal justice system will not usually pursue others employed in the system. Nevertheless, such prosecutors as Mike Nyfong, who used unacceptable methods in the Duke University lacrosse case, have been removed from office. It is here suggested that an ombudsperson is required to deal with such cases independently.

Most egregious are the special considerations given to police who beat and otherwise assault "significant others" in their lives, be they wives or girlfriends or other citizens. Neither prosecutors nor judges ordinarily prosecute police no matter their crimes against others, except when the media create a great deal of publicity in extraordinary cases. A police control board of private citizens is needed to rein in police brutality in every American jurisdiction. Such a board should have the right to hear evidence, investigate complaints, and discharge brutal or incompetent police on findings of guilt. Discharge is not the same as criminal conviction, however. Therefore, such a control board should not interfere with the rights of the accused but will, instead, protect citizens from the excesses of the police. Nevertheless, it needs to be understood that the decisions made by police officers are often made under great pressure and in frightening circumstances that can then be easily criticized by those who review such decisions later and in the comfort of their offices.

The so-called war on drugs mimics the prohibition of alcohol in the 1920s and early 1930s. Because the word "drug" excludes alcohol as formerly used, the war on drugs deals only with drugs produced in Mexico and other countries that have little prestige in the English-speaking United States. Evidently, one reason certain drugs are prohibited whereas alcohol is not is that alcohol is produced in Scotland, America, and other Western countries. In contrast, marijuana and cocaine are produced mainly in South America and Asia and are hence less prestigious products.

It is here suggested that drug addicts be supplied by physicians to the detriment of organized gangs, whose income is so huge solely because the drugs they sell are illegal.

A very important issue is the defense of the poor in American courts. Indeed, there are public defenders who try to defend the indigent. These public defenders, however, do not have nearly the resources possessed by public prosecutors, who have at their disposal the entire police department. Public defenders are thus at a disadvantage concerning their clients. The states should, therefore, spend as much money on the offices of the public defenders as they spend on prosecutions. Equal expenditure would at least furnish the community with far better representation of the defendants, guilty or innocent. At present, defendants are at an evident disadvantage vis-á-vis the prosecution.

Because juries are heavily influenced by the media and their opinions concerning a defendant, American media would be well advised, not to sensationalize, but to publish the facts concerning violent crime in the United States. The facts are that violent crime has decreased considerably since the 1970s. Yet, the media keep publishing scare stories that make it appear that crime is on the increase when the opposite is the case. Indeed, politicians welcome scare stories that tend to help elect them as they endlessly proclaim, "I am tough on crime."

The majority of American judges are elected on a local level. In small towns, the judges may be people who have no legal education whatever and make decisions based solely on their private prejudices. Therefore, it is vital that no one be eligible to serve as a judge unless he or she has graduated from a school of law. Presently, many a small town is victimized by virtual tyrants who are persistently reelected as judges even if they know nothing or care nothing about the rights of American citizens as enshrined in the U.S. Constitution.

New DNA tests have revealed that our prisons are full of innocent people who have been victimized by so-called eyewitness identification and by police and prosecutors who need convictions to maintain their incomes. Many of our prisons are also poorly run by administrators who not only need to earn a paycheck but also thrive on psychic income or the opportunity to lord it over other people. Fortunately, such prison administrators are gradually disappearing as wardens with advanced degrees in law, sociology, psychology, and social work take their place.

Our prisons are unsafe, for often the largest, physically powerful prisoners use smaller men for their sexual gratification. What is wanted are prison officials who will eliminate homosexual behaviors from prisons and who understand the necessity of giving prisoners work and providing them with an education, since a considerable number of

American prisoners have no skills with which to find work once released. In fact, the 4 percent illiteracy rate among American prisoners is twice that of the American public.

Probation and parole are far cheaper than imprisonment. For that reason alone, both means of keeping convicted offenders out of the walls of prisons should be used a good deal more than is now the case. Furthermore, probation and parole officers need a good deal more education than is now required. Sociology and psychology are of great importance in making the work of probation officers more successful, particularly if caseloads can be reduced in order to give all graduates a better understanding of human relations in their work with probationers. This kind of diversion from prisons will also reduce the crime rate, which depends, in part, on the offenders' understanding that their own lives will improve if they are more considerate of others.

Finally, it is recommended here that the president of the United States appoint a federal commission charged with making recommendations for the overhaul of the entire criminal justice system. Such a commission should exclude sitting politicians needing reelection and instead include lawyers, sociologists, psychologists, social workers, and prison officials. The need for such a revision of the system is considerable, as shown in the pages of this book.

BIBLIOGRAPHY

BOOKS

Abrams, D., and M. Hogg, eds. *Social Identity Theory.* London: Harvester Weatsheaf, 1990.

Acton, John Dalberg. In *The New Dictionary of Cultural Literacy.* 3rd ed. Ed. John Kett. 2002.

Augustus, John. *First Probation Officer.* New York: National Probation Association, 1939.

Bartlett, Robert. *Trial by Fire and Water.* New York: Clarendon Press, 1986.

Battey, Thomas. *A Quaker among the Indians.* Boston: Lee and Shepard, 1875.

Beattie, J. M. *Crime and the Courts in England.* Princeton, NJ: Princeton University Press, 1986.

Benedict, Jeff, and Don Yeager. *The Criminals Who Play in the NFL.* New York: Warner Books, 1998.

Betsey, Martin. "Violent Criminal Loses Probation." *Arkansas Matters.com* (December 23, 2007).

Bottoms, B. *Children and the Law.* Cambridge: Cambridge University Press, 2002.

Brown, Richard Maxwell. "Lawless Lawfulness: Legal and Behavioral Perspectives on American Vigilantism." *Perspectives on American Vigilantism.* New York: Oxford University Press, 1975.

Caute, David. *The Great Fear: The Anti-Communist Purge under Truman and Eisenhower.* New York: Simon and Schuster, 1978.

Cohen, Stanley, A. *Mitchell Palmer: Politician.* New York: Columbia University Press, 1963.

Connors, Edward, Thomas Lundregan, Neal Miller, and Tom McEwen. *Convicted by Juries, Exonerated by Science.* Washington, DC: Office of Justice Programs, National Institute of Justice, 1996.

Death Penalty Information Center. *Nationwide Murder Rates, 1996–2007.* Washington, DC, 2008.

Dershowitz, Alan. *The Abuse Excuse and Other Cop-Outs: Sob Stories and Evasions of Responsibility.* New York: Little Brown & Co., 1995.

Donner, Frank J. *Age of Surveillance.* New York: Vintage Books 1981.

Edwards, George J. *The Grand Jury.* Philadelphia: G. T. Bisel, 1906.

Falk, Gerhard. *Murder: An Analysis of Its Forms, Conditions and Causes.* Jefferson, NC: McFarland & Co., 1990.

Fischer, David H. *Albion's Seed*. New York: Oxford University Press, 1989.

Freeman, Lawrence M. *Crime and Punishment in American History*. New York: Basic Books, 1992.

Green, Thomas Andrew. *Verdict According to Conscience*. Chicago: University of Chicago Press, 1985.

Gurr, Ted Robert. *Why Men Rebel*. Princeton, NJ: Princeton University Press, 1970.

Hastie, Reid. *Inside the Jury*. Cambridge, MA: Harvard University Press, 1983.

Ianni, Francis A. J. *A Family Business*. New York: Russell Sage Foundation, 1972.

Inciardi, James A. *The War on Drugs: Heroin, Cocaine, Crime, and Public Policy*. Palo Alto, CA: Mayfield Publishing, 1986.

Johnson, David R. *Policing the Urban Underworld*. Philadelphia: Temple University Press, 1979.

Kalven, Harry, and Hans Zeisel. *The American Jury*. Boston: Little Brown, 1966.

Kant, Immanuel. *The Metaphysical Elements of Justice*. New York: Bobbs Merrill, 1963.

King, Gary, Robert O. Keohane, and Sidney Verba. *Designing Social Inquiry*. Princeton, NJ: Princeton University Press, 1994.

King, Rachel. "Three Decades Later: Why We Need a Temporary Halt on Executions." Washington, DC: ACLU Capital Punishment Project, 2005.

Klein, Andrew R. *Alternative Sentencing, Intermediate Sanctions and Probation*. Cincinnati: Anderson Publishing, 1997.

Lankevich, George. *American Metropolis: A History of New York City*. New York: Bronx Historical Society, 1996.

Lorber, Judith. *Gender and the Social Construction of Illness*. Lanham, MD: Rowman and Littlefield, 2002.

MacArthur, Brian. *The Penguin Book of Twentieth Century Speeches*. New York: Viking Penguin, 2000.

Michelle, Matthew T. *Probation and Parole's Growing Caseloads and Workloads Allocation: Strategies for Managerial Decision Making*. American Probation and Parole Association: Lexington, KY, 2007.

Miller, David S., and Michael Hersen. *Research Fraud in the Biomedical and Behavioral Sciences*. New York: John Wiley and Sons, 1992.

Monkkonen, Eric H. *Police in Urban America*. New York: Cambridge University Press, 1981.

Moraskin, Roslyn. *Women and Criminal Justice*. Upper Saddle River, NJ: Prentice Hall, 2000.

National Inter-religious Task Force on Criminal Justice. *Capital Punishment: What the Religious Community Says*. National Criminal Justice Reference Service, available at: http://www.ncjrs.gov/App/Publications/abstract.aspx?ID=54309.

Owen, Barbara. *In the Mix: Struggle and Survival in Women's Prison*. Albany, NY: SUNY Press, 1998.

Packard, Vance. *The Sexual Wilderness*. New York: D. McKay, 1968.

Peirce, Bradford Kinney. *A Half Century with Juvenile Delinquents*. Montclaire, NJ: Patterson and Smith, 1969.

Peterson, Arthur E., and George W. Edwards. *New York as an Eighteenth Century Municipality*. Port Washington, NY: Columbia University Press, 1917.

Platt, A. M. *The Child Savers*. Chicago: University of Chicago Press, 1977.

Powers, Edwin. *Crime and Punishment in Early Massachusetts, 1620–1692.* Boston: Beacon Press, 1966.

Preston Jr., William. *Aliens and Dissenters: Federal Suppression of Radicals, 1903–1933.* New York: Cambridge University Press, 1963.

Roadside America. *Texas Prison Museum.* Huntsville, TX, no date.

Russell, George H. *The City of Death.* Huntsville, TX: Universal Ethical Church, no date.

Sayre, Anne. *Rosalind Franklin and DNA.* New York: Norton, 1975.

Scarmuzza, Vincent M., and Paul L. Kendrick. *The Ancient World.* New York: Henry Holt, 1988.

Scott, Sir Walter. *Ivanhoe.* New York: Heritage Press, 1950.

Smith, Dwight C. *The Mafia Mystique.* New York: Basic Books, 1975.

Steinberg, Allen. *The Transformation of Criminal Justice.* Chapel Hill: University of North Carolina Press, 1989.

Stout, Martha. *The Sociopath Next Door.* New York: Broadway Publishing, 2006.

Sutherland, Edwin H., Donald R. Cressey, and David F. Luckenbill. *Principles of Criminology.* Dix Hills, NY: General Hall, 1992.

Thio, Alex. *Sociology.* 5th ed. New York: Longman, 1998.

Thomas, Keith. "Cases of Conscience in Seventeenth Century England." in *Public Duty and Private Conscience in Seventeenth Century England,* ed. J. Morrill, P. Slack, and D. Wolff. New York: Oxford University Press, 1993.

Tonty, Michael. *Crime and Justice: An Annual Review of Research.* Vol. 16. Chicago: University of Chicago Press, 1992.

Tuska, Jon. *Billy the Kid.* Westport, CT: Greenwood Press, 1983.

Udell, Gilman C. *Opium and Narcotics Laws.* Washington, DC: GPO, 1968.

U.S. Department of Justice. Bureau of Justice Statistics. *Prison Statistics.* Washington, DC: GPO, December 31, 2007.

———. *Occupational Outlook Handbook, 2008–2009.* Washington, DC: GPO, 2009.

Von Hentig, Hans. *The Criminal and His Victim.* New Haven, CT: Yale University Press, 1948.

Winslow, Robert, and Sheldon Zhang. *Criminology.* New York: Pearson, Prentice Hall, 2008.

Worchel, Stewart, and W. G. Austin, eds. *Psychology of Intergroup Relations.* Chicago: Nelson Hall, 1982.

Wright, Robert Marr. *Dodge City.* Wichita, KS: Wichita Eagle Press, 1913.

JOURNALS AND MAGAZINES

Abernethy, Thomas P. "Jackson and the Rise of South-Western Democracy." *American Historical Review* 33, no. 1, October 1927.

Anderson, K. L. "Perpetrator or Victim? Relationship between Intimate Partners and Well Being." *Journal of Marriage and Family* 64 (2002).

Antonio, Michael. "Arbitrariness and the Death Penalty." *Behavioral Sciences and the Law* 24 (2006).

Babcock, Barbara Allen. "Duty to Defend." *Yale Law Journal* 1489 (2005).

———. "Inventing the Public Defender." *American Criminal Law Review* 43, no. 4 (Fall 2006).

Baker, Newman. "The Prosecuting Attorney-Provisions of Organizing a Law Office." *Journal of Criminal Law and Criminology* 23 (1932).

Barry, John V. "Captain Alexander Maconochie." *Victorian Historical Magazine* 27 (June 1975).

Beiser, Vince. "How We Got to Two Million: How Did the Land of the Free Become the World's Leading Jailer?" *Mother Jones,* July 10, 2001.

Berger, Ken. "Grand Jury Hears Jets vs. Santa Case." *Newsday,* February 11, 2003.

Biddinotto, Robert J. "Getting Away with Murder." *Reader's Digest,* July 1988.

Biships, Jerold, and S. Auerbach. "Patrician as Libertarian: Zecheriah Chafee Jr. and Freedom of Speech." *New England Quarterly* 42 (December 1969).

Bishop, Donna M. "Juvenile Justice under Attack: An Analysis of the Causes and Impact of Recent Reforms." *Florida Journal of Law and Public Policy* 129 (1998).

Boldue, Anne. "Jail Crowding." *Annals of the American Academy of Political and Social Sciences* 478 (March 1985).

Bonnie, Richard J., and Charles Whitebread. "The Forbidden Fruit and the Tree of Knowledge." *Virginia Law Review* 56, no. 6 (October 1970).

Bowers, William C. "The Pervasiveness of Arbitrariness and Discrimination under Post-Furman Capital Statutes." *Journal of Criminal Law and Criminology* 74, no. 3 (1967).

Burke, Kevin G. "A Nurse's Dramatic Story." *Trial* 44, no. 3 (July 2008).

Butler, Paul. "Racially Based Jury Nullification: Black Power in the Criminal Justice System." *Yale Law Journal* 105 (1995).

Carson, David. "Frances Newton." Texas Execution Information Center, September 15, 2005.

———. "James Jackson." Texas Execution Information Center, February 8, 2007.

———. "Robert Hudson." Texas Execution Information Center, November 24, 2008.

———. "William Wyatt." Texas Execution Information Center, August 4, 2006.

Chapell, Richard A. "Look Back at Federal Probation: Recollections of the Early Years." *Federal Probation* 24, no. 4 (December 1975).

Cockburn, Alexander, and Jeffrey St. Clair. "The Bi-partisan Origins of the Total War on Drugs." *Counterpunch,* August 21, 2004.

Cooney, Patrick. "Death Penalty." *News Batch,* June 2008.

Daly, Rich. "Participation in Death Penalty: Where Should Line Be Drawn." *Psychiatric News* 41, no. 9 (May 5, 2006).

Daudistel, Howard. "Effects of Defendants' Ethnicity on Juries' Dispositions of Felony Cases." *Journal of Applied Social Psychology* 29 (1999).

Dodge, Mara. "A Mood of Defeat and Dejection Prevails: One Hundred Years of Reform at the Cook County Juvenile Court." *Children's Legal Rights Journal* 19 (1999).

Eady, Sandra, Norman Christopher Reinhart, and Peter Martino. "Statutory Rape Laws by State." OLR Research Report, April 14, 2003.

Finkel, Norman J. "The Insanity Defense Reform Act of 1984: Much Ado about Nothing." *Behavioral Science and the Law* 7, no. 3 (1989).

Forst, Martin, Jeffrey Fagan, and T. Scott Vivona. "Youths in Prisons and Training Schools: Perceptions and Consequences of the Treatment-Custody Dichotomy." *Juvenile and Family Court Journal* 39 (1989).

Fortier, Laura. "Women, Sex and Patriarchy." *Family Planning Perspective* 7, no. 6 (1975).

Frost, J. L. "Anonymous Juries." *Journal of Contemporary Legal Issues* 2 (1992): 263–97.

Gallagher, Mary Pat. "Criminal Lawyer Draws $500 Fine." *New Jersey Law Journal*, July 10, 2008.

Gibson, James L., Gregory L. Caldeira, and Lester Spence. "Measuring Attitudes toward the United States Supreme Court." *Journal of Political Science* 47, no. 2 (April 2003).

Green, Edith, and Kasey Weber. "Teen Court Jurors' Sentencing Decisions." *Criminal Justice Review* 33, no. 3 (September 2008).

Greenblatt, Alan. "Thinking inside the Jury Box." *Governing Magazine*, March 2005.

Gregory, Daman P. "Lionel Tate Gets Third Chance at Freedom." *Caribbean Today* 15, November 2004.

Groot, Roger D. "The Jury Presentment before 1215." *American Journal of Legal History* 26, 1982.

Gross, Samuel R. "Lost Lives: Miscarriage of Justice in Capital Cases." *Law and Contemporary Problems* 61 (Autumn 1998).

Gullion, Steve. "Sheriffs in Search of a Role." *New Law Journal* 142, no. 6564 (August 14, 1992).

Hamblett, Mark. "2nd Circuit Upsets Conviction." *New York Law Journal*, September 6, 2007.

Hannon, Joan Underhill. "The Generosity of Ante-bellum Poor Relief." *Journal of Economic History* 44 (1984).

Harger, Charles M. "Cattle Trails of the Prairies." *Scribner's Magazine* 11 (1892).

Hartley, Richard D. "Sentencing Reform and the War on Drugs." *Journal of Contemporary Criminal Justice* 24, no. 4 (November 2008).

Heward, Michelle E. "The Operation and Organization of Teen Courts in the United States: A Comparative Analysis of Legislation." *Juvenile and Family Court Journal* 53 (2002).

Hilton, Ordway. "Handwriting Identification vs. Eyewitness Identification." *Journal of Criminal Law, Criminology and Police Science* 45, no. 2 (July–August 1954).

Hornby, D. Brock. "The Business of the U.S. District Courts." *The Green Bag* 10, no. 4 (Summer 2007).

Hurnard, Naomi D. "The Jury of Presentment and the Assize of Clarendon." *English Historical Review* 56, no. 374 (1941).

Ireland, Robert M. "Privately Funded Prosecution of Crime in the Nineteenth-Century United States." *American Journal of Legal History* 39, no. 1 (January 1995).

———. "Review of Murder at Harvard." *American Journal of Legal History* 16, no. 4 (1972).

Jackson, Robert H. "The Federal Prosecutor." *Journal of the American Judiciary Society* 24 (1940).

James, Laura. "The Famous Black-McKAig Trial." *Esquire*, May 11, 2005.

James, Rita M. "Status and Competence of Juries." *American Journal of Sociology* 64 (1959).

Joh, Elizabeth E. "The Paradox of Private Policing." *Journal of Criminal Law and Criminology* 95 (2004).

Johnston, Robert. "United States Abortion Rates, 1960–2005." *Johnston's Archives*, February 17, 2008.

Kanin, Eugene. "False Rape Allegations." *Archives of Sexual Behavior* 23, no. 1 (February 1994).

Keil, Thomas J., and Gennaro E. Vito. "Race and the Death Penalty in Kentucky Murder Trials." *American Journal of Criminal Justice* 20, no. 1 (1995).

Kerr, Margaret, Richard D. Forsyth, and Michael J. Pliely. "Cold Water and Hot Iron: Trial by Ordeal in England." *Journal of Interdisciplinary History* 22 (1992): 2.

Kramer, G. P., N. L. Kerr, and J. S. Carroll. "Pretrial Publicity, Judicial Remedies and Jury Bias." *Law and Human Behavior* 14 (1990).

Kress, Jack M. "Progress and Prosecution." *Annals of the American Academy of Political and Social Sciences* 423 (January 1976).

Kury, Helmut. "Public Opinion and Punitivity." *International Journal of Law and Psychiatry* 22 (1990).

Langan, Patrick. "Between Prison and Probation: Intermediate Sanctions." *Science* 264 (1994).

Leo, Richard A., and Richard J. Ofshe. "The Consequences of False Confessions." *Journal of Criminal Law, Criminology and Police Science* 88 (1998).

Levitt, Steven D. "Understanding Why Crime Fell in the 1990." *Journal of Economic Perspectives* 18, no. 1 (Winter 2004).

Logan, Charles. "Well Kept: Company Quality of Confinement in Private and Public Prisons." *Journal of Criminal Law and Criminology* 83, no. 3 (1992).

Longaker, Richard P. "Andrew Jackson and the Judiciary." *Political Science Quarterly* 71, no. 3 (September 1956).

Lucken, Karl. "The Dynamics of Penal Reform." *Crime, Law and Social Change* 26, (1997).

Luscombe, Belinda, Wendy Cole, Maggie Sieger, and Amanda Bower. "When the Evidence Lies," *Time Canada* 57, no. 20 (May 21, 2001).

Lyman, J. T. "The Metropolitan Police Act of 1829." *Journal of Criminal Law, Criminology and Police Science* 55, no. 1 (March 1964).

Mangan, Terrence J., and Michael G. Shanahan. "Public Law Enforcement / Private Security: A New Partnership?" *F.B.I. Law Enforcement Bulletin*, January 1990.

McCoun, Robert J. "Experimental Research on Jury Decision Making." *Science*, new series 244, no. 4908 (June 2, 1989).

McElhaney, James W. "Character Matters." *ABA Journal* 94, no. 2 (August 2008).

McNamara, Donal E. H. "Sex Offenses and Sex Offenders." *Annals of the American Academy of Political and Social Sciences* 376 (March 1968).

Mokdad, Ali H., James S. Mrks, Donna F. Stroup, Julie L. Gerberding. "Actual Causes of Death in the United States." *Journal of the American Medical Association* 291, no. 4 (March 10, 2004).

Montgomery, Alicia. "Angels of Justice." *Salon*, March 17, 2000.

Mulvey, Ann, Amelia Fournier, and Teresa Donahue. "Murder in the Family: The Menendez Brothers." *Victims and Offenders* 1 (2006).

Myrciades, Lynda S. "Grand Juries, Legal Machines and the Common Man Jury." *College Literature* 53, no. 3 (Summer 2008).

No author. "Falsely Accused: Justice and the Willing Suspension of Belief." *Forensic Examiner* 17, no. 1 (Spring 2008).

No author. "HIV Infusion Clinic Administrator Sentenced to 30 Months in Prison for Health Care Fraud." *Drug Week*, July 25, 2008.

No author. "Judicial Gowns, Their Use by *Nisi Prius* (Unless before) Judges in Virginia." *Virginia Law Review* 10, no. 7 (May 1924).

No author. "Jury Recommends Death for Peterson." *Law Center*, December 14, 2004.

No author. "Mental Secquaelae of the Harrison Law." *New York Medical Journal* 102 (March 15, 1915).

No author. "Miami Jury Convicts Physician and Three Business Owners of Medicare Fraud." *Drug Week*, March 28, 2008.

No author. "White Collar Crime Convictions for January 2007." *Tracereport*, 2007.

No author. "Why Is Marijuana Illegal?" *DrugWarRant*, February 13, 2008.

Norton, Mary Beth. "Gender and Defamation in 17th Century Maryland." *William and Mary Quarterly* 44 (1987).

Panzarella, Robert. "Theory and Practice of Probation on Bail in the Report of John Augustus." *Federal Probation* 66, no. 3 (December 2002).

Pickett, Walter M. "The Office of the Public Prosecutor in Connecticut." *Journal of Criminal Law and Criminology* 17 (November 1926).

Placek, James. "Battered Women in the Court Room." *Crime, Law and Social Change* 35 (2001).

Raskin, David C., and John A. Podlesny. "Truth and Deception." *Psychological Bulletin* 86 (1979).

Redlich, Allison R., and Gail S. Goodman. "Taking Responsibility for an Act Not Committed: The Influence of Age and Suggestibility." *Law and Human Behavior* 27, no. 2 (April 2003).

Remnick, David. "One Sure Thing." *The New Yorker*, November 21, 1994.

Rister, C. C. "Outlaws and Vigilantes of the Southern Plains." *Mississippi Historical Review* 19, no. 4 (March 1933).

Robert, Paul Craig. "Guilty of Being Rich: Victimization of Hotel Magnate Leona Helsmley." *National Review*, November 15, 1993.

Roberts, J. V., and A. N. Doob. "News Media Influence on Public Views of Sentencing." *Law and Human Behavior* 40 (1990).

Rodriguez, Lisa. "Juvenile Legislation: Where's the 'Love' in 'Tough Love'?" *Florida Bar Public Interest Journal*, July 2006.

Roman, John, and Aaron Chaflin. "Does It Pay to Invest in Re-entry Programs for Jail Inmates?" *Justice Policy Center*, June 27–28, 2006.

Roper, Robert T. "Jury Size and Verdict Consistency." *Law and Society Review* 14, no. 4 (Summer 1980).

Rosenbaum, H. Jon, and Peter C. Sederberg. "Vigilantism: An Analysis of Establishment Violence." *Comparative Politics* 6, no. 4 (July 1974).

Salem, Peter, and Billie-Lee Dunford-Jackson. "Beyond Politics and Positions." *Family Court Review*, July 2008.

———. "Domestic Violence beyond Politics." *Family Court Review*, July 2008.

Sanjeez, Anand. "The Origins, Early History and Evolution of the English Criminal Trial Jury." *Alberta Law Review* 43 (2005).

Schiraldi, Vincent, and Steven Drizin. "100 Years of the Children's Court." *Corrections Today*, December 1999.

Schlosser, Eric. "The Prison Industrial Complex." *Atlantic Monthly*, December 1998, 51–77.

Scholl, Michael. "Ex-lawyer Loses $30,000 in Bond for Brief Journey." *New York Law Journal*, August 1, 2006.

Schulman, J. Neil. "Convicted by Suspicion: Why Scott Peterson May Be Innocent." *Hollywood Investigator*, November 30, 2004.

Scott, Gale. "Top Cop Targets Health Care Fraud." *Crain's New York Business*, June 25, 2007.

Scott, Marvin, and Stanford Lyman. "Accounts." *American Sociological Review* 33, no. 1 (February 1968).

Serrill, Michael S. "The 'Mob' Lawyer: Life Support for Crime." *Time*, March 25, 1985.

Shapiro, Susan P. "Collaring the Crime, Not the Criminal." *American Sociological Review*, June 1990.

Sierra, Elizabeth. "The Newest Spectator Sport: Why Extending Victim's Rights to the Spectators' Gallery Erodes the Presumption of Innocence." *Duke Law Journal* 58, no. 2 (November 2008).

Silverstein, Ken. "US: America's Private Gulag." *CorpWatch*, June 1, 2000.

Slater, David, and William Elliott. "Television Influence on Social Reality." *Quarterly Journal of Speech* 68 (1982).

Smith, Rod. "Toward a More Utilitarian Juvenile Court System." *Florida Journal of Law and Public Policy* 237 (1999).

Staff. "Dallas County Detention Center South Tower Cost: $61.7 million." *Texas Construction* 15, no. 6 (June 2007).

Stewart, Artemus. "The Legal Side of the Strike Question." *American Law Register* 42, no. 9 (September 1894).

Streeter, Holly. "The Sordid Trial of Laura D. Fair: Victorian Family Values." *Georgetown Law*, July 24, 2003.

Sunderland, Edson R. "The Sheriff's Return." *Columbia Law Review* 16, no. 4 (April 1916).

Sutherland, Edwin. "White Collar Criminality." *American Sociological Review* 5, no. 1 (February 1940).

Sykes, Gresham, and David Matza. "Techniques of Neutralization." *American Sociological Review* 22 (1957).

Talbot, Margaret. "The Maximum Security Adolescent." *New York Time Magazine*, September 10, 2000.

Taxman, F., D. Young, and J. Byrne. "Transforming Offender Reentry into Public Safety: Lessons from OHP's Recent Partnership Initiative." *Justice Research and Policy* 5, no. 2 (2003).

Taylor, Lauren R. "Has Rape Reporting Increased over Time?" *National Institute of Justice Journal*, no. 254 (July 2006).

Thompson, Roger. "Holy Watchfulness and Communal Conformism: The Functions of Defamation in Early New England Communities." *New England Quarterly* 56, no. 4 (1983).

Turner, Frederick Jackson. "The Significance of the Frontier in American History." *Report of the American Historical Association*, 1893.

Vishneski, John. "What the Court Decided in *Dred Scott v. Sandford*." *American Journal of Legal History* 32, no. 4 (1988).

Ward, John A. J. "Private Prosecution: The Entrenched Anomaly." *North Carolina Law Review* 50, 1972.

Ward, Stephanie Francis. "When Honesty Is Not Best Politics." *ABA Journal*, August 2007.

Watts, Eugene E. "Police Response to Crime and Disorder in 20th Century St. Louis." *Journal of American History* 70 (1983).

Wells, Gary L., and Elizabeth Olson. "Eye Witness Testimony." *Annual Review of Psychology* 54 (2003).

Wesely, J. K., and Edward Gaarder. "The Gendered Nature of the Urban Outdoors: Women Negotiating Fear of Violence." *Gender and Society* 18, no. 5 (2004).

West, Heather C., and William J. Sabol. "Prisoners in 2007." *Bureau of Justice Statistics Bulletin*, December 2008.

Wolfgang, Marvin E. "Victim Precipitated Homicide." *Journal of Criminal Law, Criminology and Police Science* 48, no. 1 (May–June 1957).

NEWSPAPERS

Abrams, Grady. "Quest for Justice Can Take the Longest Road." *Augusta Chronicle*, May 26, 2008.

Agee, Mark. "No Room for Sex Offenders." *Fort Worth Star-Telegram*, September 28, 2006.

Albany Times Union. "Clinton Signs Popular Taxpayers' Rights Bill," July 31, 1996.

———. "Former Enron CEO Skilling Begins Prison Sentence," December 12, 2006.

———. "2 Officers in King Case Go to Prison," October 13, 1993.

Alexander, Keith L. "Did the Crime? Watch the Time." *Washington Post*, November 8, 2007.

Amar, Akhil Reed. "A Second Chance at Justice." *New York Times*, February 6, 1997.

Anslinger, Harry. "Narcotics Rise Laid to China and Cuba." *New York Times*, June 1, 1962.

———. "U.S. Finds Heroin Big Narcotic Snag." *New York Times*, May 2, 1951.

Appleby, Julie. "Medical Claims 'Mined' to Find Fraud." *USA Today*, November 7, 2008.

Archibold, Randal C. "Ex-Congressman Gets 8 Year Term in Bribery Case." *New York Times*, March 4, 2006.

Arenson, Karen W. "Duke Grappling with Impact of Scandal on Its Reputation." *New York Times*, April 7, 2006.

Bangor Daily News. "Keeping Track of Sex Offenders," May 1, 2006.

Becker, Maki. "Newfound Evidence That Exonerates Capozzi Stored at ECMC All Along." *Buffalo News*, March 29, 2007.

Benidt, Bruce. "Ex-state Justice, Nuremberg Judge Christianson Dies." *Star Tribune*, May 28, 1985.

Bernstein, Viv, and Joe Drape. "Rape Allegation against Athletes Is Roiling Duke." *New York Times*, March 26, 2007.

Billiter, Bill. "Horror Stories about IRS Told to Congress Panel." *Los Angeles Times*, October 7, 1980.

Blankstein, Andrew. "Ryan O'Neal, Son Redmond Booked on Suspicion of Drug Possession." *Los Angeles Times*, September 17, 2008.

Block, Dorian. "Wild Torture Tale: I Was Beaten and Starved by Rich Guy, She Claims." *Daily News*, November 17, 2007.

Blythe, Ann. "Claims against Nifong to Be Heard in Civil Court." *News and Observer*, May 28, 2008.

Bohlen, Celestine. "Armed Dangerous Life of a Probation Officer." *New York Times*, December 30, 1988.

Bonner, Lynne. "Payouts to the Wrongly Jailed Get a Big Boost." *News and Observer*, July 19, 2008.

Boston Globe. Editorial. "Batterers with Badges," December 30, 2007.

Boyer, Barbara. "New Program Targets Gangs, Violence in South Philadelphia." *Philadelphia Inquirer*, January 17, 2008.

Branch, Alex. "Conviction Cleared in Death Row Case." *Star Telegram*, December 17, 2008.

Brick, Michale. "Defendant Is Convicted for His Role in 2 Killings." *New York Times*, August 10, 2007.

Bryan Eagle. "Man Had Drugs: Club," March 7, 2009.

Buettner, Russ. "New Charges for Two Accused of Embezzling Council Funds." *New York Times*, June 25, 2008.

Butterfield, Fox. "Wife Killing at Fort Reflects Growing Problem." *New York Times*, July 29, 2002.

Camp, Cheryl. "Convicted Murderer Is Freed in Wake of Tainted Evidence." *New York Times*, May 22, 2007.

Catledge, Turner. "St. Louis Combats Race Riot Rumors." *New York Times*, July 11, 1943.

Claxton, Michael, N. Sinclair, and Robert Hanson. "Felons on Probation Often Go Unwatched." *Detroit News*, December 10, 2002.

Cooper, Michale. "Hevesi's Investigation Unit Builds Prosecutable Cases." *New York Times*, December 27, 2005.

Cormier, Anthony. "Wrongfully Convicted Man's Murder Case Raises Questions." *Herald Tribune*, March 8, 2009.

Daily News. "Teen Drug Mule's Gut Full of Heroin," October 27, 2007.

Davey, Monica. "Ex-governor, Now in Prison, Sees Case End." *New York Times*, May 28, 2008.

Davis, Cary. "Officer's Undoing Began Long Ago." *St. Petersburg Times*, June 15, 2003.

Dotinga, Randy. "Ex-Disney Executive Gets Probation in Sex Case." Associated Press, Los Angeles, August 10, 2000.

Dwyer, Jim. "Trying to Give Police the Right Answer, Even When It's Wrong." *New York Times*, June 13, 2007.

Elgon, John. "Uma Thurman's Stalker Sentenced to Three Years' Probation and Treatment." *New York Times*, June 3, 2008.

Ellis, Tiara M. "Appeals Court Overturns Michael Blair's Conviction in Ashley Estell Case." *Dallas Morning News*, June 25, 2008.

Emily, Jennifer, and Steve McGonigle. "Dallas County Attorney Wants Unethical Prosecutors Punished." *Dallas Morning News*, May 4, 2008.

Episcopal Five. "An Open Letter." *New York Times*, January 9, 1920.

Esmond, Donn. "On Third Try, Justice System Gets Donahue." *Buffalo News*, May 14, 2008.

Fahim, Kareem. "Ex-legislator Is Sentenced to 2 to 6 Years." *New York Times*, June 13, 2008.

Fisher, Ian. "Stiff Sentences and Crowded Prisons." *New York Times*, January 30, 1995.

Freedberg, Sydney P. "The Stigma Is Always There." *St. Petersburg Times*, July 4, 1999.

Fried, Jospeh P. "Frank Thompson: Career in Congress Ended with Abscam." *New York Times*, July 24, 1989.

———. "Limelight Owner Is Acquitted after Long Fight in Drug Case." *New York Times*, February 12, 1998.

———. "Top Informant Denies Faking Conspiracy for Bombings." *New York Times*, April 4, 1995.

Friess, Steve. "Many Stark Contrasts as Simpson Is Convicted." *New York Times*, October 4, 2008.

Gay, Malcolm. "U.S. Judge Upholds Water Release in Flood Area." *New York Times*, March 26, 2008.

Gengler, Danile J. "The Story of Barry Beach's Innocence." *Helena (Montana) Independence Record*, January 23, 2008.

Gettleman, Jeffrey. "Montclair and Its Model School Try to Cope with a Rape Charge." *New York Times*, October 18, 2004.

Glaberson, William. "An Archetypal Mob Trial: It's Just Like in the Movies," *New York Times*, May 23, 2004.

———. "Gravano, Ever a Showman, Takes Stand Again," *New York Times*, October 18, 2003.

———. "In Tiny Courts of N.Y., Abuses of Law and Power," *New York Times*, September 25, 2006.

———. "Questioning 'Dirty Bomb' Plot, Judge Orders U.S. to Yield Papers on Detainee." *New York Times*, October 31, 2008.

Glater, Jonathan B. "Stewart Celebrity Created Magnet for Scrutiny." *New York Times*, May 7, 2004.

Goldberg, Carey. "Massachusetts High Court Backs Freeing Au Pair in Baby's Death." *New York Times*, June 17, 1998.

Goldstein, Joseph. "Meet the 2nd Circuit Court's New Judge." *New York Sun*, October 16, 2006.

Goleman, Daniel. "Studies Point to Flaws in Lineup of Suspects." *New York Times*, January 17, 1995.

Golin, Sarah. "McCloskey Labors to Exonerate Innocent Prisoners." *New Jersey Star-Ledger*, October 2, 2008.

Goodman, Brenda. "Prisoner Flees Custody in Atlanta but Is Caught." *New York Times*, November 11, 2005.

Goodman, Walter. "Bronco to Verdict: In Case You Were Out." *New York Times*, December 20, 1995.

Goodstein, Laurie. "Gotti's Lawyer Lambastes Government's Star Witness." *Washington Post*, February 14, 1992.

———. "Gotti Convicted of 13 Crimes." *Washington Post*, April 3, 1992.

Greenhouse, Linda. "Citing National Consensus, Justices Bar Death Penalty for Retarded Defendants." *New York Times*, June 21, 2002.

———. "Supreme Court: No Death Penalty for Child Rape." *San Francisco Chronicle*, June 26, 2008.

Gryta, Matt. "Inmate Indicted in 2004 Slaying." *Buffalo News*, March 7, 2009.

Hall, Christina. "Woman Admits Rape Tale Was a Lie." *Toledo Blade*, October 9, 2002.

Halley, Jim. "All-American 17, out of Jail but Facing Charges." *USA Today*, March 31, 2008, 2C.

Hanford, Desiree J. "A Newpaper Defends Naming Jurors." *New York Times*, September 17, 2007.

Hanners, David. "St. Paul Man Freed after 10 Years." *Twin Cities Pioneer Press*, October 2, 2007.

Hartocolis, Anemona. "This Season's Must-See Criminal Trial." *New York Times*, May 13, 2007.

Hastings, Deborah. "States Struggle with Cost of Execution." *Ventura County Star*, March 7, 2009.

Healy, Patrick. "Jury Tampering Claim Halts L.I. Murder Trial." *New York Times*, September 30, 2004.

Henry, Steven, and Sarah Bruce. "Family Joy as Kenny Richey Heads for Home." *Daily Mail*, December 20, 2007.

Herszenhorn, David M. "Alarm Helps to Fight Domestic Violence." *New York Times*, July 27 1999.

Hicks, Jonathan P. "From Conviction to Re-election." *New York Times*, December 9, 2005.

Hoberock, Barbara. "New Bills Require Fresh Look at the System." *Tulsa World*, July 22, 2007.

Hoffman, Morris B. "Free Market Justice." *New York Times*, January 8, 2007.

Horn, Dan. "Probation Officers to Be Disciplined." *Cincinnati Enquirer*, November 30, 2000.

Hulse, Carl. "Congress: On Prosecutors and the War." *New York Times*, March 19, 2007.

Indiana News. "Police: Woman Admits Making False Rape Claim," November 12, 2004.

Johnson, Carrie. "U.S. Targets Health Care Fraud, Abuse." *Washington Post*, July 19, 2007.

Johnson, Carrie, and Paul Kane. "Sen. Stevens Indicted on 7 Corruption Counts." *Washington Post*, July 30, 2008.

Johnson, Mark. "As Hevesi Is Sentenced, Fight Rages over His Successor." *Buffalo News*, February 10, 2007.

Kalinowski, Bob. "Driver Accused of Making False 911 Call to Avoid Arrest." *Wilkes-Barre Citizens Voice*, March 4, 2009.

Kershaw, Sarah. "New Evidence in Rape Case Frees Man after Six Years." *New York Times*, June 29, 2000.

King, Larry. "Bucks Boy, 11, Gets Probation over Burglary." *Philadelphia Inquirer*, April 4, 2007.

Ko, Michale. "Letourneau Released from Prison Today." *Seattle Times*, August 4, 2004.

Kocieniewski, David. "A History of Sex with Students." *New York Times*, October 10, 2006.

Kramer, Marcia, and Frank Lombardi. "New Top State Judge: Abolish Grand Juries and Let Us Decide." *New York Daily News*, January 31, 1985.

Krueger, Curtis, Richard Rafke, and Dong-Phuong Nguyen. "The Problem with Probation." *St. Petersburn Times*, June 13, 2004.

Lackey, Katharine. "Thieves Skim Credit Card Date at Fuel Pumps." *USA Today*, August 6, 2008.

Lardner Jr., George. "John Gotti, Modern Godfather." *Washington Post*, May 28, 1990.

Laughlin, Meg. "Years in Prison for Adults Keep a Child Frozen in Time." *Miami Herald*, October 1, 2000.

Leonnig, Carol D. "D.C. Sees Sharp Drop in Federal Prosecutions." *Washington Post*, October 21, 2007.

Leonnig, Carol D., and Yolanda Woodlee. "Barry Escapes Jail Time on Probation Violation." *Washington Post*, March 13, 2007.

Liptak, Adam. "Court Ruling Expected to Spur Convictions in Capital Cases." *New York Times*, June 9, 2007.

———. "Federal Judge Files Complaint against Prosecutor in Boston." *New York Times*, July 3, 2007.

———. "Public Defenders Get Better Marks on Salary." *New York Times*, July 14, 2007.

———. "Serving Life with No Chance of Redemption." *New York Times*, October 5, 2005.

———. "Study Suspects Thousands of False Convictions." *New York Times*, April 19, 2004.

Locke, Mandy. "Death Row Inmate to Go Free." *News and Observer*, May 2, 2008.

Los Angeles Times. "Immunity for Prosecutors," April 19, 2008.

Lozano, Juan. "Enron Victims to Speak Out." *Albany Times Union*, September 23, 2006.

Lyne, Barbara. "Giving the Bad Guys a Shot at Redemption." *New York Times*, March 28, 1993.

Madigan, Katherine G. "Videotape Interrogations, Confessions." *Albany Times Union*, February 25, 2008.

Madigan, Nick. "Woman Who Killed Spouse with Car Is Guilty of Murder." *New York Times*, February 14, 2003.

Margolick, David. "After 474 Days as a Prisoner, He Is Free." *New York Times*, October 4, 1995.

Martin, Douglas. "Barefoot Sanders Dies." *New York Times*, September 24, 2008.

McLaughlin, Abraham. "Tales of Journey from Death to Freedom." *Christian Science Monitor* 90, no. 246 (November 16, 1996).

Mcleod, Angus. "Carnegie Gave Scots a Bad Name." *Times* (London), October 26, 2006.

Mead, Julia C. "Police Arrest Sex Offender: Can Be Deported to El Salvador." *New York Times*, May 2, 2006.

Melzer, Matt. "The Arthur McDuffie Riots of 1980." *Miami Beach News*, August 12, 2007.

Meyer, Ed. "Resh Not Guilty." *Akron Beacon Journal*, April 18, 2007.

Miller, Jill. "Decisions on Expert Testimony Left to Trial Courts." *Rochester (New York) Daily Record*, May 23, 2001.

Mills, Steve, Flynn McRoberts, and Maurice Possley. "When Labs Falter, Defendants Pay." *Chicago Tribune*, October 20, 2004.

Monteagudo, Luis. "23 Probation Officers' Firings Upheld." *San Diego Union Tribune*, July 18, 2002.

Moreno, Sylvia. "New Prosecutor Revisits Justice in Dallas." *Washington Post*, March 5, 2007.

Morgenson, Gretchen. "Judge Demands Documentation in Foreclosures." *New York Times*, November 17, 2007.

Mosingo, Joe. "4 Girls Get Probation in Hate Crime Trial." *Los Angeles Times*, February 6, 2007.

Munoz, Lisa. "Black Teenagers Convicted of Beating of 3 White Women." *NewYork Times*, January 27, 2007.

Murphy, Kate. "Fraud Case Tied to Enron Ends in Prison for Three Men." *New York Times*, February 23, 2008.

———. "Judge Throws Out Kenneth Lay's Conviction." *New York Times*, October 18, 2006.

New York Post. "Black Hawk Star Jailed," February 12, 2005.

———. "Jailhouse Divorce for Koz," July 18, 2008.

———. "New Trial Agony for Yankel Kin," March 28, 2005.

———. "Probation for Woman Perv Teacher," September 27, 2003.

New York Times. Editorial (no title), July 7, 1892.

New York Times. "Actor Is Ordered to Pay $30 Million in Killing," November 19, 2005.

———. "Brown Draws Probation," October 6, 1999.

———. "A Chronology of Events in the Watergate Case: An Election Scheme That Backfired," May 1, 1973.

———. "Day in Jail for Ex-Duke Prosecutor," September 1, 2007.

———. "Eugene Nickerson, Ex-Nassau Politician and Judge in Louima Trial," January 3, 2002.

———. "Ex Teacher in Sex Case Freed," February 18, 2005.

———. "Graft Rap for Housing Big," July 11, 2008.

———. "Great Lengths Taken to Fill the Jury Box," July 29, 2007.

———. "The Hell's Kitchen Riots," August 7, 1898.

———. "Injured Reach 600," June 22, 1943.

———. "John M. Mitchell Dies at 75; Major Figure in Watergate," November 10, 1988.

———. "Makes Race Riot Charges," July 29, 1943.

———. "Negroes Accuse the Police," August 22, 1900.

———. "New Duke DNA Tests Are Reportedly Inconclusive," March 13, 2006.

———. "Police Accused of Inciting Race Riots," July 20, 1905.

———. "Police Chief Indicted in Cicero Race Riots," September 19, 1951.

———. "The Private Detective Abuse," Janaury 25, 1889.

———. "Private Police Equals McAdoo Force in Numbers," January 22, 1905.

———. "Probation Officer Is Cleared by Judge," March 5, 2004.

———. "Race Riot on West Side," August 16, 1900.

———. "Race Riots Laid to Lax Police Rule," July 8, 1917.

———. "Rochester Police Battle Race Riot," July 25, 1964.

———. "Senator Williams Exits Unrepentant," March 14, 1982.

———. "Suggests 59 Means to Curb Race Feeling," September 25, 1922.

———. "Teacher Arrested in Two Sex Attacks," June 24, 1993.

———. "Texas Killer Is Executed," March 12, 2009.

———. "Tulsa Race Riot Jury Indicts Police Chief," June 26, 1921.

———. "2 Bodies Found at Residence of U.S. Judge," March 1, 2005.

———. "Young Sniper Is Sentenced to Six Life Terms," November 9, 2006.

Newman, Andy. "Seating Jurors for Child Murder Case Raises Questions That All Parents Face." *New York Times*, January 12, 2008.

Newman, Maria. "Man Freed after Serving Seven Years for Rape." *New York Times*, June 3, 1992.

Ngowi, Rodrique, and Anne D'Innocenzio. "11 Charged in What May Be the Biggest ID Theft Case Ever." Associated Press, August 6, 2008.

Noble, Kenneth B. "The Endless Rodney King Case." *New York Times*, February 4, 1996.

Nordheimer, Jon. "In New Jersey, Slip-ups Show Autopsy Deficiencies." *New York Times*, October 20, 1993.

O'Connor, Anahad. "Sex Offenders See New Limits for Halloween." *New York Times*, October 26, 2005.

O'Shaughnessy, Patrice. "Ex-cop Terrorized Her, Afraid She'd Die." *Daily News*, February 25, 2008.

Ott, Dwight. "Some Charges Dropped against Temple Students Accused of Hate Crime." *Philadelphia Inquirer*, April 30, 2008.

Perry, Tony. "Release of Widow Ends Bizarre Case." *Los Angeles Times*, April 19, 2008.

Philadelphia Inquirer. Editorial. "Prison Reform Always Misses the Point." February 5, 2007.

———. "In Cincinnati Blacks Say Racial Inequality Has Been Years in Making," April 15, 2001.

Pignataro, T. J. "Zarbo Gets Three Years' Probation in Domestic Violence Case." *Buffalo News*, June 18, 2003.

Possley, Maurice. "Always Knew I Was Innocent." *Chicago Tribune*, November 24, 2006.

Pressley, Sue Anne. "Sheriff's Specialty: Making Jail Miserable." *Washington Post*, August 25, 1997.

Raab, Selwyn. "A Mafia Family's Second Wind." *New York Times*, April 29, 2000.

Rahn, Richard. "Stopping IRS Misconduct." *Washington Times*, July 25, 2007.

Rankin, Robert A. "More IRS Abuses Revealed on Final Day of Senate Hearings." *Buffalo News*, September 26, 1997.

Rashbaum, William K. "A Closer Eye of the Worst Sex Offenders." *New York Times*, February 25, 2009.

Raskin, A. H. "GM Doubles Force to Curb Sabotage." *New York Times*, April 5, 1942.

Reinhold, Robert. "How Lawyers and Media Turned the McMartin Case into a Tragic Media Circus." *New York Times*, January 25, 1990.

Rimer, Sara. "Unruly Students Facing Arrest, Not Detention." *New York Times*, January 4, 2004.

Rose, Derek, and Jimmy Vielkind. "Wife's Attorney in Slay: He Had It Coming." *Daily News*, November 13, 2006.

Ross, Barbara, and Dave Goldiner. "Who Will Protect Me Now?" *Daily News*, May 7, 2008.

Ruiz, Albor. "Court System Is Another Abuser." *Daily News*, May 15, 2009.

Sanders, Rob Ray. "The First to Die by Injection." *Fort Worth Star-Telegram*, December 3, 2007.

Sandoval, Stephanie. "Local Officials Seek State 'Safe Zone' Law." *Dallas Morning News*, August 18, 2006.

Santos, Fernanda. "Trenton Man Killed by Police Was Wanted on Parole Violation." *New York Times*, November 14, 2005.

Saunders, Debra J. "Willie Horton, 2008." *San Francisco Chronicle*, November 27, 2007.

Schiffman, John. "Long Sentence in Vast Pill Selling Case." *Philadelphia Inquirer*, December 10, 2007.

Schlosser, Gretchen. "Teen, Already in Sex Offender Treatment Faces New Sex Charges." *Willmar (Minnesota) West Central Tribune*, February 26, 2009.

Seelye, Katharine Q. "Freed Reporter Says She Upheld Principles." *New York Times*, October 4, 2005.

Shea, Kathleen Brady. "2 Jailers Charged in Inmate Attack." *Philadelphia Inquirer*, June 12, 2007.

Shellem, Pete. "Guest Shot: How Justice Gets Done in Spite of the Justice System." *Harrisburg Patiot News*, September 14, 2007.

Stacy, Mitch. "Teacher in Sex Case Spared Second Trial." *Buffalo News*, March 22, 2006.

Stark, Louis. "Riot Photos Force Police Admission." *New York Times*, July 1, 1937.

Sullivan, John. "Cutler, Gotti's Lawyer, Gets Three Months' Contempt Sentence." *New York Times*, December 14, 1996.

Surro, Roberto. "Ripples of a Pathologist's Misconduct in Graves and Courts of West Texas." *New York Times*, November 22, 1992.

Teltsch, Kathleen. "Alternative to Prison in New York: Six Months of Counseling and Therapy." *New York Times*, February 1, 1988.

Thompson, Don. "Controversy Follows Ex-Radicals Parole." *Internatonal Business Times*, March 28, 2008.

Toronto Star. "U.S. Appeals Court Refuses to Reconsider Black Case," August 22, 2008.

Tulsky, Frederic M. "Last Chance, Little Help." *San Jose Mercury News*, January 26, 2006.

Urbina, Ian. "Judge Guilty in Kickback Is Accused of Fixing Suit." *New York Times*, February 21, 2009.

Valenzuela, Beatriz E. "Illegal Alien Arrested for Carrying an UZI." *Victoria Daily Press*, February 14, 2009.

Warner, Gene. "Donahue's Denial Was Backed by Lie Detector." *Buffalo News*, October 2, 2007.

———. "False Allegations Take Toll on Teacher." *Buffalo News*, June 7, 1996.

Washington Post. "Catholic Bishops Plan Drive against Death Penalty." March 21, 2005.

———. "Reputed Crime Boss Gotti Acquitted in Conspiracy Trial." February 10, 1990.

Watson, Debra A. Skok. "Polygraph Test Can Do More Harm than Good." *Buffalo News*, August 23, 2001.

Whiteley, Peyton. "Woman Pleads Guilty to False Rape Report." *Seattle Times*, March 19, 2008.

Wilson, Duff. "New Timeline by Prosecutor in Duke Case." *New York Times*, September 23, 2006.

Woodall, Martha. "The Assault Broke the Teacher's Neck." *Philadelphia Inquirer*, April 6, 2007.

Worth, Robert F. "Juror in First Crown Heights Trial Remains Bitter about Ordeal." *New York Times*, May 1, 2003.

Zenike, Kate. "The Siren Song of Sex with Boys." *New York Times*, December 11, 2005.

DOCUMENTS

Berger v. United States, 295 U.S. 78 89 (1935).

Biemel v. State, 71 Wisconsin 444, 37 N.W. 244, 245–48 (1888).

Branzburg v. Hays, 408 U.S. 665 (1972).

Chisholm v. Georgia, U.S. (2 Dall) 419 (1793).

Coker v. Georgia, 433 U.S. 584 (1977).

Death Penalty Information Center (DPIC). "Innocence Cases." Available online at http://www.deathpenaltyinfo.org.

———. The Innocence Protection Act of 2004. Available online at http://www.deathpenaltyinfo.org.

Ford v. Wainwright, 477 U.S. 399 (1986).

Gideon v. Wainwright, 372 U.S. 335 (1963).

Hale v. Henkel, 201 U.S. 43, 65 (19060.

Judiciary Act of 1789, Chap. 20, Section 1.

Judiciary Act of 1789, Section 35.

Leeke v. Timmerman, 454 U.S. 83 (1981).

Marbury v. Madison, 5 U.S. (1 Cranich) 137 (1803).

Massachusetts Court System, "Violent Criminals on Probation in Bay State Increase by 200 Percent." Office of the Commissioner of Probation, January 26, 2002.

Meister v. People, Michigan 99, 103–104 (1875).

Morrissey v. Brewer, 408 U.S. 471, 477 (1972).

Niets, Marcus. "Probation Camps and Ranches." Sacramento, CA: California Research Bureau, November 2008.

Oyler v. Boles, 368 U.S. 448, 82 S. Ct. 5017 L Ed. 2d 446 (1962).

People v. Baum, 231 N.W. 95, 96 (Mich. 1930).

People v. Ford, 19 Illinois 2d 466, 168 N.E. 2d 33 (1960).

People v. Woodruff, 272 N.Y.S. 2ns 286 (1966)

President's Commission on Law Enforcement and the Administration of Justice. *Task Force Report: Organized Crime*. Washington, DC: GPO, 1967.

Prison Reform Trust. *Prison Privatization Report International*. London, 2007.

Puzzanchera, Charles, and Melissa Sickmund. "Probation as a Court Disposition." *Juvenile Court Statistics, 2005*. Washington, DC: Office of Juvenile Justice and Delinquency Prevention, 2008.

Rompilla v. Beard, 545 U.S. 374 (2005).

Snyder v. Louisiana, 128 S. Ct. 1203 (2008). No. 06–10119.

State v. Funicello, 60 N.J. 60, 286 A.2d 55 (1971).

Thompson v. Oklahoma, 487 U.S. 815 (1988).

U.S. Census, *The American Community*. Washington, DC: GPO, 2004.

U.S. Constitution, Article 1.

U.S. Constitution, Article 3, Sections 1 and 2.

U.S. Constitution, Fifth Amendment.

U.S. Constitution, First Amendment 1.

U.S. Constitution, Fourth Amendment.

U.S. Constitution, Sixth Amendment.

U.S. Department of Health and Human Services, Administration on Children, Youth and Families. "Child Maltreatment." Washington, DC: GPO, 2007.

U.S. Department of Justice, Bureau of Justice Statistics. "Capital Punishment Statistics." *Summary Findings*. Washington, DC: GPO, March 26, 2009.

———. "Characteristics of State Supervising Agencies, 2006," by Thomas P. Bonczar. Washington, DC: GPO, 2007.

———. "Contents of Homicide Trends in the United States." Washington, D.C.: GPO, no date.

———. "Crime in the United States, 2006." *Uniform Crime Reports*. Washington, DC, GPO, September 2007.

———. *Criminal Sentencing Statistics*. Washington, DC: GPO, May 24, 2007.

———. *Criminal Victimization, Number and Rates, 2006*, by Michael Rand and Shannan Catalano. Washington, DC: GPO, 2007.

———. *Prior Abuse Reported by Inmates and Probationers*, by Caroline Wolf Harlow. Washington, DC: GPO, 1999.

———. "Prison Statistics." Washington, DC: GPO, June 30, 2007.

———. *Prison Statistics*. Washington, DC: GPO, 2008.

———. *Prisoners in 2006: Drug War Facts*, by William J. Sabol, Heather Couture, and Page M. Harrison. Washington, DC: GPO, December 2007.

———. "Probation and Parole Statistics." Washington, DC: GPO, December 14, 2008.

———. "Probation and Parole in the United States, 2007 Statistical Tables," by Lauren E. Glaze and Thomas P. Bonczar. Washington, DC: GPO, 2008.

———. *Sentencing in the Federal Courts*, by D. C. McDonald and K. E. Carlson. Washington, DC: GPO, 1993.

———. *Violent Victimization Rates*. Washington, DC: GPO, September 10, 2006.

U.S. Department of Justice, Drug Enforcement Administration. "In the Matter of Marijuana Rescheduling Petition." Docket 86–22, September 6, 1988.

U.S. Department of Justice, FBI. "Expanded Homicide Data." *Uniform Crime Report, 2006.* Washington, DC: GPO, 2007.

———. *Uniform Crime Reports.* Washington, DC: GPO, 2007.

———. *Uniform Crime Reports,* Washington, DC: GPO, 2008.

U.S. Department of Justice, Special Prosecution Force. "Jaworski Memorandum on Prosecuting Nixon," by Carl M. Feldbaum and Peter M. Kreindler. Washington, DC: August 9, 1974.

U.S. Department of Labor, Bureau of Labor Statistics. "Probation Officers and Correctional Treatment Specialists." *Occupational Outlook Handbook, 2008–2009,* http://www.bls.gov/oco/ocos265.htm.

U.S. Public Health Service. *Statistical Abstract of the United States.* Washington, DC: GPO, 2008.

———. *Vital Statistics of the United States.* Washington, DC: GPO, 2008.

U.S. v. Smyth, 104 F. Supp. 283, 298 (1952).

Wiles v. Wood, 98 Eng. 489 (C.P. 1763).

Witherspoon v. Illinois, 391 U.S. 510 (1968).

INDEX

About the Author

Gerhard Falk, PhD, is professor of sociology at the State University of New York, College at Buffalo, in Buffalo, New York. He is the author of 19 books and 40 journal articles. Dr. Falk is the recipient of the New York State University Research Foundation's Award for Excellence in Scholarship, the State University College President's Award for Excellence in Creativity, and the State University of New York Chancellor's Award for Excellence in Teaching.